Invitations to Love

Invitations to Love

Literacy, Love Letters, and Social Change in Nepal

LAURA M. AHEARN

Ann Arbor
THE UNIVERSITY OF MICHIGAN PRESS

For Rick,
my in-house editor
and favorite correspondent

Copyright © by the University of Michigan 2001
All rights reserved
Published in the United States of America by
The University of Michigan Press
Manufactured in the United States of America
⊗ Printed on acid-free paper

2012   2011   2010   2009   8   7   6   5

A CIP catalog record for this book is available from the British Library.

Library of Congress Cataloging-in-Publication Data

Ahearn, Laura M., 1962–
     Invitations to love : literacy, love letters, and social change in Nepal / Laura M.
Ahearn.
         p.   cm.
     Includes bibliographical references and index.
     ISBN 0-472-09784-9 (cloth : alk. paper) — ISBN 0-472-06784-2 (pbk. : alk. paper)
     1. Magar (Nepalese people)—Marriage customs and rites.   2. Magar (Nepalese
people)—Social conditions.   3. Love letters—Nepal.   4. Literacy—Nepal.   I. Title.

     DS493.9M3 A54   2001
     306.81'089'954—dc21   2001053049

ISBN 978-0-472-09784-5 (cloth : alk. paper)
ISBN 978-0-472-06784-8 (pbk. : alk. paper)

Contents

Illustrations

Tables

Preface

On June 1, 2001, shortly before this book went to press, Nepal's Crown Prince Dipendra opened fire with a machine gun, killing ten members of the Royal Family, including himself. While accounts of the tragedy differ, and while many Nepalis still refuse to believe that their beloved Crown Prince could have perpetrated such a heinous crime, an official government investigation concluded that Dipendra was solely to blame for the murders. According to widespread reports, Dipendra killed his parents, siblings, and other family members because they disapproved of his choice of a bride. His parents, King Birendra and Queen Aishwarya, allegedly wanted to arrange a match for Dipendra with a "more suitable" woman, and they wanted to postpone his marriage for several more years until an astrologically auspicious date.

In murdering his parents and other members of his family, Dipendra committed a crime that would be unthinkable to the vast majority of Nepalis, who regularly bow down to their parents in respectful greeting. Even before the tragic massacre occurred, however, Dipendra's life was completely foreign in almost every way to the experiences of most Nepalis. Educated at Eton, Dipendra enjoyed the same material comforts that royal family members in Western countries do, and, unlike most other residents of Nepal, he even had access to machine guns and illegal drugs. Nevertheless, although Dipendra's social circumstances were as extraordinary as his response to parental pressure, the tensions that he faced were similar, if not identical, to those of the ordinary Nepali villagers I describe in this book.

At all levels of Nepali society, a shift is occurring away from arranged marriage and capture marriage toward love marriage. This transformation in marriage practices is both the outcome of, and a contributing factor to, the dramatic political, economic, and social changes taking place in Nepali society as a whole. These changes include—to name only a few—the People's Movement of 1990, which ushered in a democratic system of government that has encouraged Nepalis to view themselves as individuals in the political sphere; the monetization of the Nepali economy, which has rendered the younger generation less dependent on their elders for their livelihood; an influx of "development discourse," the rhetoric that accompanies economic development programs, emphasizing self-sufficiency, free choice, consumerism, and individualism; and a sharp increase in levels of education, which has led to a whole array of new literacy practices, including love letter writing.

All of these changes have facilitated an alteration in the way many Nepalis are conceiving of their own actions and personhood. Increasingly, they are viewing themselves more individualistically, placing their own interests above those of their families or communities. More and more Nepalis are associating being "modern" or "developed" with being able to choose a "life friend" for a companionate marriage. The meanings of marriage, romantic love, and "life success" have changed significantly over recent years for many Nepalis, especially those who are young. With these modifications in meaning, the values and life goals of many Nepalis—not just the Crown Prince—are being reconfigured.

Such remarkable changes have the potential to transform Nepal profoundly. It is my hope that readers will come away from this book with a deeper understanding of the complexities involved in social change, not only in Nepal, but wherever and whenever it occurs.

Acknowledgments

I have incurred many debts as I researched and wrote this book, but most of all I want to thank the family of Jiba Kumari and Lila Bahadur Rana for taking me in as their daughter almost twenty years ago and teaching me about village life. I am also grateful to the residents of Junigau, who were unfailingly generous teachers, neighbors, and friends. I had other homes in Nepal as well, which provided me with warm company, great food, and unparalleled hospitality, including the home of Brian, Judy, Jesse, and Sonya Hollander and the home of my old Peace Corps friends, Ann Hendrick and Mark Keener, and their two children, Jed and Rae. I will never be able to thank these dear friends enough for all the hot showers, good conversation, and excellent dental care they provided. During my visits to Tansen, I appreciated the hospitality of Bimal Shrestha and enjoyed the culinary skills of Mark Countryman and Patrick Greene.

Several organizations have funded my research. A Foreign Language and Area Studies (FLAS) Fellowship supported me while I completed my coursework. My research on the Tij festival during the summer of 1990 was funded by a Margaret Wray French Anthropology Scholarship from the University of Michigan. For my dissertation research in 1992–93, I received a Fulbright-Hays Doctoral Dissertation Research Abroad Fellowship and a National Science Foundation Doctoral Dissertation Improvement Grant. A Mellon Foundation Doctoral Dissertation Fellowship supported me as I wrote my dissertation. In 1996–97, a National Endowment for the Humanities Fellowship for University Teachers enabled me to return to Nepal for several months and then to spend the remainder of the year writing the first draft of this book. A College of Liberal Arts Scholarship Support Grant from the University of South Carolina funded another trip to Nepal in 1998, during which I showed a draft of the book to those whose stories appear in it in order to receive feedback from them.

While writing this book, I benefited enormously from the suggestions and encouragement I received from Rick Black and Peter Laipson, who read the manuscript countless times. The following people also read the entire manuscript and commented on it: Kamal Adhikary, Beki Bishop, Karl Heider, Callee Kaiser, Laura McFarland, Melissa Schwartz, and Laura Von Harten. In addition, I owe thanks to the chair of my dissertation committee, Tom Fricke, and my other committee members, Bruce Mannheim, Sherry Ortner, and Tom Trautmann, for providing me with an excellent education and a lot of wise advice. A number of others also read various chapters or earlier incarnations of parts of this book and commented thoughtfully, including Anne Blackburn, Coralynn Davis, Lessie Jo Frazier, Michele Gamburd, Lisa Gezon, Dorothy Hodgson, Ann Kingsolver, Laura Kunreuther, Charlene Makley, Krista Van Vleet, Julia Thompson, Anne Waters, Mark Whitaker, and John Zimmerman. Members of the Linguistic Anthropology Lab at the University of Michigan and students in my Understanding Other Cultures classes at the University of South Carolina also read sections of the book. In addition, I received encouragement from members of the Agency Reading Group at the University of South Carolina, especially Marcia-Anne Dobres and Alice Kasakoff. I am also grateful for the detailed feedback provided to me by the two reviewers from the University of Michigan Press: Mary Des Chene and Stacy Pigg. The book is far better for their input, and of course I alone remain responsible for any weaknesses that remain. In the field I was fortunate to be aided by two extremely competent research assistants, Harkha Bahadur Thapa and Gun Bahadur Thapa. I also drew on the insight and skills of Devendra Shrestha and Dilli Ram Dahal, Nepali scholars who were on postdoctoral fellowships at the University of Michigan during 1993. I had help from Grant Jackson in creating the map of Nepal.

Finally, I would like to thank my parents, Fred and Eileen Ahearn, my sisters, Peggy and Kerry, and my other family members, whose love and support have sustained me throughout this project. I dedicate this book to my husband, Rick Black, whom I first met through letters, and whose warm insight and keen editorial eye shine through every page of this book.

A Note on Transliteration, Transcription, and Pronunciation

Throughout this book, a Sanskrit Roman font is used for Nepali words that appear in the text. I follow Turner ([1931] 1990), except in the following cases:

- Nasalization is indicated by a tilde over the letter, as in ã.
- The unaspirated "ch" sound is indicated by *ch*, not *c*, while the aspirated "ch" sound is indicated by *chh*.
- *s* is used for all three sibilants, as they are not distinguishably different in pronunciation to Junigau villagers.

The dialect of Nepali spoken in Junigau differs in some important phonological, lexical, and morphological respects from the dialect spoken in Kathmandu. Thus, the spelling of some words in this book, or even the grammatical construction of entire phrases, might seem unfamiliar to speakers of a more standard dialect of Nepali. For example, Junigau residents call the sitting place under a banyan tree a *chaupārī*, not a *chautārā*, and call "developed" people or ideas *bikāsī* or *bikāse*, not *bikāsit*. Similarly, villagers often use the ergative marker *le* at the end of subjects preceding a verb in the present or future tense, not just the past tense, as is common in standard Nepali.

In transcribing conversations, I generally follow the conventions prescribed by Schiffrin (1994). Latching (the lack of a pause between utterances) is indicated by an equal sign (=) at the end of one person's utterance and the start of another's. Brackets are used for implied meanings. A pause in the conversation is indicated by three dots in a row, while omitted utterances are indicated by three dots with spaces between them. Ellipses that appear in the love letters themselves are indicated by a series of six dots (......).

The pronunciation of some Nepali words can pose challenges for the native English speaker. The main vowels are pronounced roughly as follows:

a	as in *fun*
ā	as in *cot*
i	as in *peek*
ī	as in *peek* (*i* and *ī* are pronounced the same in Junigau)
u	as in *pool*
ū	as in *pool* (*u* and *ū* are pronounced the same in Junigau)
e	as in *pay*
ai	as in *guy*
o	as in *moan*
ou	as in *sew*

The consonants are pronounced approximately the same as their English counterparts, with the exception of the *t*s and *d*s, which have dental aspirated and unaspirated phonemes (represented by *th, dh, t, d*) and retroflexed aspirated and unaspirated phonemes (represented by *ṭh, ḍh, ṭ, ḍ*). These will sound alike to most native English speakers. Several other consonants come in aspirated and unaspirated phonemes; these are differentiated in this book by the presence of an *h* (as in *gh* or *bh*), which indicates that more breath should be added to the consonant.

PART ONE

Arrivals, Introductions, & Theoretical Frameworks

Invitations to Love

Sarita, I'm helpless, and I have to make friends of a notebook and pen in order to place this helplessness before you. Love is the sort of thing that anyone can feel—even a great man of the world like Hitler loved Eva, they say. And Napoleon, who with bravery conquered the "world,"[1] united it, and took it forward, was astounded when he saw one particular widow. Certainly, history's pages are colored with accounts of such individuals who love each other. In which case, Sarita, I'll let you know by a "short cut" what I want to say: Love is the union of two souls. The "main" meaning of love is "life success." I'm offering you an invitation to love.

In June 1992, Bir Bahadur,[2] a twenty-one-year-old man who at the time often sported flashy jeans, a gold chain, and a winning smile, wrote these words in his first love letter to Sarita, whose long, black hair, fashionable Punjabi outfits, and demure giggles had caught his eye. Sarita, a twenty-one-year-old woman from the Magar village of Junigau, and Bir Bahadur, who was from another Magar village in western Palpa District, were both studying at the college campus in Tansen, the district center. They had met only once very briefly two months earlier when he had sought her out to deliver a message about some books she wanted to borrow from a relative. That one brief encounter, however, was enough to prompt each of them to inquire about the other's family, personal qualities, and marriageability. Two months later, Bir Bahadur sent his "invitation to love," and when Sarita replied a complex, tumultuous courtship ensued.

Courtships such as this one involving love letters became possible for the first time in the early 1990s as a result of increasing female literacy rates in the village. Since it was still not considered appropriate for young men and women to date or spend time alone together (though many managed to do so occasionally despite close parental supervision), love letters provided them with a way to keep in touch with their sweethearts. Love letters such as Bir Bahadur's

not only kept young people in touch with one another, however; they also prolonged courtships, enabling the participants to get to know each other better.
Moreover, the mere sending and receiving of love letters marked someone as a
particular kind of person—a "developed" (*bikāsī*) as opposed to a "backward"
(*pichhyāḍī*) individual,[3] someone who was capable of creating a particular kind
of companionate marriage with a "life friend." Together, the two would try to
create a future made brighter by love and "life success."

Although Sarita and Bir Bahadur were among the first young people in
their villages to court through love letters, they were not by any means the first
to experience romantic love. Indeed, expressions of romantic love in Junigau
can be found in old folk songs, poems, and stories, not to mention in villagers'
narratives of elopements that occurred decades ago. And yet Bir Bahadur and
Sarita's courtship differed in many respects from those of their parents' generation. The few older Magars in Junigau who eloped rather than taking part in
arranged or capture marriages carried on extremely brief courtships, often
eloping the day after meeting someone at a songfest or wedding. While these
few elopements were frequently triggered by romantic love, and while romantic love sometimes developed between spouses who had had arranged or capture marriages, most Junigau courtships that took place in the 1990s differed
significantly from those that occurred in previous decades with regard to the
way romantic love was conceptualized.

Not only did courtships leading to elopements look different in the 1990s;
there were also many more of them in Junigau than there had been in earlier
time periods. The number of elopements rose steadily in the village during the
last decades of the twentieth century, whereas the number of arranged and
capture marriages declined. More and more emphasis was placed on obtaining
the woman's "consent" (*mañjur*) to the marriage. What this consent looked like
in various types of marriage; how brides, grooms, and others felt about it; and
how this consent affected villagers' notions of action and responsibility will be
explored in the chapters that follow. In the case of the love letter correspondences that will be analyzed in depth later in the book, consent becomes a key
trope as the young men attempt to persuade their sweethearts to consent to
their proposals of marriage. According to Junigau gender ideologies that remained dominant through the 1990s, men had the power to initiate actions or
make suggestions, while women could only consent or object to them. As is always the case, however, actual behavior was considerably more complex than
this simple dichotomy.

There is a common Nepali saying in Junigau: *bhāvīle lekheko, chhālāle
chhekeko*—"It is written by fate but covered by skin." This adage reflects a belief not only among the Magars who populate Junigau but also among many
other South Asian ethnic groups and castes that at birth a person's fate is writ-

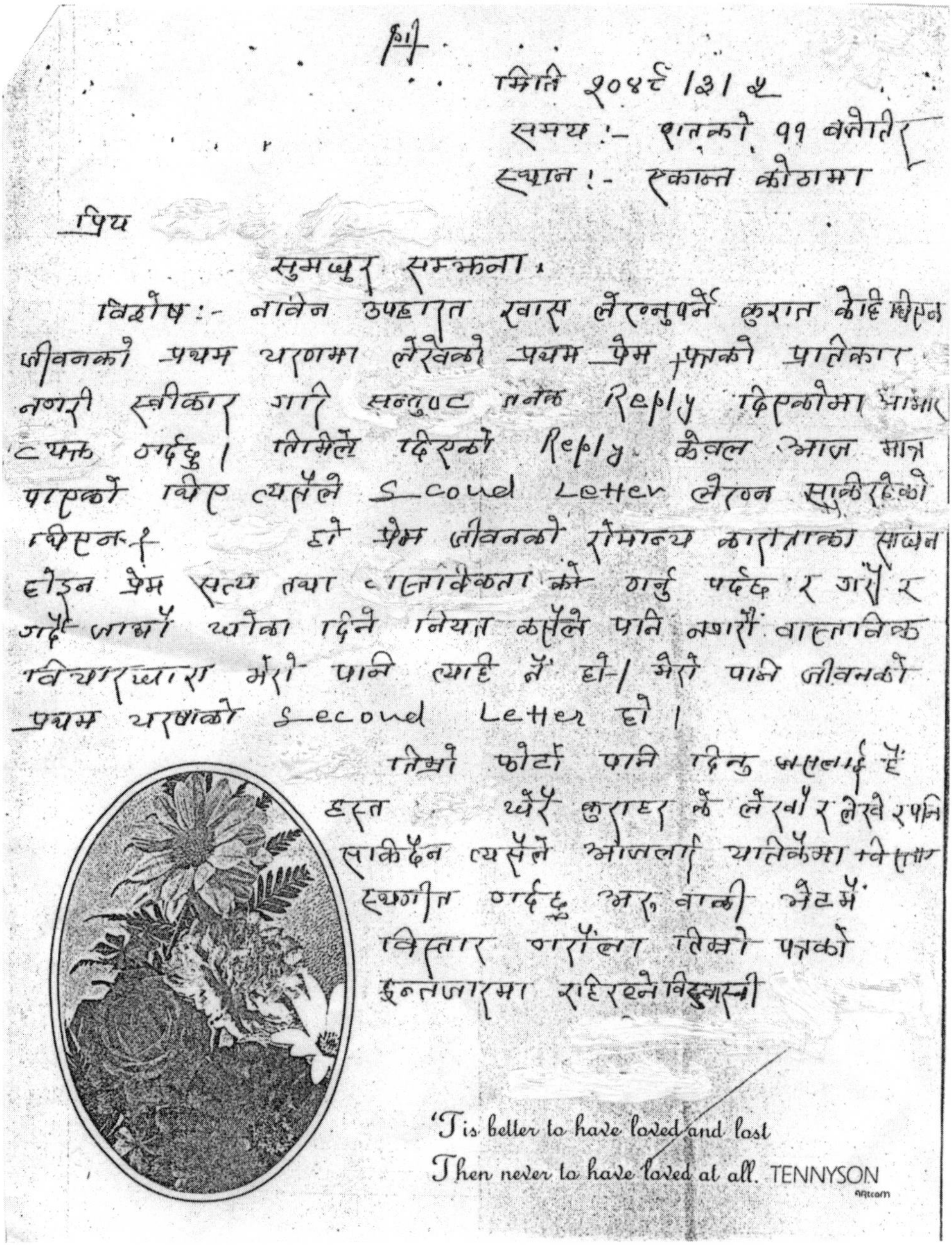

श्री

मिति २०४८ /२/८
समय :– रातको ११ बजेतिर
स्थान :– एकान्त कोठामा

प्रिय

सुमधुर सम्झना।

विशेष :– नौलेन उपहारात खास लेख्नुपर्ने कुरात केहि छैन जीवनको प्रथम चरणमा लेखेको प्रथम प्रेम पत्रको प्रतिकार नगरी स्विकार गरी सन्तुष्ट तनले Reply दिएनौमा आभार व्यक्त गर्दछु। तिमीले दिएको Reply केवल आज मात्र पाएको बिए त्यसैले Second Letter लेख्न साहिरहेको छैनन्। हे प्रेम जीवनको रोमान्य नाताताका साथन छोड्न प्रेम सत्य तथा बास्तविकता को गर्नु पर्दछ र गर्ने र जुने जाऊँ धोका दिने नियात कसैले पनि नगरौं। बास्तविक विचारधारा मेरो पनि त्यही नै हो। मैले पनि जीवनको प्रथम चरणको Second Letter हो।

तेस्रो फोटो पनि दिनु जरुलाई हुँ
हस्त   धेरै कुराहरु ले लेर्ने र नेरे रुचि साकिदैन त्यसैले आजलाई यातेकैमा ने त्याग स्वगीत गर्दछु अरु बल्ली भेटमा विस्तार गर्ला तिम्रो पत्रको इन्तजारमा रहिरहने विश्वासी

'Tis better to have loved and lost
Then never to have loved at all. TENNYSON

Plate 1   A love letter written by a Junigau man

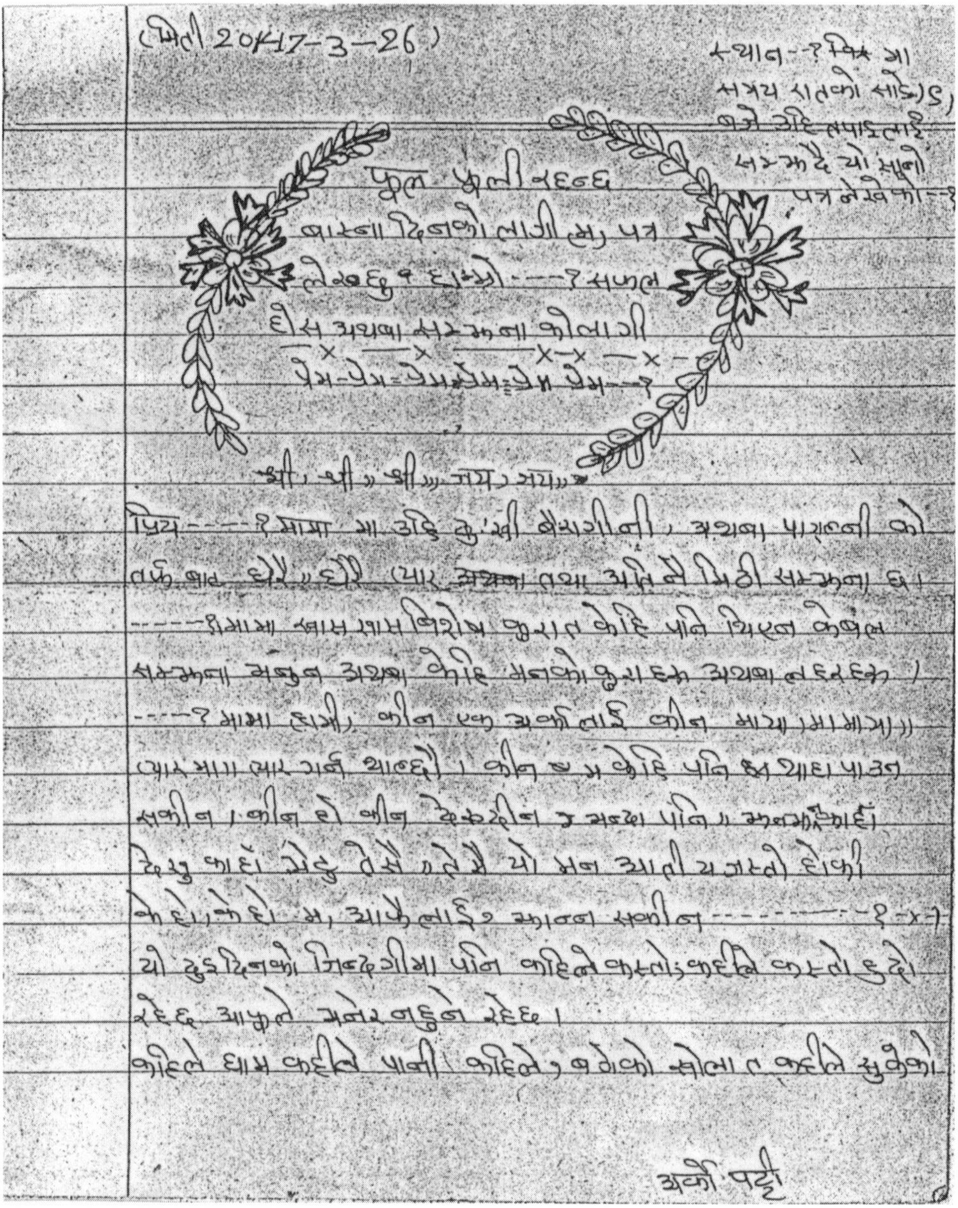
(मिति 2047-3-26)

Plate 2 A love letter written by a Junigau woman

ten underneath the skin of the forehead, making it impossible to ascertain what will happen.[4] According to this view, fate is responsible for events that befall the individual, for it is fate, or, in a different translation, God or the gods, that has the power to write. Two other common sayings in Junigau are corollaries of this: *dekheko mātrai hunna, lekheko hunu parchha*—"It is not enough just to see something; it must also be written [i.e., fated]"—and *bhaneko mātrai hunna, lekheko hunu parchha*—"It is not enough just to say something; it must also be written [i.e., fated]." Given these connections between fate and the written word, it becomes important to ask what happens when villagers in an incipiently literate community such as Junigau acquire the power to write and the power to read what others write. How do conceptions of agency, gender, fate, and development shape and reflect new literacy practices? What new "structures of feeling"[5] emerge with these practices?

In this ethnography, I investigate how villagers have applied their literacy skills to the new courtship practice of love letter writing in Junigau.[6] I discuss the implications of the emergence of love letter correspondences for social relations in Nepal and trace out the broader ramifications for conceptions of agency (which I define as the culturally constrained capacity to act), literacy, gender, love, and social change. The central argument of this ethnography is that a close examination of marriage practices and love letters in Junigau reveals the microprocesses of social transformation as it is occurring. I contend that the transition under way in Junigau involves not only a shift away from arranged and capture marriage toward elopement facilitated by love letters but also a change in how villagers conceive of their own ability to act and how they attribute responsibility for events—developments with potential ramifications that extend far beyond the realm of marriage and well past the Himalayas.

In addition to offering us valuable insights into the rapidly changing marriage practices in this one community, these love letter correspondences also provide us with a deeper understanding of the social effects of literacy. While the acquisition of literacy skills may open up new opportunities for some individuals, such skills can also impose new constraints, expectations, and disappointments. As will become apparent in the chapters that follow, the increase in female literacy rates in Junigau in the 1990s made possible the emergence of new courtship practices and facilitated self-initiated marriages, but it also reinforced certain gender ideologies and undercut some avenues to social power, especially for women. Thus, this study reminds us that literacy is not a neutral, unidimensional technology but rather a set of lived experiences that will differ from community to community.

In order to enable the reader to assess in a more informed manner the following account of these complex, ongoing social transformations occurring in Junigau, I present in detail the cultural contexts surrounding love letter writing in the village. In particular, I analyze (1) the culturally specific means by which villagers experience and express romantic love; (2) the ways in which Junigau residents themselves conceive of their own actions, how they attribute responsibility for events, and how they accord romantic love the power to enable them to achieve "life success"; and (3) how villagers' ideas about their own personhood have been changing as a result of Western-influenced development discourse, which has saturated everything in the village from school textbooks to village council meetings, radio programs, and love letters.[7] Development projects, many of which have been in existence for half a century or more in Nepal, carry with them not only new agricultural, educational, or social practices; they also disseminate new ways of speaking, thinking, being, and behaving. I leave the study of particular development programs, policies, and practices to other scholars; instead, I focus in this work on the cultural life of ideas surrounding development in one particular Nepali village in one particular time period. Talk about development is ubiquitous in Nepal. As Stacy Pigg notes, "The salience of development in Nepali national society cannot be overemphasized: the idea of development grips the social imagination at the same time its institutional forms are shaping the society itself" (1996:172). This ethnography demonstrates how this "idea of development" is taken up, changed, or challenged by Junigau residents, who thereby create what Arjun Appadurai has called "alternative, interactive modernities" (1996:65), many of which are evident in the language of the love letters as well as in the actions of the letter writers.

Overview

I have divided this ethnography into three parts. The first, "Arrivals, Introductions, and Theoretical Frameworks," consists of three chapters, including this one. In the remainder of this chapter, I describe who the Magars are as an ethnic group and provide a brief overview of some of the recent changes in Junigau social life, especially those involving gender relations and literacy. In chapter 2, "Juggling Roles: Daughter, Development Worker, and Anthropologist," I situate myself in Junigau by describing how I came to live there, how the villagers positioned me within their social world, and how over time I became disillusioned with my initial role as a development worker. The chapter concludes with a discussion of my research methods and some thoughts on the challenges of translation. In chapter 3, "Key Concepts and Their Application," I define five "keywords" that are central to the theoretical concepts of this study and explain how a "practice theory of meaning constraint" can help us narrow the range of possible interpretations that people (villagers, ethnographers, readers of ethnographies) might take away from an event. I conclude the chapter by citing three examples of "literate agency" designed to illustrate how the theoretical concepts I have introduced can be applied in an illuminating way to the ethnographic and linguistic data I present.

The second part of the book is entitled, "Transformations in Gender and Marriage" and contains chapters 4, 5, and 6. In chapter 4, "Gender and Marriage over Time in Junigau," I introduce the reader to Junigau's gender ideologies and recent trends in marriage practices in the village, drawing upon the results of a survey I conducted. In chapter 5, "Narratives of Marriage," I supplement these quantitative figures with qualitative data in the form of villagers' narratives of their arranged marriages, capture marriages, and elopements. In chapter 6, "Meeting by Way of a Letter: Shila Devi and Vajra Bahadur's Courtship," I present the first of two case studies involving love letter correspondences, this one between two Junigau residents I call Vajra Bahadur and Shila Devi. I follow them through their courtship, drawing on letters, narratives, and events at which I was present in order to provide as multidimensional a picture of their courtship as possible.

The final section, entitled "Love, Literacy, and Development," consists of the final four chapters of the book. In chapter 7, "Developing Love: Sources of Development Discourse in Nepali Love Letters," I examine what love meant to young Junigau residents in the 1990s and then analyze the textbooks, magazines, and novels that constitute some of the main sources of the development discourse found in Junigau love letters. All of these texts contain messages, both explicit and implicit, about agency, nationalism, development, and personhood that villagers are absorbing, resisting, and reconfiguring. In chapter 8, "The Practices of Reading and Writing," I place these texts in their social contexts, discussing how literacy practices in the village have changed over the years and exploring some of the settings in which reading and writing take place in Junigau and Tansen. In chapter 9, "Wearing the Flower One Likes: Sarita and Bir Bahadur's Courtship," I present the second of two case studies, picking up the story of Sarita and Bir Bahadur with which this book began and drawing on as many different kinds of linguistic and cultural data as possible in order to facilitate an understanding of their courtship. In the final chapter, "Love, Literacy, and Agency in Transition," I explore the ways in which Junigau residents are transforming their understandings of agency, causality, and personhood and suggest how these changing notions have both shaped and reflected new structures of feeling and social relations in the village, especially regarding literacy and marriage. I also argue that development is much more than a set of economic programs; it is a set of ideas about how to think and act. In the case of Junigau, development programs, and the ideas accompanying them, have not necessarily led to better lives for village residents, especially women. Finally, I emphasize the importance of examining actual literacy practices in particular societies at

Plate 3   Junigau as seen in the winter

particular historical moments in order to guard against simplistic overgeneralizations about the allegedly universal results of literacy.

Mary Louise Pratt (1986:31–32) points out that many ethnographies open with the trope of arrival, and my ethnography, in this sense at least, is no different. To begin with, then, I invite the reader to accompany me as I arrive in Junigau in December 1982 for the first time as a young, enthusiastic, and naive Peace Corps volunteer.

Arrival in Junigau

While I had not chosen Nepal for my Peace Corps service, I did choose Junigau as a post, sight unseen, because it was a village populated by Magars, a Tibeto-Burman ethnic group reputed to be friendly, easygoing, and not as strict as higher-caste groups about certain Hindu concepts such as pollution (or so the post report said). In fact, so attractive did living among Magars seem that I ended up having to flip a coin with another volunteer for the privilege of living in Junigau.

Surprised and delighted that I had won the coin toss, I set off for Junigau on foot from Tansen, the thriving bazaar and district center of Palpa District, and arrived in Junigau after what should have been an easy morning's walk but ended up being an arduous, full-day trek because I got lost. I remember feeling extreme embarrassment at my sweaty, bedraggled, pink-faced appearance when I met the headmaster of the school in which I was to teach. The headmaster and other village elders (all male) had rejoiced when they received a cable a week or two earlier notifying them that their request for a Peace Corps teacher had been granted, but all had assumed that the volunteer would be a man, not a woman. When I showed up all by myself and was evidently not only female but young and unmarried, I caused the village elders great consternation. How could they place a twenty-year-old unmarried woman alone in the house they had set aside for a male volunteer? Certainly, their responsibilities to protect me (and my reputation) precluded such an arrangement. As I learned many years later during my anthropological fieldwork, the protection of a daughter's reputation and the preservation of their virginity are duties that parents take extremely seriously in Junigau, and when I showed up in the village the elders took it upon themselves to act in loco parentis.[8]

I still have a vivid memory of sitting in the school's office by a window with a glorious view of the Himalayas. My sweat dried in the cool December air as a dozen or so men discussed my fate in a dialect of Nepali that bore little resemblance to the language I had just spent three months intensively learning. Every once in a while I would try to interject and make clear my preference for a house, or at least a room, of my own. Only later did I come to realize the logistical difficulties involved in this request. In the early 1980s, most Magar houses in Junigau consisted of one main room downstairs and sometimes an attic for storing grain upstairs. Family members cooked, worked, ate, and slept either in the main room or out on the veranda. Providing me with my own room was therefore extremely difficult. As inappropriate as the village elders considered it to place me alone in a house, however, they also realized I would need some space of my own. Eventually, the elders decided to place me in a tiny hut adjacent to the main house of a family that lived only a minute or two from the school. The location offered not only proximity to where I would be teaching but relative peace and quiet, since the family at the time consisted of a mother and father, a son, a daughter, and a new daughter-in-law. With the son away in the Nepali Army, the four members of the family who remained constituted a household considerably smaller than average in Junigau.[9]

When the headmaster and village elders took me there to show me where I would live, we arrived in the courtyard accompanied by every child in the neighborhood to find Bhauju,[10] the new, sixteen-year-old daughter-in-law of the family, busily cleaning out the debris and firewood that had been stored in the hut. I learned my first lesson about the lowly status of daughters-in-law when the assembled crowd roared in laughter after I used the honorific form of "you" (*tapaī*) to ask Bhauju her name. I later discovered that my audience considered my question humorous not only because they deemed the honorific too respectful for a woman of Bhauju's status but because asking the name of almost anyone, especially a new daughter-in-law, was unheard of in a village like Junigau, where virtually all people (including myself) were addressed using kinship terms. Over the years, Bhauju has taught me many, many other lessons and has become one of my closest friends. When I think back to how sad and shy she was as a new bride and compare that demeanor to her present one of considerable self-confidence almost twenty years later, I am also reminded of how a Nepali woman's role and status evolve over her lifetime.

On that first day, just after I arrived in the courtyard of my new home, a short, wiry woman of about fifty came over to me and began gesturing enthusiastically, grabbing my arm painfully, and speaking loudly in a dialect utterly unintelligible to me. Nowadays whenever Didi and I reminisce about our first meeting we never fail to chuckle over how crazy she seemed to me and how dumb I seemed to her on that first day. Didi also boasts (with a great deal of truth) to anyone who will listen that she was the one who taught me everything I know. At the time, however, I was not sure I wanted to live two or three years with people who not only seemed crazy but who would undoubtedly take it upon themselves to keep me company and "protect" my reputation. Fortunately, within a month I had grown close enough to the women of the family to rule out any other living arrangement, and, indeed, I have lived with the same family every time I have returned to Junigau since 1982, for a total of about six years' residence.

The Magar Village of Junigau

To reach Junigau from Kathmandu in the early 1980s, it used to be necessary to spend two days on several different buses before arriving in Tansen, the district center of Palpa District in western Nepal. By the late 1990s, however, it became possible to take a direct bus from Kathmandu to Tansen, arriving in about ten hours. From Tansen, Junigau is approximately half a day's walk, depending on the weight of one's load, the length of one's legs, and the strength of one's cardiovascular system. Quick walkers with no loads to carry can make it in under two hours, but the fastest I have ever done it is in about three hours. A tractor road to Junigau has been planned for years, but as of this writing it has yet to be completed. One therefore must arrive in Junigau on foot.

On clear days, the views from Junigau northward toward the Annapurna Range of the Himalayas are spectacular. Junigau's location a thousand or so feet above the Kali Gandaki river valley allows for even more breathtaking views—and cool breezes in the warm months. Despite the relative proximity of a river, however, village households do not have running water. Indeed, water is so scarce that it is rationed carefully, the few village taps being unlocked for only a couple of hours each day. Electricity has been sporadically available in Junigau since 1996, but the supply is barely enough to enable families to put a few light bulbs in their houses.

Partly because of the dim interiors of Junigau mud and stone homes and partly because people's daily activities often take them out to the fields, social life in Junigau takes place outdoors to a large extent—on verandas, in the sitting places (*chaupārī*) under large trees, at the water tap, or in one of the public buildings in the middle of the village. These include: several school buildings; a temple to Kali, a Hindu goddess; a building for village meetings; a health post; a youth club building; and a half dozen tea shops that sell cigarettes, matches, soap, alcohol, and sometimes tea. It is indicative of the rapid pace of social change in the village that none of these buildings existed in 1982 except for the temple and the main school building.

Comprising four of the nine wards of a Village Development Committee (formerly called a *panchāyat*),[11] Junigau is spread out along the side of a ridge at an elevation of about 4,500 feet. Although the four wards of Junigau are in some sense arbitrary political divisions, for the most part they conform to existing social divisions among the patrilines in the village. Ward boundaries are used to determine not only political representation but everything from volleyball teams to wedding guest lists. In the 1990s, Junigau had a population of approximately 1,250 people, almost all of whom were from the Tibeto-Burman ethnic group known as Magars.[12] While villagers uniformly claim that no Magars are higher or lower than any other Magars in any of the four wards, there are nonetheless important distinctions made among subclans (*thar*) as to appropriate marriage alliances. There are also differences in wealth, status, gender, and age that set Junigau residents apart from one another. As tightly knit and multiply related through kinship as the villagers are, therefore, the village is not without its internal divisions. Moreover, it is a challenge to determine the boundaries of the village, for they extend as far as its residents' marital and economic ties—that is, to distant villages in Nepal and India and to places like Hong Kong, Singapore, Korea, the Middle East, and Great Britain.

I conducted most of my research in Junigau's central ward, where the school and tea shops are located. I knew many of the ward's 320 residents from my years living and teaching there while in the Peace Corps, and it seemed advisable to make the most of these earlier contacts. I therefore came to know this ward the best, since I surveyed it twice myself and elicited narratives of marriage and love letters from its residents. Throughout my research, however, I made attempts to branch out to the other wards, attending weddings and visiting friends there. I also had Harkha Bahadur Thapa and Gun Bahadur Thapa, my Junigau research assistants, collect survey information on marriage practices from two other wards. Thus, I can say with relative certainty that the observations contained in this ethnography apply equally to all four wards of Junigau.

Magars as an Ethnic Group

The Magars of Junigau, like many other Magars in Palpa District and elsewhere in Nepal, do not speak the Magar language except for isolated words found most notably in kinship terminology. For all but some women who marry into Junigau from distant Magar-speaking villages, the first language of Junigau residents is a dialect of Nepali. Like many other peoples throughout the Indian subcontinent, the Magars of Junigau have become Hinduized, fitting themselves into the Hindu caste system about three-quarters of the way down the hierarchy, well below high-caste Brahmans and Chhetris but above untouchable castes such as tailors and blacksmiths. Junigau residents also observe most Hindu holidays and hold strong Hindu beliefs about pollution and gender relations. This process of Hinduization must have occurred long ago, for even among the oldest living villagers no one recalls Junigau residents ever having spoken anything but Nepali or having practiced any religion other than Hinduism. Nevertheless, Junigau Magars retain an identity and many cultural practices that distinguish them from their neighbors of other castes or ethnic groups. Even the ways in which they observe certain Hindu festivals, such as Tij, differ from the customs of Brahmans, Chhetris, or untouchables (cf. Ahearn 1998).

Like all subaltern groups, Magars have a complicated history and ethnic identity.[13] No one is certain exactly when Magars arrived in what is now Nepal, or even where their place of origin was, but most scholars agree that it was somewhere north of the Himalayas, probably northeast of Tibet. Numbering approximately 1.3 million in the 1991 Nepali census, Magars comprise over 7 percent of the population—a figure some Magar politicians consider an underestimate by perhaps half.[14] Magars reside all over Nepal, but their settlements are concentrated in the middle and western parts of the country. Far from homogeneous as a group, Magars have been divided by John Hitchcock into two broad subgroups, the southern and the northern Magars, representing, Hitchcock claims, two waves of migration from the north (1966:4). Although both groups call themselves Magars, the languages they speak are not mutually intelligible. Gary Shepherd conducted a linguistic survey and discovered "at least five different groups who spoke different languages, yet each claimed they were the Magars" (1982:11). Shepherd suggests that as successive waves of immigrants arrived those who settled near them might have taken on the Magar name.

Most Magars in Junigau told me they had no idea when their ancestors settled there or what their origins had been. Members of one subclan in Junigau, however, described how three of their ancestors were high-caste, sacred-thread-wearing Thakuris who gave up their high status when hunger forced them to accept food prepared by people of lower castes. The three brothers then reportedly threw their sacred threads into the holy Kali Gandaki River just below Junigau and became Magars.

Despite the uncertainty as to the origin of Magars, all scholars agree that they must have arrived centuries ago. Kamal Adhikary concludes that since Magars must have come from their place of origin by way of Tibet and since they show no traces of Buddhism in their religious activities, they most likely arrived in Nepal before Buddhism was introduced to Tibet in the seventh century C.E. (1993:11). Once Nepal had become a nation and was in the process of attempting to incorporate the many peoples within its borders under one main law, the Muluki Ain, in 1854, Magars were inserted into the Hindu caste hierarchy as "water-acceptable, non-enslavable alcohol drinkers" (Höfer 1979). This meant that higher castes could accept water but not food from them and, unlike other Tibeto-Burman groups, they could not be enslaved. Their alcohol drinking, however, relegated them to a relatively low placement in the hierarchy.

In the current political climate in Nepal, questions of ethnic origin, identity, and religion are far from academic. Magar politicians and historians such as Gore Bahadur Khapangi and M. S. Thapa claim that Magars used to be Buddhist before other groups arrived from the south and imposed their Hinduism on them (Ahearn 2001b; Thapa 1993). In a political speech in Junigau in early 1993, Khapangi urged villagers to cast off Hinduism and return to their "Buddhist roots," thereby also overturning their social, religious, and economic oppression at the hands of high-caste Brahmans and Chhetris. Although Khapangi disagrees with Adhikary's contention that Magars were most likely never Buddhist, both Khapangi's observations and my own echo Adhikary's conclusions regarding the continuation of economic hardship for most Magars: "In sum, the social structure of domination and subordination that enchained the Magars for a long time has to some extent been dismantled, but there has been very little change in their actual standard of living" (1993:39). Magars are still discriminated against and are at a disadvantage in most social and economic arenas in Nepal. These broad political, historical, religious, and economic concerns have direct relevance when one is seeking to understand the day-to-day actions of Junigau residents.

Magars as Nepali Citizens

The Magars are only one of dozens of different ethnic, linguistic, religious, and caste groups in Nepal. Although Nepal is a relatively small country of about 23 million people in a mountainous land roughly the size and shape of Tennessee, it has received a disproportionate amount of attention from anthropologists.[15] While Nepal was never formally colonized by any country, its close proximity to India (which borders Nepal on three sides) has led to a significant amount of influence from that country, both while it was a British colony and subsequently. This colonial and postcolonial influence can be seen in Junigau as men join the Indian and British Gurkha regiments, as villagers walk into Tansen, the district center, to see Hindi films, and as Indians increasingly travel up into the hills of Nepal to peddle goods.

Others have written comprehensive accounts of Nepal's history,[16] so I will only give a brief overview of those recent developments in Nepali politics and history that are most salient to this study. From the mid-1800s to the mid-1900s, Nepal was ruled by a series of prime ministers from the Rana family who made the monarchs of the time into figureheads, kept the country closed to most outsiders, and prohibited all but the most elite, high-caste families from educating their children. When the monarchy regained control from the Ranas in the 1950s, a brief period of party democracy ensued before a "partyless democracy" was instituted in which people (both men and women) voted for members of local councils (*panchāyats*). Political parties were illegal during this *panchāyat* era.

When the People's Movement of 1990 reestablished party democracy in Nepal, it marked a significant change in the way many Nepalis conceived of themselves as political and personal actors. In the case of Junigau, while no one took part in the demonstrations in 1990, the mere fact that "democracy has arrived," as radios, teachers, and magazines continuously tell them, means that villagers are beginning to think and talk about the importance of individual actions and choices. Indeed, many villagers have defined democracy to me as the ability to act according to one's own wishes (*āphno ichchā*).[17] Their conceptions of their own and others' agency—in both the political and personal realms—have begun to change, as people attribute responsibility for events more often to individuals rather than to fate. I believe it is no coincidence that elopements have skyrocketed in Junigau, as villagers are being inundated with political rhetoric and development discourse that emphasizes individual choice, "progress," and "success."

There is also an increased sense of nationalism among many Junigau residents since the 1990 revolution. While villagers have always been aware of their nationality and indeed consider their king to be an incarnation of the Hindu

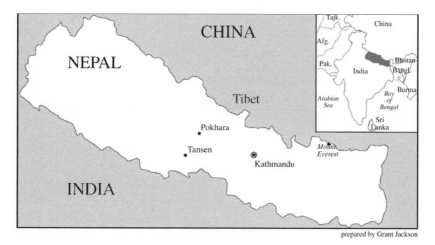

prepared by Grant Jackson

Plate 4   Map of Nepal

god Vishnu, the advent of formal schooling and the growth of various kinds of literacy practices in the village have contributed to the development of a new awareness of themselves as citizens of Nepal.

In 1996, Maoist revolutionaries initiated an armed insurrection that has spread to many districts throughout Nepal, causing the deaths of over one thousand Maoists, police officers, and government officials (Kumar 2000). In Gorkha District, newly literate women have been joining the Maoist ranks in record numbers (Machanda 1999). As of this writing, however, Junigau remains unaffected by the Maoist insurgency; indeed, most villagers are unaware of its existence. Nevertheless, the popularity of the Maoist movement among newly literate women in Gorkha District and the novel courtship practice of love letter writing in Junigau represent two fascinating examples of the unexpected consequences of female literacy.

Changes in Junigau

I observed a number of changes in Junigau from 1982 to 2000 that point to on-going, complex processes of social transformation. More and more villagers have been able to afford battery-operated radios and so have begun to listen to programs on "rural women's development," romantic songs from Hindi and Nepali movies, and serialized weekly soap operas. Even more influential are the Hindi and Nepali films themselves, which villagers view at the cinema hall in Tansen (cf. Dickey 1995). On many occasions, I have accompanied village friends and family members to see the latest film, walking as quickly as possible into the bazaar in order to be on time for a matinee, then trudging several hours to get back home before dark. Many of the plots, the details of which are secondary in the minds of most viewers to the characters' romantic songs and dances, seem to be variations on a *Romeo and Juliet* theme. In addition to being a popular surreptitious meeting place for courting couples, therefore, the cinema hall in Tansen exposes Junigau residents to images and narratives of romantic love unlike anything they have ever seen before.[18]

Another major change Junigau is undergoing is the increased monetization of its economy. All villagers engage in farming and no Magar families are landless in Junigau, but very few households are able to subsist solely on what their fields and livestock produce. As Junigau has no irrigation system and thus no rice paddies, villagers must rely on the three months of monsoon rain every year to moisten the soil enough to grow corn, millet, wheat, and vegetables. Households are joint until their size becomes unwieldy or there is intrafamilial conflict, at which point the family's land and property are divided equally among all sons. Under Nepali law, daughters cannot inherit their parents' land or property unless they remain unmarried until the age of thirty-five (Gilbert 1992:746–47). As a result of this pattern of inheritance, landholdings have grown significantly smaller over the generations, to the point that almost all families must rely on the earnings of male family members who work abroad or elsewhere in Nepal. While no Junigau residents have been in danger of starving since the famines of the 1930s, many families are nevertheless unable to make ends meet simply through the remittances sent home by sons and husbands. Most families are therefore in debt to Chhetri moneylenders from nearby villages. Paradoxically, many are at the same time owed money by their relatives. I have often seen the money brought home from abroad by male family members lent out to relatives instead of being used to repay high-interest loans from moneylenders. Social obligations in these cases outweigh the need to pay off debts.

For as long as the oldest villagers can remember, Junigau men have enlisted in foreign armies as a means of supplementing the meager living their families can extract from Junigau's dry and rocky soil. Known as "Gurkha soldiers," these men have served or are serving in the armies of Great Britain and India and in police or Gurkha Reserve units in former British colonies such as Malaysia, Hong Kong, and Brunei.[19] Foreign army service is common throughout Nepal's rural areas, especially among Tibeto-Burman groups such as the Magars, Gurungs, Rais, and Limbus. John Hitchcock's comment about a Magar community he calls Banyan Hill in the 1960s applies equally well to Junigau in the 1990s: "The most important nonlocal source of income in Banyan Hill is army service, a source that is part of a long-standing hill tradition" (1966:17).

Plate 5   Ratna Bahadur Rana, a retired Indian Army soldier

In addition to joining foreign armies, Junigau men also enlist in the Nepali Army, or, if they are unable to serve in any military capacity, they travel to India, Korea, Singapore, or the Middle East in order to find work as manual laborers. A few Junigau men have now become educated enough to work as teachers or engineers locally or elsewhere in Nepal, but most villagers consider military service to be preferable to other occupations because of the relative wealth and status that accrue to the *laure* (foreign soldier). The major drawback to foreign army service is the amount of time a man must reside abroad before becoming eligible for at least a partial pension: in both the British and the Indian military, the minimum period of service is fifteen years.[20] In nonmilitary jobs, where there is no possibility of a pension, men often remain abroad indefinitely. Every couple of years servicemen are allowed to come home to Junigau on a few months' leave, but in general most of the village's male population between the ages of eighteen and forty-five or so are simply gone.

According to the survey I conducted in 1993, among the forty-six households in Junigau's central ward, all but three had some income from male family members working outside the village. Of these three households, one was an untouchable Damai tailor family that lived for a few years in Junigau, earning money and food by sewing clothes for villagers. The family has since moved. The other two households without access to foreign remittances were headed by extremely poor, sonless widows. These two households were the poorest in Junigau—and yet their residents still had enough to eat and a house to live in. The wealthiest households were the ones that had multiple members in the Indian or British armies. (As is evident in table 1, more than one member of many Junigau households earn money nonlocally.) Since this survey was taken in 1993, several of these wealthier households have moved to Tansen or the Terai (the southern part of Nepal). Such out-migration to urban areas in search of an easier life and greater educational opportunities for children is common in Nepal and elsewhere in the world.

Whereas Junigau men in the past tended to join the Nepali Army most often, in the 1990s a greater number of villagers succeeded in enlisting in the more lucrative Indian and British armies (including the militaries and police forces of former British colonies). Furthermore, the 1990s saw many more men than in the past leaving to work outside the village, mostly in menial factory jobs in India, Korea, or the Middle East. The net result of this employment trend has been an increasingly monetized economy in Junigau in which people rely on cash to a larger extent than on land to provide them with a living. One indisputable effect of greater monetization has been a shift in power, auton-

TABLE 1.   Nonlocal Occupations of Eighty-Four Men in the Forty-Six Households of Junigau's Central Ward, 1993

	Nepali Military (current)	Indian Military (current)	British Military[a] (current)	Nepali Military Pension	Indian Military Pension	British Military Pension	Indian Non-military	Other Away
Number of households with at least one member working nonlocally								
	2	21	5	8	16	2	11	7
Total number of men working nonlocally								
	3	28	5	8	16	2	14	8

[a]Because Junigau residents are lumped together in service in the military and other security forces in Britain and its former colonies, this figure includes one man who is in the Singapore police force as well as four who serve in the British Gurkha Brigade.

omy, and status away from the older generation and toward the younger generation of Junigau men. The relevance of this shift for this ethnography is that when young men know they need not rely on their elders to inherit land in order to make a living they tend to act more freely in the choice of a marriage partner. At the very least, they expect to be consulted when their parents arrange a marriage for them.[21]

Junigau Literacies

Education is another area—and one that is particularly relevant to the subject of love letter writing—in which Junigau has experienced significant change in the past few decades. While I describe Junigau's literacy practices in much greater detail later in the book, I provide a brief overview here to introduce readers to education and literacy in Junigau. Throughout Nepal, Magars have only recently begun to acquire formal education (Adhikary 1993). Magars in Junigau and elsewhere in Nepal were usually only able to provide schooling for their sons, and, with few exceptions, daughters were simply not sent to school at all in Junigau until the late 1970s. Even then, most daughters were sent only for a year or two. As a result, literacy skills are distributed unevenly across the Junigau population according to gender and age.

The patterns of this distribution can be traced to historical shifts in political and educational policy in Nepal as a whole. Before 1951, Nepal was closed to outsiders, and very few Nepalis besides the Rana elites in Kathmandu were afforded an education (Bista 1991:118–21). There was no school in Junigau in those years, but many of the men learned how to read and write after enlisting in the military. Although these men often let their literacy skills lapse upon retirement, even the oldest retired soldiers in Junigau are able to sign their names to documents.

During the 1950s and 1960s, a national education program was instituted, and many schools were constructed throughout Nepal. It was during this era that Junigau got its first school. Like most other schools of the time (cf. Bista 1991:123–24), Junigau's Nepal Rastriya Primary School, opened in 1959, was established upon the initiative of community members. Villagers vividly remember the structure that served as the school's home for its three years of existence. Lacking walls and furniture, the Nepal Rastriya Primary School had only one teacher, a *pandit* from the only Brahman family in Junigau, who taught the assembled Magar boys basic literacy and numeracy skills using Hindu scriptures.

In 1962, Junigau's primary school was moved and renamed the Sarvodaya Primary School. It offered only three grades of schooling until 1969, when grades four and five were added. In 1980, Sarvodaya became a middle school offering grades one through eight, and in 1982 it became a full high school by adding grades nine and ten.[22] In Sarvodaya's early years, most of its high school students were Brahmans from villages up to two hours' walk away; local Junigau Magars comprised only a minority of the students in the more advanced grades.[23] In the early 1990s, however, several high schools were constructed in neighboring villages, so by 1998 most of Sarvodaya's students were Junigau Magars, and a substantial number of them, at least in the lower grades, were girls. As of 1998, Junigau girls were almost all being sent to school for at least a few years, and, although most of the students in the upper grades continued to be boys, a handful of Magar girls, including Sarita, whose courtship was briefly described at the outset of this ethnography, have graduated from high school and gone on to study at the college campus in Tansen (the district center three hours' walk from Junigau).

In Junigau, then, there is the following pattern: almost all men are literate, with those below the age of twenty usually having continued in school at least through the tenth grade. Women have significantly lower levels of formal education, and many of the older women cannot even sign their names on documents. In the early 1980s, however, informal female literacy classes began to be offered sporadically in the evenings, taught initially by another teacher and myself and then later by Junigau high school graduates (all male, with one exception). The targets of these classes were women who had married into Junigau families without having had much, if any, formal education in their natal villages. Because women found it difficult to go to a class after a hard day of work, however, and because many of their in-laws failed to see the point of allowing them to study, most women managed to attend only off and on. In fact, many attended the first few sessions of each new literacy class, only to drop out, forget their skills, and have to start from square one the next time the class was offered a few months or years later.

Gender Relations in Junigau

Accompanying the changes in literacy rates have been changes in gender ideologies and practices. Two examples are particularly illustrative to this study. First, when I arrived in Junigau in 1982, Didi informed me that I should tell her when I was menstruating and she would make sure I had "everything I needed."[24] In other words, during the four days when I would be "untouchable" (*nachune*) every month, unable to go inside the main house, touch males, or go near the temple, Didi would see to it that I was brought food to eat. I could eat it either in my hut or outside on the veranda—but not in the family's main house, where the cooking took place. When the other women in the family were menstruating, they, too, were prohibited from entering the house and had to eat and sleep outside on the porch, in the cowshed, or in my hut. After being "untouchable" for three days, we bathed on the morning of the fourth day and sprinkled *sun pānī* (water into which something gold has been dipped) over ourselves and our bedding for the sake of purification. When I returned to Junigau in 1990, however, I noticed that the family had reduced the required number of "untouchable" days from four to three, and over the course of my anthropological fieldwork during the following years the three days were reduced to two, then eliminated altogether. The reasons the women in the family gave were ones of practicality: it was difficult to spare Bhauju, the daughter-in-law, from cooking and other chores inside the house for so many days each month. Didi therefore consulted her husband and did away with the *bāḍne*[25] custom of prohibiting menstruating women from entering the house. By the end of 1993, many other households in Junigau's central ward had done the same thing, although some women expressed regret that they were unable to continue the practice. Now, when most Junigau women start menstruating each month all they do is bathe the front strands of their hair perfunctorily,[26] sprinkle themselves with *sun pānī* for purification, and refrain from taking part in religious ceremonies. No longer must they sleep outdoors or be treated as untouchable.

A second practice that is becoming less common in Junigau is a woman's daily washing of her husband's feet. In this ceremony, before a woman can eat anything in the morning she must drink the water that falls from her husband's feet and then touch her forehead to his hands and feet as a gesture of worship, respect, and obedience. One's husband is a god, several older women told me. When I first arrived in Junigau, Didi would perform this ritual on Saila Dai, her husband, every morning before she ate. Bhauju, her sixteen-year-old daughter-in-law, worshipped her own husband in this manner whenever he was home from the Indian Army. When he was off in India, she performed the ritual using *sun pānī* instead of water from his foot bath.[27] In the mid-1980s, however, Didi stopped washing Saila Dai's feet when he hit her with the stick from his hookah while he was drunk. For a while, she continued to touch her forehead to his hands and feet every morning, but in 1993 she discontinued even that sign of respect. After moving to Tansen to take care of her grandchildren, who were attending school there, Didi would occasionally resume this perfunctory worship of her husband when she was back in the village, depending on her mood and Saila Dai's level of intoxication. Still, she did not resume the complete foot-washing ceremony. As for Bhauju, during 1990–91 she lived with her

Plate 6   Daily obeisance by a daughter-in-law, Kalpana Rana, to her mother-in-law, Jiba Kumari Rana

Plate 7   Kalpana Rana ritually washes her husband's (Krishna Bahadur Rana's) feet in
the early 1980s

husband in India, and during that time she stopped washing his feet and
touching her forehead to them because, she said, it became inconvenient to
have to wait to eat in the mornings until her husband returned from his irreg-
ular hours of duty. Other Junigau women who accompanied their husbands to
India mentioned their embarrassment at having to perform the ritual as the
reason why they stopped doing so. Many of these women left off the practice
after their husbands told them not to do it anymore—it was too *jangalī* (un-
civilized, as if one lived in a jungle) and *pichhyāḍī* (backward), the men said.

As is evident from these two examples, gender relations are among the many things in Junigau that are changing, but the ongoing processes of transformation do not point unidirectionally to simplistic outcomes. Throughout this ethnography, I trace the transformations influencing—and being influenced by—Junigau's new courtship practice of love letter writing, exploring the complexities of changes that are still very much in progress.

CHAPTER TWO

Juggling Roles

Daughter, Development Worker, and Anthropologist

The longer I have worked on these love letters, the clearer it has become to me that who I was, how I got to Junigau, and what I did there had an enormous impact on the kinds of information I was able to collect and the kinds of understandings I developed. My different roles—as a daughter in a Junigau family, as a Peace Corps volunteer directly involved with the processes of development discussed throughout this book, and as a researcher who shared intimate confidences with many Junigau residents—deeply shaped my interpretations of social change in the village. It was not always easy to switch back and forth among these roles or to reconcile their sometimes conflicting obligations. For example, although I was careful to remind people frequently that I was conducting research, there were still things I learned by virtue of being a family member or a friend rather than a researcher. In these cases, I either asked later for permission to include the information in the book or omitted the information altogether.

Reflecting on my experiences and the reactions of the villagers to me has been instructive. The stories that follow help to illustrate how villagers conceive of my agency, not just their own. People were often puzzled as to why I would want to write about something as inconsequential or even foolish (*murkha*) as love letter writing, but all agreed that the many social changes, of which love letter courtships were just one example, were more than worthy of a researcher's attention. As many ethnographers are now realizing, the process of conducting fieldwork is an intersubjective one; ethnographies, therefore, must describe the researcher's relationships with the people who are the subjects of the inquiry.

It is with some hesitation, however, that I focus here on positioning myself in relation to the people about whom I write, for it seems to me that the important critiques of the absence of the ethnographer in some previous ethnographies have led to works that are not just self-reflexive but self-centered. In this chapter, and, indeed, throughout the book, I therefore seek to insert myself into the text as unobtrusively as possible and yet in a fashion that indicates to readers the ways in which this ethnography is partial in both senses of the word (Clifford 1986:7). I want to convey how the meanings that are present here emerged dialogically as I interacted with the women and men of Junigau. "Western feminist scholarship," Chandra Mohanty writes, "cannot avoid the challenge of situating itself and examining its role in such a global economic and political framework" (1991b:54).

Kinship Terms

As kinship is so central in Junigau, I will start the process of situating myself by indicating the ways in which family members and other villagers have inserted me into the extraordinarily complex web of Magar kinship relations. From the day I arrived in Junigau, no one has ever called me by my name alone, though some people have used it in conjunction with a kinship term. Many villagers, in fact, do not even know what my name is. Within the family with which I stay whenever I am in the village, the kinship terms by which I am addressed are somewhat inconsistent, testifying both to my acceptance as a family member and to a recognition of my outsider status.[1] For example, although Didi and I have a relationship that most closely resembles a mother-daughter bond, instead of calling her by the kinship term meaning "mother," I call her *didī*, which means "older sister," and she calls me *bahinī*, meaning "younger sister." Early on in my stay, Didi told me she preferred that term instead of the term for "mother" because, she said, being called "mother" by me would make her feel old (even though she has a son who is older than I am and she herself is older than my own mother). In the years since we first established our fictive kinship, however, Didi has frequently referred to me as her *ṭhulī chhorī*, her oldest daughter. Didi's husband I call *sāilā dāī* (third-eldest brother). Consistent with my daughterly status but inconsistent with the terms I use to address Didi and Saila Dai, I call their son, who is six months older than I am, *sāno dāī*, (little older brother). His wife I address as *bhāuju* (wife of older brother), and she calls me *didī*. Their two children (who were not yet born during my Peace Corps stay) call me *ninī*, the Magar term for father's younger sister. I call Didi and Saila Dai's daughter, who is ten years younger than I am, *nānī* ("little girl," which is her nickname) or *bahinī* (younger sister), while she calls me *didī*. Most of the rest of the villagers call me by the kinship term appropriate for their relationship to a daughter of Didi and Saila Dai. Because I was a teacher for the first two years I was in the village, many of my former students and their parents still call me *mis* (Miss), the term used in Nepal to address unmarried female teachers, but over the years many of these people have shifted to addressing me using one or another kinship term.

I describe the kinship terms by which I am addressed in Junigau not only to illustrate my position in the family and the village but also to emphasize the point that kinship terms have affective as well as denotative content, as Margaret Trawick (1990) and Mary Des Chene (1991) have so convincingly demonstrated for Tamils and Gurungs, respectively. As part of an organized system of kinship, these terms provide an abstract mapping of villagers' relations as well as a way of both signaling and (re-)creating affective ties. Kinship terms used to address me are not the only examples of how a system that seems rigid and impersonal in the abstract can actually allow for the expression of strong emotional ties, for in Junigau people are often related to one another in a number of different ways and may therefore choose the terms that best suit their feelings. Conversely, the mere use of particular terms is often enough to trigger behaviors or sentiments appropriate to them. This point was brought home to me when Didi encouraged a man who came by our house frequently to call me *sālī* (mother's brother's daughter), the appropriate term for him to call a daughter of hers. I, in turn, was told to call him *bhenā* (father's sister's son). In a society such as Junigau's, where there is preferential cross-cousin marriage between exactly these two kinds of cousins, simply using these terms was enough to establish a humorously flirtatious relationship between the two of us, despite the fact that he was a grandfather in his sixties. It is important to remember, therefore, that, as Trawick writes, "the selective use of kin terms is a powerful way of conveying, igniting, or engendering certain sentiments" (1990:152). This will become even more apparent when we examine how young villagers choose to address each other in their love letters.

Being Part of "Development"

Soon after I arrived in Junigau as a Peace Corps volunteer (PCV), I started to become aware of the contradictions and difficulties inherent in my position as a development worker. These contradictions and difficulties emerged even more forcefully when I helped the villagers procure a grant from the Peace Corps Partnership Program for an addition to the school. Initially naive and idealistic, I declared in a letter to my parents dated 7 May 1983 that I wanted to be "an agent for development" in the village, and, while I had some concerns about how to become such an agent, I was not yet questioning the desirability of playing such a role:

> Now, there are several issues that arise—for me, anyway—because of this ready availability of funds. First, I really want to be an agent for development in this village, but I'm not sure how best to do that. I also don't want

to be seen as the typical American with pockets stuffed full of money just ready to be thrown at the "natives." These concerns have made me conclude that the impetus for, and type of, development must come from these villagers—all of them, not necessarily just their leaders. So, I've talked to people at the place I'm most involved in: school. According to the students, teachers, and Headmaster, their needs are for: books, a place to put them, lab equipment, a room for lab equipment, a new office (bigger), and a hostel (room for students who live far away to sleep in). Not necessarily in that order. My tentative thoughts are to use Partnership funds to build a four-room annex to the school (rooms for lab, hostel, library, and office), and possibly, depending on the cost of construction and other sources of funds, also for books in Nepali and lab equipment. (They haven't got even a magnet, never mind a microscope.) The Headmaster is reading the Partnership pamphlet this weekend, and we'll discuss this again tomorrow. The application process is quite involved. It usually includes quite a bit of villager input (like student essays, letters from villagers, descriptions of daily life and how it will be changed, all translated by the PCV—also, usually pictures). I'll have to see if enthusiasm is that high.

In this excerpt, I can hear myself echoing Peace Corps rhetoric about the importance of community involvement, and while I had concerns from the start about how to make the project reflect the needs of the entire community I was still optimistic that such development projects could benefit everyone. The delays and conflicts that occurred as the project slowly moved forward disillusioned me, however. There were contradictory goals and local politics that I had only dimly perceived at the outset. The community was required to contribute at least 25 percent of the cost of the project in labor or in-kind supplies, and this burden became an onerous one that the headmaster and other village leaders had difficulty enforcing because villagers were already stretched too thin by their agricultural work, which often had to be done without the labor of sons or husbands, who were away in the military. I began to question to what degree this was "everyone's" project if the village leaders were forcing people to carry sand, rocks, and other supplies or to do other menial labor. The situation was exacerbated by poor rainfall during those years; the water that was needed to make mud and cement had to be carried from a long distance—when it was available at all. At the time, I only caught snippets of conversations complaining about the project, but I imagine that many more took place out of my earshot. The addition to the school was supposed to take six months to build; it ended up taking over two years. I had already left the village and was spending my third year in the Peace Corps conducting teacher trainings in other areas of Nepal by the time the project was finished.

One result of my involvement in the Peace Corps Partnership Project to build an addition to the school was that my relationship with some villagers was adversely affected when I came to be seen as "an agent of development." A few people, mainly male village leaders, did come to see me as an endless source of money, as I had feared, and asked me for help with numerous other personal and community projects. Other Junigau residents, when addressing me, referred to the school as "your school," and no amount of reminding them about all the labor they themselves contributed to the project could convince them that the addition to the school was the result of their actions, not mine. This left me with an enduring ambivalence toward development projects, even so-called community-initiated ones. For all that villagers were striving to become "developed" as individuals during this time period, when it came to formal development projects they attributed agency to outsiders (cf. Pigg 1992, 1996).

While my participation in development projects as a Peace Corps volunteer undoubtedly contributed to the kinds of transformations Junigau underwent in the 1980s, I was actually only a small part of much larger forces at work in Nepali society. A new school building might not have been built so quickly, if at all, had I not been posted in Junigau, but most of the changes I report in the following chapters would have occurred even if I had not been present in the village. At times, I was unaware of how my presence was being used by villagers for their own purposes, such as when village leaders used the visit of my program officer to further their plans to get the school accredited. The pervasiveness of development discourse and the prestige associated with development projects did not result merely from my presence in the village; indeed, looking back I now realize that I was sometimes a pawn in local political maneuverings.

Although my presence had little impact on the larger processes of social change under way in the village, I can point to several cases in which my presence or my actions did have a direct impact on individuals' lives. For example, when I moved in with my Nepali family in 1982 my Nepali sister, Nani, had just failed the fourth grade. Her parents were not planning to have her continue in school, but when they ended up housing the new female teacher they reconsidered and decided that it would be too embarrassing not to have their daughter in school. Nani ended up being the top student in her class for the next three years, and she went on eventually to attend college in Tansen. I often wonder whether Nani has any regrets about the way her life turned out, since her schooling seems in many ways to have complicated her life rather than simplified it. Although she sometimes seems less than content, she has never said that she would have preferred to be taken out of school.

In addition to my involvement as a teacher in the village school and as an instructor in evening female literacy classes, my presence during critical moments in Junigau residents' lives also had an impact on village attitudes and practices, such as when Sarita was trying to decide how to broach the subject of marriage with her father (described in greater detail in chapter 9). My mere presence in the village as a single, educated woman who had a career and eventually chose her own husband served as an example of other ways of being, thinking, and acting. Although I conformed to village norms in many respects (such as dress, language, and behavior) and refrained from advocating my way of life as the best way for everyone, when my village friends confided in me about their lives I reciprocated, and my own values and preferences became well known among Junigau residents. I happily wore a *lungī* (sarong) or a long skirt, never pants, in the village but more grudgingly went along with menstrual seclusion practices that made me feel paradoxically like a queen and a leper at the same time. Like many other ethnographers before me, I faced ethical dilemmas when I witnessed women being verbally abused by their husbands or saw children being disciplined in ways that made me uncomfortable. For the most part, I refrained from interfering, not wanting to impose my views on people who had been so tolerant of me, but when close friends and family members asked me what I thought I was often quite frank. From these conversations, many villagers learned about, and perhaps were influenced by, my values.

To what degree young people aspired to imitate me I do not know. From time to time, young women would tell me that they wished they could remain independent and unmarried well into their thirties as I had done. But at other times my life evoked pity among the villagers. One time in particular will remain in my memory forever. I had spent the afternoon with a close friend, hearing about the horrific ordeal of her illegal, and nearly fatal, abortion, which she had undergone when she got pregnant too soon after giving birth to her first child. She and her husband had decided that her body was just not ready for another pregnancy, and they were not ready for another child, she said. After telling me all about the pain and infection that followed the illegal abortion, she turned to me and asked whether I thought I would every marry and have children. I answered truthfully that I did not know. She started crying. I assumed that she was thinking back on her ordeal, but it soon became clear to me that she felt incredibly sorry for me. After all the pain she had experienced in her abortion and the rest of her life, she pitied *me*. Thus, although I was considered by many villagers to represent "modernity" and "development" (cf. Pigg 1996:161), I was not always considered to be an unambiguously positive role model that villagers sought to imitate.

After spending two years teaching English and math in Junigau, I spent a third year traveling around Nepal conducting teacher trainings, and it was during that year that my relationships with my Junigau family and other villagers became cemented, for during my periodic visits to the village I no longer had to spend most of the day at the school and could instead be doing whatever the other women were doing. Moreover, the fact that I returned regularly during that year caused many villagers, I think, to consider me more as a daughter home on vacation than a teacher who belonged with the outsider teachers, almost all of whom were high-caste Brahman and Chhetri men. As a result, when I returned to the village for another half-dozen visits, for a total of six years of residence between 1982 and 2000, most Junigau residents simply accepted my presence as a matter of course and were sometimes even skeptical of my allegedly work-related reasons for being there. My transition from Peace Corps volunteer to anthropologist was therefore a relatively painless one.[2]

Gender relations, in particular the frequent separation of the sexes, have had an undeniable impact on how I have positioned myself and how I was positioned by villagers as I conducted my research. Over the years, it has become increasingly evident to me that my relationships with women in Junigau are in general much stronger and more intimate than my relationships with most Junigau men. One reason for this is that in a society like Junigau's, which segregates women and men much of the time, it has seemed more "natural" for me to spend time with the women rather than the men, and this has become even more the case now that I am no longer the token female teacher at the school. Furthermore, because almost all Junigau men between the ages of twenty and forty-five are away in the military or in other jobs abroad, very few adult men are present in the village. In addition, I greatly prefer the company of almost any Junigau woman to all but a few Junigau men because I am more comfortable with the way Junigau women relate to me and am usually more interested in their topics of conversation.

One way, therefore, in which this ethnography is partial is in my close association with Junigau women and rather more distant relationship with most Junigau men. In an attempt to balance my sources of information somewhat during my fieldwork, I attended the almost all male village meetings whenever they were called and included as many men as I could in my interviews. Ironically enough, because women were the sources of most of the love letters I collected, many more of the letters I have analyzed were written by men than by women. This provided me with important insights into Junigau men's thoughts and feelings. As a supplement to these letters, several Junigau men in their late teens or early twenties were extremely helpful to me. Because these young men were my students in the early 1980s, they felt less awkward around me than did some of the senior men, who, though also eager to be of assistance, tended not to know exactly how to relate to me. My research assistants, for example, Harkha Bahadur Thapa and Gun Bahadur Thapa, both young men, are former students of mine who have become good friends.[3] While I cannot pretend to be perfectly balanced in my treatment of Junigau women and men in this ethnography,

therefore, I do try to do justice to some of the complex gender dynamics oper-
ating in the village.

Field Methods

Whenever I give a talk on the subject of Nepali love letters, one of the first
questions I am inevitably asked is, "How did you gain access to so many love
letters?" The answer attests to the importance as a research method of spending hours, weeks, months, even years "just chatting" (*gaf garnu*)—what anthropologists call participant observation. I had no idea that Junigau residents
were sending love letters to one another when I began my dissertation fieldwork on the subject of marriage practices. I had known even before I had become an anthropologist that "love marriages" were becoming more and more
popular in the village, but I did not know how most courtships were carried
out until I was "just chatting" one day with a young man and two young
women whom I knew very well. We were discussing elopements, and I asked
them how, if at all, those who eloped managed to court before marriage, since
I knew that dating was frowned upon by virtually all Junigau parents. In response to my question, the three told me for the first time about the increasingly common practice of love letter writing. We compared what might be
found in hypothetical Nepali and American love letters, discussed who generally starts a correspondence (in Nepal, the man almost always does), and ex-
amined what roles the letters play in courtships. Later on, one of the young
women asked if I would like to see a letter she had received from the man who
eventually became her husband. Not wanting to invade her privacy, I was reluctant to ask her if I could take notes on it. Before I could even do so, however, she offered me the letter to take home and copy. She was already married,
she explained; the letters were old history to her, and they could no longer ruin
her reputation if they fell into the wrong hands. Eventually, I borrowed not
only her letters but those of many other villagers and took them to Kathmandu
to photocopy before returning them to their owners. In all, I collected over 200
letters, of which roughly 170 were written by men and the rest by women.
Whenever I stop to think about it, I am overwhelmed by the generosity and
trust of my friends, who shared their intimate correspondences with me. I
hope that I have done justice to their stories.

In addition to participant observation, I employed a variety of other methods in the field. Although my emphasis was on collecting qualitative data, I also
gathered quantitative data through a census and survey. In order to understand
Junigau's love letters in terms of their relation to the social system and shifting
attitudes and behaviors, I sought both qualitative and quantitative information

about the community's history and demographics, individuals' life experiences, and the microprocesses of social and linguistic interactions. The following were the main field methods I used to obtain these different kinds of data:

1. *Participant observation.*   As mentioned, participant observation can yield enormous insights. Like many ethnographers, I find that much of what I have learned has been from the process of taking part in, and standing somewhat apart from, the life of the village. Although my first years in the village were not as an anthropologist, in some sense the participant observation on which this book is based began the day I walked into Junigau. Over the course of the six total years or so of my residence in the village from 1982 to 2000, I attended countless wedding ceremonies and related events, observed courting couples, heard stories about love letter correspondences, attended songfests and other social gatherings, and participated in family life. This book would be much poorer if the residents of Junigau had not involved me so willingly in their daily lives.

2. *Census.*   When I returned to Junigau in 1992 to begin my dissertation research, the first task I set myself, apart from attending all the weddings that were then taking place, was to conduct a census of the village's central ward. As I visited all forty-six households in this central ward, I reacquainted myself with the villagers, determining kinship relations, making a count of the ward's 320 residents, and attempting to ascertain residents' marriage types. The main benefit of the census, besides providing some basic raw data, was to teach me how not to ask about marriage. Having identified a trend away from arranged marriage toward elopement, I mistakenly assumed that these were the only two forms of marriage practiced in the village. Only halfway through conducting the census did I discover that capture marriage had been very common in the past and continued to be practiced through the early 1990s, though rarely. Needless to say, I had to start over again on the census.

3. *Survey.*   During 1993, I designed a survey to collect more thorough information on marriage types and decision-making processes, kinship relations, levels of education, occupations, details of wedding ceremonies, and courtship practices. I myself administered the survey to all 161 ever-married residents of Junigau's central ward, and my research assistants, Harkha Bahadur Thapa and Gun Bahadur Thapa, administered it in two other wards. In 1998, I updated the survey, including 33 newly married individuals in the central ward of the village. Even more valuable than the quantitative data the survey produced was the opportunity it provided me to talk at length with people I did not normally see on a daily basis. It also enabled me to select individuals for the recording of narratives of marriage.

4. *Narratives of marriage.*   In thirty-six in-depth conversations with women and men from Junigau's central ward, I attempted to elicit information

and attitudes about marriage in general as well as narratives of marriage describing individuals' own experiences. These taped conversations lasted anywhere from half an hour to three hours, and, although most were with one individual at a time, several were with married couples who spoke together of their marriages. (I also interviewed married individuals separately whenever possible.) Overall, I elicited formal, tape recorded narratives of marriage from twenty-seven women and nine men; among the narrators, some of whom had been married more than once, the following numbers of marriage types are represented: twelve arranged marriages, 9 capture marriages, and twenty elopements. I present excerpts from these narratives, and draw on many more informal stories involving love, marriage, and literacy, throughout the book.

In all but one case, the narrators gave me permission to use their names when quoting the excerpts.[4] After considerable thought, however, and many ethical debates with villagers and other anthropologists, I have decided to use pseudonyms in the text for the names of the village and its residents, and real names in the captions accompanying photographs. Although I believe that the use of village's and informants' real names in the text could provide assistance to future ethnographers of the area and also afford the subjects of the ethnography with "coevalness" (Fabian 1983) to the extent that they are portrayed as living contemporaneously with the ethnographer, I have no way of guaranteeing the subjects of this study that the knowledge they have shared with me might not one day be used by someone else to cause them distress, embarrassment, or worse. It is my hope that using pseudonyms for the village and its residents in the text will not make their voices any less audible or their stories any less credible. Throughout the narratives of marriage, I have removed only those few minor details that would definitively identify the speaker; I do not use composites of individuals, nor have I made up fictitious stories to accompany their narratives.

5. *Interviews.* During my most recent stints of fieldwork in the mid- to late 1990s, I conducted countless structured, semistructured, and unstructured interviews with Junigau residents about love, love letters, and social change. While I recorded relatively few of these interviews, I took copious notes during and/or after them. These were the discussions in which I learned the most about villagers' perceptions of social change and their part in it.

6. *Naturally occurring conversations.* Over the course of my fieldwork in Junigau, in addition to the narratives of marriage, I recorded (with the permission of the participants, of course) over thirty hours of naturally occurring conversations and twenty hours of songfests. My family members and most other villagers did not at all mind being recorded; indeed, they all loved to hear their own voices on tape, laughing uproariously no matter what they had been recorded as saying. For the most part, these conversations (and many others

Plate 8   The author interviews Pemi Sara Thapa

that I did not record) merely provide background information for the chapters that follow. Occasionally, however, I draw on excerpts from them to illustrate attitudes toward love letter correspondences, female literacy, social change, and other issues.

Conversations and events from my Peace Corps years also appear from time to time in the chapters that follow. Luckily, I did not have to rely solely on my memory of those preanthropologist days, for, although my journal was ruined during the first monsoon (never write with felt-tipped markers in a tropical climate!), my parents saved all 104 of the letters I sent home from 1982 to 1986. They also saved the two cassettes on which I had recorded my thoughts about living in the village and greetings to them from my Nepali family members. Because these letters and cassettes contained accounts of my first impression of the villagers, my experiences teaching female literacy classes, and other interactions with Junigau residents, they proved to be an invaluable resource while I was writing this book.

7. Ethnography by phone.   With the exception of the periods of time I have

Plate 9   Ghani Sara Rana listens to her own interview on tape

actually spent in Nepal, I have called my Junigau family on the first of every Nepali month since 1993. Because there are no phones in Junigau, I call either a fabric store or a granary in Tansen at a prearranged time. Didi now lives in Tansen, taking care of her grandchildren, who go to school there, so she is always there to receive the call. Frequently, other Junigau residents make the three-hour walk into Tansen on the appointed day to talk to me. One time in 1999 I was even able to reach people in Junigau itself by dialing the number of a satellite phone owned by a wealthy Brahman from a neighboring village. The battery on the phone died, however, and it also turned out that my Junigau friends and family members had to pay for that phone call, so I have since gone back to calling Tansen instead. I also exchange letters with the younger, literate residents of Junigau, but the phone calls enable me to keep in touch with older,

Plate 10   Gun Bahadur Thapa, Harkha Bahadur Thapa (my research assistants), and
Maya Thapa sit in front of a Junigau tea shop

illiterate villagers such as Didi and to have lively conversations with my
younger friends on occasion. In the 1980s, I never would have believed it possible to talk regularly to people in Nepal by phone, but now I am very grateful
for the opportunities the phone calls have given me for checking details, asking follow-up questions, and keeping up with the news. Didi and Bhauju, who
before 1993 had never spoken on the phone in their lives, now give me regular
transcontinental updates on village births, deaths, and marriages. In addition
to helping me with follow-up research questions, the phone calls are one of the
ways in which I try to act like the daughter my Nepali family members consider
me. Most Junigau daughters remain close to their natal families after they move
to their husbands' homes, and Didi often uses this analogy to remind me to
stay in touch with them. *Māyā namārnus,* she says—"Don't kill your love." I assure her that I couldn't do so even if I tried.

The Challenge of Transcription and Translation

To conclude this chapter, I would like to say a few words about how I sifted
through and analyzed field data because it is a process that is often overlooked

as a site for the construction of meaning. It is well recognized by anthropologists that researchers exercise their power when they include, exclude, and arrange materials in their ethnographies. In the case of recorded narratives and conversations, however, even before such decisions can be made the ethnographer must render oral language into written language, and if a foreign language is involved it must be translated. The transcription and translation of recorded materials presented me with choices that influenced the content, not just the form, of this ethnography. During the countless hours I have spent transcribing and translating conversations and interviews, I have come to believe that the choices I have made and some of the dilemmas I have faced should be stated explicitly here. Jane Edwards remarks, "To the degree that transcription conventions influence perceptions of the data, it seems important to consider them explicitly, and to systematically enumerate their underlying assumptions and implications for research" (1993:4).

One decision I have made involves the placement of quotation marks around statements attributed to Junigau residents. I have decided to use quotation marks only when I have the words on tape or in verbatim notes taken during the conversation or shortly thereafter because I have no desire to put words in my friends' mouths. When I do not have the exact words from a conversation or interview, I paraphrase them without using quotation marks. In all cases, I have drawn on Deborah Schiffrin's compilation of transcription conventions to transcribe conversations, narratives, and interviews (1994:422–33). I have opted not to show lengths of pauses or changes in intonation, however, since including such information might very well distract the reader from the focus of my analysis. Another omission that perhaps requires fuller explanation is my decision not to include what linguists call "backchanneling"—the often unconscious utterances, such as "mmhmm" or "uh huh" in English, that act as signals to the speaker that the listener is still listening. While transcribing conversations in Junigau, I became conscious of the much greater frequency of backchannel responses in Nepali than in English. At first I transcribed every one, but eventually I realized that to present these utterances, which were only subconsciously registered by the participants themselves, created a transcription that appeared far more disjointed than the narratives actually felt at the time. I therefore follow linguists such as John DuBois and Stephan Schuetze-Coburn (1993:246) in omitting most backchannel responses.

If transcription is challenging, translation is even more so. In fact, as the great poet and scholar A. K. Ramanujan noted, "The chief difficulty of translation is its impossibility" (1989:47). How, then, should we go about it? In his classic piece on "The Task of the Translator," Walter Benjamin warns against too slavish an emphasis on literal translation, a warning that applies especially well to Junigau love letters, which are often poetic in tone and sometimes even in form:

Fidelity in the translation of individual words can almost never fully re-produce the meaning they have in the original. For sense in its poetic sig-nificance is not limited to meaning, but derives from the connotations con-veyed by the word chosen to express it. ([1923] 1992:79)

Similarly, José Ortega y Gasset writes:

The simple fact is that the translation is not the work, but a path toward the work. If this is a poetic work, the translation is no more than an apparatus, a technical device that brings us closer to the work without ever trying to repeat or replace it. ([1937] 1992:109)

I cite these important theoretical works on translation partly to dispel the myth that perfect translation is possible and partly to deflate expectations of graceful, easily understood renderings of the villagers' words. I have attempted to retain the somewhat formal style of the Nepali in the love letters while also rendering them easy for English speakers to understand. I present here a "har-vest of voices" (Parish 1994:8), but I fear this harvest may not always be so eas-ily reaped by the reader. One difficulty in translating the Nepali spoken in Ju-nigau into written English deserves special mention. In the love letters and conversations that I include in the following chapters, subjects and objects often remain unspoken, left ambiguous or presumed to be understood. Be-cause the Junigau dialect tends not to conjugate verbs (relying on the -e or -eko endings), the elimination of subjects in particular can make meaning obscure, especially when taken out of context. When contextual information enables me to infer the intended subject, I insert it; when it does not, I have retained the ambiguity in the English translation.

An even more challenging feature of Junigau love letters is the use of el-lipses. Letter writers will often insert ellipses instead of completing their thoughts, resulting in sentences such as the following, written by Vajra Ba-hadur: "If we do meet and speak, the villagers will certainly......" Sometimes the implied meaning is clear, as in this sentence, in which Vajra Bahadur is warn-ing Shila that villagers will certainly spread rumors about them if their courtship goes on long enough for them to figure out what is going on. (He urged a speedy elopement to prevent this.) In other letters, however, I can only guess at the implied meaning. When I am fairly certain, I place the omitted phrase in brackets after the ellipses; when I am unsure, I leave the ellipses to speak for themselves.

Also difficult to render in English is the Nepali ergative particle *le*, which de-notes agency when appended to a noun or pronoun. In standard Nepali, *le* is re-quired for the past tense, but in the dialect spoken in Junigau it is often used for other tenses as well. When a person appends this particle to a pronoun such as *I* when speaking of the present or future, the effect is an emphasis on agency. I have translated such statements by italicizing the pronoun in question.

The love letters that I present in this ethnography were particularly difficult to translate because they contained a mixture of the Junigau dialect of Nepali and more formal standard written Nepali. (Interested readers can find the entire Nepali and English texts of the letters on the Internet at <http://www.press.umich .edu/webhome/ahearn/index.html>.) Writers also sometimes incorporated Hindi, Sanskrit, and English words into their letters in order to impress their sweethearts.[5] Ambiguous or totally absent pronouns or punctuation rendered meanings even more indeterminate. Take, for example, these lines from one of Bir Bahadur's letters to Sarita, transliterated from the Devanagari script with spelling and punctuation exactly as they appeared in the letter, except that instead of Devanagari script the words are transliterated here using English letters:

> *ke garne, Sarita keṭāharulāī jati kaṭhināī keṭiharulāī bhognu pardaina yahinai chāhanchhu hāmro bichhoḍ nahos. hāmī jīvanmā kunai pani samājmā basetā-pani "down" hunu naparos bhanne bhāvanamā linu nitānta āvasyek hunchha.*

One way to translate this passage is as follows:

> What to do, Sarita? Girls don't have to endure as much difficulty as boys do. This is all I want: may our separation not occur. In life, whatever society we happen to live in, may we not end up "down"; it's absolutely necessary to feel this way.

Because of the lack of punctuation, however, it could also be read like this:

> What to do, Sarita? That girls don't have to endure as much difficulty as boys do—this is all I want. May our separation not occur. in life, whatever society we happen to live in, may we not end up "down"; it's absolutely necessary to feel this way.

The completely opposite meanings in the first sentence of these two translations are striking. Does Bir Bahadur feel that girls do not have to endure as much difficulty as boys do or does he feel the reverse? From contextual clues, such as the rest of the letter, Bir Bahadur's personality, the character of his relationship with Sarita, and gender relations in general in Junigau, I believe the first translation is most likely to be closest to what Bir Bahadur intended to convey. As with all statements, however, some indeterminacy necessarily remains.

There is additional ambiguity in the last sentence of the passage. Because there is no pronoun mentioned in connection with the "down" statement, the referent could be "we," as already suggested, but Bir Bahadur could also be referring to "it," meaning the society. As for what he means by the English word *down* (written using English letters), I am not at all sure. Moreover, he has thrown in a Hindi word, *nitānta* (absolutely) that would not be familiar to most villagers. When I went through each of Bir Bahadur's letters with Sarita in order to get some assistance in translating them, it became clear that she, too, was uncertain of the meanings of many words. In the tape recorded session in which we discussed each letter, when faced with (to me) ambiguous passages such as the one just quoted, Sarita many times would shrug, giggle, and say, "Oh, that just means he loves me." Of course, on one level she was completely correct. In fact, Bir Bahadur himself might not have been sure of the meaning of some of the words he used, especially the English ones. (In one letter, he even wrote in English script, "so that no because by other letter," which remains opaque to me—and to Sarita.) Nevertheless, important meanings *were* conveyed in these letters: that he loved her, that he was someone who had mastered the prestigious skill of writing in English and Hindi, and that he was willing to commit himself to the relationship by putting everything down in writing.

For all transcriptions and translations in the chapters that follow, it is my hope that they will serve as the "path" Ortega y Gasset mentioned, bringing the reader closer to the experiences of Junigau residents. In every case, however, some degree of indeterminacy of meaning remains, for we as researchers or participants can never discern with absolute certainty what meanings might emerge from a text or a conversation. It is the job of the linguistic anthropologist to apply a *practice theory of meaning constraint* to the analysis of any discursive event in order to narrow the range of possible interpretations that participants might take away from the event. While we can almost never know what a text or a verbal interaction "really means" to someone, with careful ethnographic and linguistic analysis we should be able to rule out the least likely interpretations and settle on the meanings participants most probably took away from the interaction (Ahearn 1998).

My approach to written and oral texts derives inspiration from the work of Niko Besnier, Brian Street, and others who have explored the manifestations of various literacies in their social contexts. I consider this ethnography to be an example of what Besnier calls an "event-centered study" of literacy, which he defines in the following passage:

An event-centered approach to literacy typically focuses on one particular social setting where literacy plays a key role and investigates how the social characteristics of the context shape the nature of literacy as it is practiced in that setting. . . . In all cases, the central object of ethnographic investigation is the way in which literacy derives its meaning from the broader context in which it is practiced, and how other aspects of the situation acquiring meaning from acts of reading and writing. (1995:9)

In other words, this study does not treat Nepali love letters in isolation from the contexts in which they are composed and read, nor does it explore Nepali marriage practices without considering the significant impact literacy has had on gender relations and courtship customs in Junigau. Texts and contexts are integrally interwoven throughout this ethnography.

CHAPTER THREE

Key Concepts and Their Application

Throughout this book, I attempt to interweave theory and ethnography in mutually illuminating ways. In order to make this intermingling of data and analysis work, this chapter first introduces the main theoretical concepts that inform the rest of the book, then spells out a *practice theory of meaning constraint,* an approach to the interpretation of cultural and linguistic data. The chapter closes with three case studies of "literate agency" to show how events in Junigau can be understood more clearly by looking at them through the lens of theory. My goal here is to avoid jargon that would make the discussion inaccessible to nonspecialists, while at the same time presenting complex theoretical ideas about social practice, emotion, and cultural transformation that will both enrich the ethnographic data in subsequent chapters and interest scholars whose own research might be far afield of the Himalayas.

For my theoretical discussion, I have taken as my model Raymond Williams's 1983 classic, *Keywords: A Vocabulary of Culture and Society.* In this work, which Williams describes as "not a dictionary but a vocabulary" (26), he defines and discusses more than 130 words of particular salience in the study of culture and society. In compiling the entries and exploring the interconnections among them, Williams found that many social issues "could not really be thought through, and some of them, I believe, cannot even be focused [on] unless we are conscious of the words as elements of the problems" (16). As both a cultural and a linguistic anthropologist, I would like to draw attention in this section to the words scholars use to talk about social processes since the words themselves are implicated in the ways we conceptualize reality (Sapir [1929] 1985:162).

In the following sections, I present five key concepts: *literacy, love, gender, social change,* and *agency.* All of these terms carry traces of scholarly and everyday usages, making them at least "half someone else's," to borrow M. M. Bakhtin's felicitous phrase (1981:293). Bakhtin further reminds us that "there are no 'neutral' words and forms—words and forms that can belong to 'no one'; language has been completely taken over, shot through with intentions and accents" (ibid.). As I discuss each term, I attempt to clarify some of these intentions and accents and indicate how each is central not only to this study of the significance of love letter writing in Nepal but also to many other cultural analyses.

Literacy

Love letter writing in Junigau has become possible only because Junigau women have become literate. But what does it mean to be literate? Definitions of literacy and illiteracy are hotly contested. Often it is not at all clear what scholars mean by a "literate person" or an "illiterate society." One widely accepted definition of *illiteracy* used by the United Nations Educational, Scientific, and Cultural Organization (UNESCO) and the World Bank reads: "Adult illiteracy is defined here as the proportion of the population fifteen years and older who cannot, with understanding, read and write a short, simple statement on their everyday life" (World Bank 1996:229). So ambiguous is the definition, however, that UNESCO has changed it several times over the years. Arguments still abound over the meanings of phrases such as "with understanding," "short, simple statement," and "everyday life."

Rather than impose UNESCO's, or any other outsider's, definition of *literacy* on Junigau villagers, I instead asked them how they defined *literacy* and what meanings and values they attributed to being able to read and write. Villagers considered someone literate if he or she could sign his or her own name to a document instead of marking it with a thumb print. They further explained that there are other kinds of literacy as well—the kind one acquires as a result of formal schooling, the kind one learns in adult female literacy classes, and the kind one demonstrates in the process of reading love stories in magazines or making lists of people for feast invitations, for example. To these I would add cultural literacy, which people acquire for the most part unconsciously as they absorb and enact practices and behaviors (Bourdieu 1977). Cultural literacy skills predispose people to read situations and texts in certain ways and constrain the types of interpretations they are likely to construct. Another set of literacy skills people acquire can be considered visual literacy skills. As I learned in Junigau when Didi could not recognize herself or anyone else in the first photographs I brought back for her, interpreting photographs, pictures, or films requires practice. Not only are there many different kinds of literacy skills, but the types of literacy practices in which people engage vary over the course of their life span, with many Junigau residents repeatedly acquiring, losing, then regaining literacy skills over the years.

By exploring the specificities of the advent of literate practices in one particular place, I enter into a theoretical debate that has been taking place as to how literacy should be defined and studied.[1] On one side of the issue are scholars like Jack Goody, who was an early proponent of what Brian Street has called the "autonomous" model of literacy (Goody 1986; Goody and Watt 1963). Goody and other supporters of the autonomous model maintain that the advent of literacy in a society will cause the *same* social and psychological effects, no matter which society is being studied. These scholars "conceptualise literacy in technical terms, treating it as independent of social context, an autonomous variable whose consequences for society and cognition can be derived from its intrinsic character" (Street 1984:5). Walter Ong, another proponent of the autonomous model, asserts boldly that, "without writing, human consciousness cannot achieve its fuller potentials, cannot produce other beautiful and powerful creations. In this sense, orality needs to produce and is destined to produce writing" (1982:14–15). Ong, Goody, and others who espouse the autonomous model see a "Great Divide" separating "oral" societies from "literate" ones—a gap similar to the one turn of the century anthropologists used to claim existed between "primitive" and "civilized" societies. I find this approach to studying literacy untenable.

On the opposing side of the issue are those scholars, such as David Barton (Barton and Hall 2000; Barton and Hamilton 1998; Barton, Hamilton, and Ivanič 2000), Keith Basso ([1974] 1989), Mike Baynham (1995), Niko Besnier (1995), Jonathan Boyarin (1993), Ruth Finnegan (1988), and Brian Street (1984, 1993), who favor an "ideological" model for studying literacies. Besnier describes the goals of this approach as follows: "Rather than seeking an overarching and context-free characterization of the cognitive and social consequences of literacy, proponents of the ideological model focus on the activities, events, and ideological constructs associated with particular manifestations of literacy" (1995:5). This approach examines the specific ramifications of the advent of literacy in each society and claims that there are no universal attributes of literate societies. I fall into this latter camp and maintain that it is impossible for literacy skills to be acquired neutrally. I (and many other anthropologists) support the following remarks by Mike Baynham about the importance of studying the specificities of different literacies. Baynham writes:

> It is important to study from the linguistic base, as the analysis of texts, but we also need the further dimension of literacy as strategic, purposeful activity in social interactions. Beyond this we need to understand literacy as social practice, the way it interacts with ideologies and institutions to shape and define the possibilities and life paths of individuals. (1995:71)

Thus, in this ethnography, I attempt to explore the interconnections between text and context—between the love letters and the social environments in which they are written and read.

Love

Throughout this ethnography, I argue that love, like all other emotions, accrues meanings (note the plural here—meaning*s*) only in specific sociocultural interactions, in particular places, and at given moments in history (cf. Seidman 1991:2–3). Junigau love letters both shape and reflect changing notions of romantic love, thereby demonstrating that there is no universal, ahistorical experience of romantic love that all humans share. Context is absolutely crucial. While every human being might possess the capacity for romantic love (and Jankowiak's 1995 volume suggests that they do), emotions do not exist as fully formed feelings, identical across all cultures and time periods. Rather, emotions are constructed in and through linguistic and social interactions. They are inherently cultural and linguistic in their manifestations. Discourse is therefore central to any understanding of emotions. As Abu-Lughod and Lutz argue, "the most productive analytical approach to the cross-cultural study of emotion is to examine discourses on emotion and emotional discourses as social practices within diverse ethnographic contexts" (1990:1). Similarly, Jankowiak, a strong believer in the universality of romantic love, nevertheless notes:

> The relative frequency with which members of a community experience romantic love may very well depend upon that culture's social organization and ideological orientation. What is obviously needed are many more close, fine-tuned analyses of the phenomenon of love as it is experienced and expressed in a variety of social settings, as well as ethnographic and historical contexts. (1995:13)

In this ethnography, I attempt such a fine-tuned analysis of the phenomenon of love. What did "love" mean to the young people of Junigau, Nepal, in the 1990s? What claims did villagers make about the effects of romantic love? To answer these questions, I look not only at their love letters but also at how they discussed romantic love in their everyday conversations with friends and in formal or informal taped interviews with me.

Young people in Junigau constructed romantic love in a culturally and historically specific way in the 1990s. They came to perceive love as happening *to* them. It afflicts and torments them, they said. It catches them in a web, makes them feel like they're going crazy.[2] Yet it also empowers them, giving them a sense of agency in other realms of their lives and connecting them up with "development discourse" (cf. Escobar 1995; Grillo and Stirrat 1997; Pigg 1992, 1996) and Western, commodified notions of "success." It should not be surprising that romantic love is tied up with economic development in Nepal, for Eva Illouz has found a similar connection in the United States. "Far from being a 'haven' from the marketplace," she writes, "modern romantic love is a practice intimately complicit with the political economy of late capitalism" (1997:22). While ideologies of romantic love in Nepal, the United States, and elsewhere disavow any association with crude materialism or economic realities, postulating instead a utopian vision of true love unfettered by mundane economic necessities, such ideologies of love mask the degree to which ideas about romantic love have always both been influenced by and had an impact on the economic structures of particular societies at particular historical moments.[3]

Ideas about love are tied up not only with economic practices in any given society but also with other social institutions and everyday practices such as political movements, educational opportunities, gender ideologies, and kinship-based activities. All of these aspects of life in Junigau are therefore described in this ethnography. Many Westerners automatically associate romantic love with sexual desire and marriage, and yet these connections are neither inevitable nor necessarily desirable to many Nepalis (cf. Lindholm 1995; de Munck 1998). The culturally and historically specific ways in which Junigau villagers came to interconnect romantic love, sexual desire, and marriage in the 1990s will be the focus of the remaining chapters of this ethnography.

Finally, let me discuss the particular words Nepalis use to talk about love. First of all, *māyā*, a noun, is a catchall term for many different emotions that English speakers would call love—love for one's parents, love for a husband or wife, love for a child. It would be inappropriate to use it to say something like "I love rice and lentils," but otherwise it is similar to the English word *love* in that it can describe platonic, filial, or romantic love among human beings or sometimes supernatural beings or animals.

The usual translation of the verb *to love* in Nepali is *māyā garnu* (*māyā* meaning "love" and *garnu* meaning "to do or make"—with no sexual connotations). While sentences containing this phrase are common, it is equally possible and much more common in Junigau love letters to construct a sentence about love that uses the verb *lāgnu* instead. The difference is an interesting one, for in the first case there is grammatical agency; *garnu* is a transitive verb. With *lāgnu*, on the other hand, there is an eschewing of agency, especially in the construction that appears most commonly in the love letters, *māyā lāgyo*. The literal translation of *māyā lāgyo* is something like, "Love befell," with the understood object being "me" (*malāī*).

Other words are also used by Junigau villagers to describe feelings akin to what we would term love. Although *māyā* is by far the most common word for love in conversational Nepali (at least in the dialect spoken in Junigau), *prem* is also used, though much less commonly because it carries a more formal connotation. Prem is also a fairly common first name for both girls and boys in Junigau, as Maya is for girls.[4] *prem* shows up much more often in recent Junigau love letters than in conversations, usually in the compound *māyā-prem* or *prem-māyā*. The same is true of the Hindi word *prītī*, which, as far as I have been able to tell, occurs only in love letters and only in the compound word *māyā-prītī*.

One more word is used in Junigau to describe romantic love—and romantic love only—and that word is the English loanword *lav*.[5] It is used by many villagers in the phrases *lav merej* (love marriage) or *lav garnu* (to love romantically). The word *lav* is found very often in Junigau love letters, written in either Devanagari or Roman script. This association is part of the constellation of meanings Junigau villagers associate with love these days, meanings that link romantic love with economic development, progress, and the ability to speak English.

Gender

One of the central concerns of this ethnography is gender. By "gender," I do not mean only women. Instead, I will be looking at gender as a set of socioculturally constructed relationships, symbols, behaviors, and identities that involve men as well as women and that are crosscut by other dimensions of difference, which in the case of Junigau include age, caste, wealth, and education level. While each element is important, the particular content of, and relationships among, them will vary in any given society at any given historical moment, and this is what I will be exploring with reference to Junigau in the chapters that follow.

As feminist anthropologists have been arguing for the past quarter century, gender is not the same as sex.[6] Although biological differences may exist among people, what makes them salient in any given situation will depend on cultural norms and expectations. Sherry Ortner and Harriet Whitehead write, "What gender is, what men and women are, what sorts of relations do or should obtain between them—all of these notions do not simply reflect or elaborate upon biological 'givens,' but are largely products of social and cultural processes" (1981:1). As a result, Michelle Rosaldo notes, "Gender in all human groups must, then, be understood in political and social terms, with reference not to biological constraints but instead to local and specific forms of social relationship and, in particular, of social inequality" (1980:400).

In her now classic essay, "Gender: A Useful Category of Historical Analysis," Joan Wallach Scott presents a thoughtful definition of gender that has guided me in my analysis of social change in Junigau. Scott's definition consists of two interrelated parts and several subparts. First, she claims, "gender is a constitutive element of social relationships based on perceived differences between the sexes" (1986:42). This first aspect of gender involves four subparts: (1) culturally available symbols that evoke multiple (and often contradictory) representations, (2) normative concepts that set forth interpretations of the symbols, (3) a notion of politics and a reference to social institutions, and, (4) subjective identity (or identities) (43–44). Scott argues in the second part of her definition that gender is always "a primary field within which or by means of which power is articulated" (45). As such, an analysis that incorporates an examination of gender dynamics and relationships will reveal a great deal more about a society than simply "what women are doing."

By analyzing the intersections between gender dynamics and other social fields in Junigau, I hope to demonstrate two things: (1) the usefulness of considering other dynamics of difference and power alongside gender, and (2) the necessity of incorporating gender into analyses of social transformation. While gender alone is rarely the only social dimension that matters, it is even more rarely irrelevant.

Social Change

This ethnography is a study of social change as it is occurring. Its main contribution to social theory, therefore, is that it provides a close look at the microprocesses of a major cultural shift that is under way in one particular society. In the remarks that follow, I draw on practice theory, defined by Sherry Ortner as "a theory of the relationship between the structures of society and culture on the one hand and the nature of human action on the other" (1989:11), and show how it helps us to understand a crucial aspect of social change in Junigau: that love letter writing embodies revolutionary ideas about agency and personhood even as it reinforces some long-standing gender hierarchies and ideologies.

Because similar changes are occurring in many societies, and because all societies are continually transforming themselves, this ethnography contributes to the body of social theory concerned with questions of social reproduction and social transformation—why, in other words, things sometimes change and sometimes remain the same or why things sometimes change even as they remain the same. The central question for practice theorists, Ortner remarks, is determining how "loosely structured" actors manage at times to transform the systems that produce them (1989:14).

I ground my discussion of social change in the work of Raymond Williams, a cultural Marxist. For Williams, to understand culture one must understand hegemony, which he defines as "in the strongest sense a 'culture', but a culture which has also to be seen as the lived dominance and subordination of particular classes" (1977:110). Emphasizing the processual nature of any "lived hegemony," Williams reminds us that "it does not just passively exist as a form of dominance. It has continually to be renewed, recreated, defended, and modified. It is also continually resisted, limited, altered, challenged by pressures not all its own" (112). In other words, Williams concludes, while any lived hegemony is always by definition dominant, it is never total or exclusive (113).

Social systems—hegemonies, habitus, structures, cultures, or whatever we choose to call them—are created and re-created, reinforced, reshaped, and re-configured by the actions and words of particular individuals, groups, and institutions acting in socioculturally conditioned ways. In other words, cultures emerge dialogically in a continuous manner through the social and linguistic interactions of individuals "always already situated in a social, political, and historical moment" (Mannheim and Tedlock 1995:9). Neither structure nor practice, therefore, should be seen as analytically prior to the other. Instead, each should be seen as being embedded in the other. It is necessary, therefore, as Gloria Raheja notes, to attend carefully to praxis (another word for practice), for, "Attention to the emergent properties of praxis and discourse opens cultural and linguistic meanings to the circumstantiality of everyday life, the multiple interpretations, indeterminacies, and ambiguities therein, and the differing speech strategies of variously positioned speakers" (1994:22).

Such attention to everyday life does not merely lead to indeterminacies and ambiguities, however; it also leads to the identification of patterns. We can seek guidance in the pursuit of an understanding of cultural patterns and how they change by examining Williams's concept of "structures of feeling." According to Williams, this concept provides researchers with a way to talk about the inchoate, often unconscious stirrings that signal potential changes in the status quo. Because culture and society should be considered not as formed wholes but as forming and formative processes, and because social forms are actively lived by individuals, tension may be created when the received interpretations of social forms clash with the individuals' own personal experiences, ideas, or feelings. When such tension between the received interpretation and practical experience arises, it is often "an unease, a stress, a displacement, a latency: the moment of conscious comparison has not yet come, often not even coming" (1977:130). The tension cannot yet (if ever) be termed resistance or social transformation; rather, it is an embryonic phase, a social and material kind of thinking and feeling that is not (yet) fully articulated or explicit (131).

Williams's concept of structures of feeling perfectly describes the attitudes, experiences, and emotions surrounding the new practice of love letter writing in Junigau because he is talking about qualitative changes in the way people experience and interpret events, changes that are subtle but nonetheless strong enough to exert palpable pressures and set effective limits on experience and action (1977:132). Furthermore, the nascent changes in meanings and values that constitute structures of feeling can be discovered upon analysis to be patterned sets. Williams explains:

> We are then defining these elements as a "structure": as a set, with specific internal relations, at once interlocking and in tension. Yet we are also defining a social experience which is still *in process,* often indeed not yet recognized as social but taken to be private, idiosyncratic, and even isolating, but which in analysis (though rarely otherwise) has its emergent, connecting, and dominant characteristics, indeed its specific hierarchies. (132; emphasis in the original)

By proposing the term *structures of feeling,* Williams seeks to call to our attention a change in "meanings and values as they are actively lived and felt" by real individuals (1977:132). It is important not to misinterpret Williams's phrase, however. He explicitly states that the "feeling" in "structures of feeling" does not merely refer to emotions; rather, it encompasses changes in thoughts *and* feelings, as well as the gray area between the two. He writes, "We are talking about characteristic elements of impulse, restraint, and tone; specifically affective elements of consciousness and relationships: not feeling against thought, but thought as felt and feeling as thought: practical consciousness of a present kind, in a living and interrelating community" (132). Similarly, the "structures" in "structures of feeling" must not be taken to be rigid, preexisting social forms but as patterns in the process of being formed. As long as these cautions are noted, "structures of feeling" is a robust notion that should help to clarify the relationships between social reproduction and social transformation that exist in Junigau, thus pinpointing the location of patterned microprocesses of social change as they are occurring. In particular, the chapters that follow explore the ways in which Junigau practices and attitudes regarding love, literacy, courtship, and marriage are changing and how these practices and attitudes both influence and are influenced by other aspects of Junigau culture, which are also changing, such as concepts of individual responsibility, gender relations, economic success, and social hierarchies.

Agency

Having identified the patterned spaces in which social transformation takes place, we must now explore the contours of action, resistance, and accommodation—what social theorists call "agency."[7] Human beings are neither free agents in the Western sense of atomic individuals nor culturally determined automatons. What, then, are they? The concept many scholars are calling agency can help us answer this question, although what scholars mean by it—*the culturally constrained capacity to act*—can differ considerably from everyday usages of the word. When I did a keyword search in our university library catalog for *agency*, for example, the system returned with 24,728 matches (and that's just books, not articles). Among these were books about travel agencies, the Central Intelligence Agency, social service agencies, collection agencies, the International Atomic Energy Agency, and the European Space Agency. Few, if any, of these book use *agency* in the way scholars do. In fact, ironically enough, the commonsense notion of the term in English often connotes a *lack* of what scholars would call agency because the everyday definition of *agency* involves acting on behalf of someone else, not oneself.

All too often, anthropologists who use the term *agency* fail to specify what they mean by it. As Robert Desjarlais notes, "In general, although many contemporary anthropologies draw on a concept of human agency, they often lack a thorough understanding of the cultural underpinnings of the concept as well as any theoretical specificity on what agency is, how it comes about, and how and why it varies from place to place" (1997:202). Agency is a concept that *is itself context-dependent.* Moreover, agency is tied up with culturally and historically variable notions of personhood that can be influenced by such things as capitalism, the Industrial Revolution, and Western development endeavors. "Agency," Desjarlais concludes, "poster-child of capitalism, is a political creature through and through" (205).

The concept of agency gained currency in the late 1970s as scholars across many disciplines reacted against structuralism's failure to take into account the actions of individuals. Inspired by activists who challenged existing power structures in order to achieve racial and gender equality, some academics sought to develop new theories that would do justice to the potential effects of human action. Feminist theorists in particular analyzed the ways in which "the personal" is always political—in other words, how people's actions influence, and are influenced by, large social and political structures. In the late 1970s and early 1980s, sociologist Anthony Giddens popularized the term *agency* and, along with Pierre Bourdieu and Marshall Sahlins, focused on the ways in which human actions are dialectically related to social structure in a mutually constitutive manner, although each did so in a different way. These scholars followed earlier writers such as Berger and Luckmann (1966) in noting that human beings make society even as society makes them. As mentioned earlier, this loosely defined school of thought has been called "practice theory" by Sherry Ortner, a theorist who has herself carried forward this program of study.[8] The riddle that practice theorists seek to solve is how social reproduction becomes social transformation—and they believe agency is the key.

The field is wide open for theorists to explore and distinguish among various types of institutional and collective agency exercised by entities such as states, corporations, anthropology faculties, unions, lineages, families, or couples. Similarly, we might also be able to talk about agency at the subindividual level, thereby shedding light on things like internal dialogues and fragmented subjectivities. The level of analysis appropriate for scholars interested in agency should not automatically be considered to be the individual since such a tight focus on individual agency is likely to render invisible larger social structures such as gender, race, and class, which shape possibilities for, and types of, agency. Scholars analyzing agency must also decide whether it can act below the level of awareness. What sorts of actions are truly "agentive" (or "agentic" or "agential")? Must an act be fully, consciously intentional in order to be agentive? How could a scholar ever know one way or the other?

Note that agency in these formulations is not synonymous with free will. Rather, practice theorists recognize that actions are always already socially, culturally, and linguistically constrained. Agency is emergent in sociocultural and linguistic practices (Ahearn 2001a). Furthermore, although some scholars use *agency* as a synonym for *resistance,* it is important to note that agentive acts may also involve complicity with, accommodation to, or reinforcement of the status quo—sometimes all at the same time (Ortner 1995; cf. Rao 1998; J. C. Scott 1985, 1990). Lila Abu-Lughod attests to the complexity of the concept in her work on Bedouin women's lives, remarking on how they both embrace and resist male domination (1986, 1990, 1993). Arlene Elowe MacLeod (1992) goes even further, suggesting that actions such as the renewed practice of veiling on the part of Egyptian women be viewed as "accommodating protest," behavior that inextricably intermixes both acceptance and rejection of existing power relations. The most fruitful approach in seeking to understand such multivalent practices therefore requires transcending the resistance-accommodation dichotomy and realizing that elements of both resistance and accommodation are likely to be present in most actions. MacLeod argues persuasively that

> women, even as subordinate players, always play an active part that goes beyond the dichotomy of victimization/acceptance, a dichotomy that flattens out a complex and ambiguous agency in which women accept, accommodate, ignore, resist, or protest—sometimes all at the same time. Power relationships should be viewed as an ongoing relationship of struggle, a struggle complicated by women's own contradictory subjectivity and ambiguous purposes. (534)

Such complex power relationships and the nature of Junigau women's—and men's—conceptions about their own ambiguous agency form the core of this book. For the remainder of this ethnography, instead of attempting to measure who has "more agency" or philosophizing about what might constitute agency, I search for the theories of agency that Junigau villagers themselves espouse. I analyze Nepali marriage narratives and love letters in order to ascertain how people in Junigau interpret actions and assign responsibility for events—by blaming or crediting others, attributing the events to fate, or naming a supernatural force. Instead of attempting to locate, label, and measure agency myself, I try to discover how people in Junigau conceptualize it. Who do they believe can exercise agency? Do they view it as differentially or hierarchically distributed somehow? The chapters that follow attempt to answer these questions.

A Practice Theory of Meaning Constraint

Together, the five terms just discussed—*literacy, love, gender, social change,* and *agency*—form the core of an approach to the study of people's words and actions that I call a practice theory of meaning constraint. The question of how we know what a text like a love letter or an event like a songfest means to those involved is a central question of this ethnography. As noted in the previous chapter, and as I have argued elsewhere in reference to song lyrics,[9] it is the task of the linguistic or cultural anthropologist to identify the *constraints* on the range of interpretations that might emerge from any discursive event, regardless of whether it involves reading, writing, or speaking. We must shift our focus away from searching for definitive interpretations and instead concentrate on looking for information that constrains the type and number of meanings that might emerge from an event such as a song performance, a conversation, or an individual's reading of a love letter. We must acknowledge the inevitability of a certain degree of interpretive indeterminacy while also recognizing that indeterminacy is not limitless. To give a mathematical example, although there is an infinite number of real numbers between one and two, these numbers do not include plus three or minus four. Similarly, although people might come up with an infinite number of possible interpretations of any discursive event, by examining many different kinds of social and textual evidence the anthropologist should be able to rule out some of these interpretations and identify emergent patterns that might constitute new structures of feeling. As Umberto Eco notes, "If it is very difficult to decide whether a given interpretation is a good one, it is, however, always possible to decide whether it is a bad one" (1990:42)

A practice theory of meaning constraint thus demands a significant re-

thinking of epistemological possibilities. Instead of producing conclusive interpretations, such a theory encourages us to look closely at both texts and
contexts for those factors that limit interpretive indeterminacy. Neither textual
analysis nor ethnographic fieldwork alone can generate a sufficient understanding of potential meanings. Both text and context must be taken into con-
sideration, and they must be understood to be intrinsically interwoven. In the
case of a love letter, for example, close attention to the contents, along with
knowledge of the social contexts of its reading, personal histories, relevant cultural meanings and values, spatial configurations, the contents of similar texts,
and relationships among the readers will at best lead to a bounded range of
possible interpretations that the readers might construct. This indeterminacy
results from the fact that every interaction contains emergent qualities that are
not predictable a priori from knowledge of the text and/or its performance. In
other words, text and context influence each other reflexively, creating a potentially infinite range of possible interpretations upon which participants, audience members, and scholars may draw, both during the performance and
over time (cf. Goodwin and Duranti 1992).

I hasten to add, however, that such indeterminacy, or what Eco calls "unlimited semiosis," by no means precludes analysis. Indeed, Eco argues that "the
notion of unlimited semiosis does not lead to the conclusion that interpretation has no criteria. To say that interpretation (as the basic feature of semiosis)
is potentially unlimited does not mean that it 'riverruns' for the mere sake of
itself" (1990:6). It is therefore the job of the anthropologist to identify these interpretive criteria in particular discursive events by looking for textual, temporal, sociocultural, and spatial constraints on meaning. The main task of a practice theory of meaning constraint consists of the determination of a
constrained range of possible meanings associated with situated speech events.
My approach is therefore similar to what Arjun Appadurai has called for: a new
"theory of reception" that incorporates an understanding of intertextuality and
situatedness (1991:472). In calling my approach a practice theory rather than a
theory of reception, however, I emphasize how individuals, including scholars,
actively construct and constrain—rather than passively receive—interpretations that are both socially mediated and intertextually situated within a
bounded universe of discourse.

As discouraging as it may seem to give up on the possibility of ascertaining
definitive meanings, such a focus on constraining interpretive indeterminacy
has the advantage of directing our attention toward the multivocal nature of all
linguistic exchanges. Language *is* social practice, and when it is understood to
be fundamentally dialogic and social in nature meaning can be viewed as
emerging from particular social interactions. M. M. Bakhtin writes the following about the dialogic nature of the word:

The word, directed toward its object, enters a dialogically agitated and tension-filled environment of alien words, value judgments and accents, weaves in and out of complex relationships, merges with some, recoils from others, intersects with yet a third group: and all this may crucially shape discourse, may leave a trace in all its semantic layers, may complicate its expression and influence its entire stylistic profile. (1981:276; cf. Mannheim and Tedlock 1995).

A single utterance, a line from a love letter, or an article in a film magazine can take on a multitude of meanings depending on who speaks or reads it, when, where, how, why, and to whom. Thus, a practice theory of meaning constraint must include detailed analyses of written and spoken language as it is situated in—and inextricably part of—social interactions. Only through such detailed investigations can the complex way in which discursive forms are related to cultural meanings and social practices be understood.

Literate Agency

I turn now to three examples of "literacy events" in order to demonstrate how the five key concepts discussed in this chapter, when accompanied by a practice theory of meaning constraint, can provide a robust foundation for constructing an understanding of the processes involved in social transformation in Junigau and elsewhere.

Shirley B. Heath defines a literacy event as "any action sequence, involving one or more persons, in which the production and/or comprehension of print plays a role" (1983:386). Heath further suggests that "literacy events have social interactional rules which regulate the type and amount of talk about what is written, and define ways in which oral language reinforces, denies, extends or sets aside the written material" (ibid.). The following three literacy events, all involving letters (but not always love letters) occurred in recent years in Junigau. From these case studies, we can begin to explore how the five phrases defined in this chapter, when combined with a practice theory of meaning constraint, are important tools for understanding Junigau villagers' practices and attitudes during the 1990s.

Pema Kumari's Letter

When Pema Kumari's marriage was arranged in 1988, she was in the ninth grade, the next to last year of high school in Nepal. She and the other young women in her class, all of whom I had taught in the fifth grade, were by then the most educated females in the village. The ideas to which Pema Kumari was exposed and the literacy skills that she gained during her formal education helped her to use a culturally sanctioned space available to arranged marriage brides for expressions of ineffectual resistance in a manner that was unique in the village's history.

Pema Kumari, upon learning that she had been given away in marriage, retreated crying to the attic—the expected token resistance of the bride of a soon to be arranged marriage. Once there, however, she composed a letter to her father, threatening to have him put in jail if he made her go through with the marriage—an act unheard of in Junigau.[10] Others who were there at the time recounted to me how Pema Kumari's father cried as he read the letter aloud to the assembled guests at the prewedding feast, after which he reportedly went upstairs to the attic and pleaded with his daughter not to throw away the family's honor. According to differing versions of the story, she either agreed to drop her threat to have her father jailed for marrying her off against her will or her father proceeded without such an assurance. One woman maintains that it was her own reminders of the inauspiciousness of such actions that convinced Pema Kumari to relent. In any case, the wedding went forward on schedule.

As a teenager, then, Pema Kumari was married to her father's sister's son, who was in the Indian Army.[11] What no one told her at the time, fearing she would become even more upset, was that after his leave he was to be sent to fight in Sri Lanka. Within a year of her marriage, Pema Kumari was a widow. Recalling the scene at Pema Kumari's prewedding feast, many villagers remarked that she had brought her own bad luck upon herself by using her literacy skills to bring dishonor (*beijjat*) to her family.

After the customary six months of mourning, Pema Kumari was unwilling to remain any longer in the extremely subservient role allotted to her as a widow.[12] She moved back to her natal home and, without consulting either her parents or her in-laws, she informed the headmaster that she would be returning to school. Since that time, Pema Kumari has passed the School Leaving Certificate exam and is now enrolled in classes at the Tansen campus of Tribuvan University. She lives alone in the bazaar, supported by the generous pension provided to her by the Indian Army. Once a year, on the anniversary of her husband's death, she returns to her husband's home to perform rituals, but otherwise she has almost no contact with her in-laws and very little more with her parents. Pema Kumari is ambivalent about the prospect of ever marrying again; what she wants in order to secure her future (in addition to the pension) is a college degree and a job. Pema Kumari explicitly strives to be "independent" and "developed."

Although Pema Kumari's literacy event did not succeed in preventing her arranged marriage from taking place, through a confluence of factors she did manage to use her literacy skills in a completely novel way, one that challenged the practice of arranged marriage as no actions before ever had, thus demonstrating how cultural transformation develops. Moreover, in her narrative of marriage, which I recorded in 1993, Pema Kumari constructs herself as actively resisting the arrangement and criticizing her parents and in-laws even as she explicitly recognizes their power over her life. As Junigau girls become increasingly educated and literate, more cases like Pema Kumari's are likely to occur.

Jiri's Graffiti

Before Jiri dropped out of the eighth grade in order to help her mother with the farming and housework, she briefly exchanged letters with another student, a young man named Tek Bir. Jiri told me right before her wedding in 1995 that her responses to Tek Bir's ardent letters always discouraged romance, as she preferred that both of them devote their time and energy to their studies rather than to a love letter correspondence. Nevertheless, Tek Bir persisted, and even after he enlisted in the Indian Army he continued to send Jiri long letters full of love and promises of marriage. The only problem was that Jiri never received these letters—they were all intercepted by Tek Bir's male relatives. In Junigau, it is understood by all that any letter addressed to an unmarried woman will be opened by whoever first finds it among the pile of Junigau letters at the makeshift post office an hour and a half's walk uphill from the village. Then the letter may or may not be passed on to the intended recipient. Correspondents have developed various ways of dealing with this inconvenience. Many villagers will, if possible, have a trusted go-between (the *hulākī*, literally, "post office worker") deliver love letters. If the post office must be used, a masculine pseudonym is sometimes created for the woman or a feminine one for the man in the hope that no one will recognize the names before the woman picks up her mail.

In Jiri's case, no such prior arrangements had been made, and so Tek Bir's relatives continued to intercept his letters to her without her knowledge. As a further practical joke, they then decided to send a forged response to Tek Bir in Jiri's name. I do not know what they said in their letter, nor do I know when Tek Bir discovered it was not sent by Jiri.[13] Jiri soon found out about their actions, however, and she was livid. Marching all the way up the hill to Tek Bir's side of the village, she took some white chalky stones and used them to write all over the walls of the main perpetrator's house. What did her graffiti say? She was too shy to tell me, but others reported that she used some curse words, including *mardār*, or "dead body," an obscenity rarely spoken by women in Junigau and even more rarely written. None of this dimmed Tek Bir's ardor, though, for when he came home on leave after two years in India he had his parents negotiate with Jiri's parents an arranged marriage. Jiri had no say in the matter, as is common in Junigau arranged marriages, and she did not even find out about her imminent marriage until shortly before the betrothal ceremony, only two weeks or so before the wedding itself. Such was not the outcome Jiri had tried to create, she told me, as I kept her company during the wedding in my role as bridal attendant. She did not love Tek Bir and never had. Moreover, her graffiti on the house of one of Tek Bir's relatives almost ensured that the initial settling-in period of being a daughter-in-law up in that part of the village would be rockier than usual. Thus, just as in Pema Kumari's case, the use to which Jiri put her literacy skills seems to have benefited her very little, if at all, and indeed may have made things worse for her. Like Pema Kumari, however, Jiri used her literacy skills to attribute to a particular man the responsibility for an unwelcome act. It is hard to imagine such an event taking place in Junigau without both literacy skills and particular structure of feeling regarding human agency. That these are intertwined is not, I believe, coincidental.

Durga Kumari's Two Love Letter Correspondences

It was not the sort of wedding gift Mirgun Dev had expected: a pillowcase full of incriminating letters that his new bride, Durga Kumari, had written to another man. The three youths who delivered it were relatives of the jilted former boyfriend, and they insisted on presenting their "gift" to Mirgun Dev in person. It was the eve of the postwedding *ḍhobheṭ* feast in the summer of 1995, and the courtyard at Mirgun Dev's house was full of people preparing food and alcohol to take to Durga Kumari's parents' house for the blessing ceremony the next day. Upon looking inside the pillowcase and realizing what it contained, Mirgun Dev flew into a rage, storming up to the attic to escape the prying eyes of neighbors and family. Once there, he quickly downed two bottles of *raksī,* the rice alcohol that the women of Mirgun Dev's family had distilled to take to the feast. Thus fortified, he returned to the courtyard and searched out Durga Kumari, threatening within earshot of everyone to kick her out of his house because of her correspondence with another man prior to her marriage. Following her into the tiny room they had occupied during the two weeks since their elopement, Mirgun Dev accused her of not being a virgin when he married her and, half-crying and half-shouting, he shoved her against the wall. I was worried that the violence would escalate, but fortunately Mirgun Dev's sister and mother were able to calm him down. "This is your wife!" they reminded him. "She's yours now, no matter what happened in the past! Just forget it!" The scene ended with Mirgun Dev sobbing himself to sleep.

As shocked as Mirgun Dev appeared to be when he discovered what the pillowcase contained, he had received a hint of Durga Kumari's previous relationship from Durga Kumari herself, although he may not have realized it at the time. Mirgun Dev and Durga Kumari had had a very brief courtship consisting of an exchange of several love letters and a single meeting in person. The brevity of the courtship was atypical for the 1990s in the village of Junigau, but Mirgun Dev was under extreme pressure from his elders to find a wife during his two-month leave from the Indian Army. They were so desperate for the labor of a daughter-in-law that they were prepared to arrange a marriage for Mirgun Dev if he failed to bring home a bride himself.

Mirgun Dev had to act quickly, therefore, but his shyness put him at a disadvantage. Unlike other young men in Junigau, who had started relationships before enlisting as Gurkha soldiers in the Nepali, Indian, or British armies, Mirgun Dev had been too shy to initiate a correspondence with anyone, and so he had had to start a relationship from scratch when he arrived home on leave. Another villager's wedding feast provided him with the opportunity to meet unmarried young women, and Durga Kumari, a pretty, vivacious high school student from the other side of the village, caught his eye.[14] Emboldened by their brief conversation at the wedding feast, Mirgun Dev wrote Durga Kumari a letter. He asked one of his male relatives to act as a go-between and deliver his declaration of lifelong love to Durga Kumari.

Durga Kumari's response was heartening. She spoke of her happiness at having received Mirgun Dev's letter and hinted that his feelings of love were reciprocated. She ended the letter, however, with a stern warning to Mirgun Dev not to back out of the relationship before marriage; after all, such a breakup would carry heavy consequences for Durga Kumari's reputation. A woman who carries on a relationship with one man before marrying another—even if the relationship takes place solely in writing and not in person—risks being labeled a *rāḍī* (literally, "widow," but when used as a term of abuse it means "slut"). So Durga Kumari made the following appeal to Mirgun Dev at the end of her first letter to him:

> One thing that I hope you will promise is that you will love me truly and that when you think about the future you will continue to want to do so and won't break up with me in the middle of our relationship. Okay?
>
> I do not want to go against your happiness; your happiness alone is my happiness.
>
> If you think that loving me will bring happiness into your life, then I will certainly accept your happy words. Not just in this life but in hundreds of lifetimes will I accept and love you.
>
> Later on in the middle of our relationship you are not to do anything [i.e., break up]—understand?

I want you to love me without causing me suffering, okay?
Finally, if you love me, send a "reply" to this letter, okay?

For now farewell,
Your
Durga Kumari

Moving quickly to reassure her, Mirgun Dev responded in his next letter that his intentions were honorable. Indeed, he wanted to elope with her as soon as possible—ideally, he would bring her home to his house as his bride in the next couple of weeks. In Durga Kumari's second letter to Mirgun Dev, she states that he has completely won her over. She agrees to elope with him but tells him that they cannot elope until after she has finished her final exams. Her education is important to her, she writes, but she just as clearly declares her eternal love for Mirgun Dev in passages such as the following:

Mirgun Dev, to find a husband like you would be my good fortune. In this world thousands of people love, but many do so for "fashion" and change their love as if love were a thing to be auctioned off. But I consider my love to be like clear water, as pure, immovable, and immortal as the Himalayas.

It is in this second (and final) letter from Durga Kumari to Mirgun Dev that the incident with the pillowcase full of letters from Durga Kumari to another man is foreshadowed. Durga Kumari guesses that Mirgun Dev has been hearing rumors about her involvement in another love letter correspondence—and indeed such rumors were swirling about the village at the time, for I heard them from at least two sources. In the following passage, Durga Kumari urges Mirgun Dev to ignore such gossip:

Mirgun Dev, it seems that I have become caught up with you in a web of pure love. I don't want to give you any hopes based on lies. There are thousands of people who will speak ill of me. In this world people are prepared to do anything for selfish reasons. They don't do anything but speak ill of others. The world is like this. Villagers or your friends may speak ill of me to you, but please don't believe such talk, okay? Between us there should only be honesty in this life. There may have been many other men who wrote me letters—this is true, but I hate all of them and don't accept any of them—and never have.

I haven't loved any man because I've stayed at home respectfully living with my mother and father. But today I love you because I see that your love is boundless. And I accept your proposal.

Mirgun Dev believed Durga Kumari's assertion that she had never loved another man, and so with great happiness he went forward with the elopement, bringing Durga Kumari home to live with him and his extended family. A Brahman priest was brought in from a neighboring village to conduct a short Hindu wedding ceremony, and all of Mirgun Dev's relatives welcomed their new daughter- or sister-in-law.

It was two weeks later, just before the newlyweds were to return to Durga Kumari's parents' home for the first time since the elopement for the *dhobhet* blessing ceremony, that Mirgun Dev received the pillowcase full of letters in which Durga Kumari declared her love for another man. After his rage was spent, Mirgun Dev reluctantly went forward with the ceremony, and gradually the relationship between the spouses regained its warmth. By the time Mirgun Dev had to return to the Indian Army, they had put the incident behind them.

Six months or so later, after Mirgun Dev had returned to India, Durga Kumari found herself miserable in her marital home. The stigma of her previous love letter correspondence had not disappeared, and she felt mistreated by her husband's relatives, especially his mother. She had not been allowed to continue her schooling, as she had been promised, and she was being given all the most arduous tasks in the fields and the house. Once again she resorted to letter writing, this time to complain to Mirgun Dev about her treatment and to urge him to return home and intervene on her behalf with his mother. Such letters from newly married women to their distant husbands are becoming more common in Junigau. In several recent cases among villagers, including Mirgun Dev's and Durga Kumari's, the men have indeed come home and have taken their wives' sides in the disputes. Life improved for Durga Kumari after that, but Mirgun Dev's mother felt betrayed when her son accused her of mistreating his wife. Such an act represented further proof, she claimed (as if any were needed!), that the *chhucho jovāna,* a selfish, mean, or backbiting time period, had arrived.[15] For Durga Kumari and other new daughters-in-law, however, their use of their literacy skills in this manner gives them an advantage over their mothers-in-law, who are members of a generation of females who were rarely taught to read or write. Still, certain engendered notions, such as the importance of a bride's virginity and the assumption that men are more capable than women of taking effective action, persist even as literacy practices surrounding love and marriage change in Junigau.

In the following chapter, the ongoing shift in gender relations, courtship practices, and types of marriage will further illuminate the themes introduced in the preceding pages.

PART TWO

Transformations in Gender & Marriage

CHAPTER FOUR

Gender and Marriage over Time in Junigau

Junigau Gender Roles in Transition

When a boy is born in Junigau, villagers rejoice, firing off shotguns and hosting feasts to celebrate. A girl's birth, on the other hand, is usually greeted with silence and resignation. As stark as this contrast is, however, it elucidates only part of the gendered life trajectories of Junigau residents, for, although girls and women are socially devalued in some of their roles, particularly as daughters-in-law, they are beloved as daughters and sisters. Ortner's remarks on the status of Polynesian women hold true for Junigau:

> Thus most of the negative ideology concerning women centers upon their sexual and reproductive activities as lovers, wives, and mothers; kinswomen, who are neither sexual nor reproductive from the point of view of their kinsmen, escape the problematic associations of such activities and functions. (1981:395)

Lynn Bennett (1983) identifies the same tensions in the roles of the high-caste Nepali women she studies. Indeed, although she writes of Brahman and Chhetri women, much of her discussion describes equally well the dominant gender ideologies of Junigau. According to Bennett, the strain of Hindu thought that advocates purity and asceticism for men clashes with the part of Hinduism in which men seek salvation through marriage and the production of offspring, especially sons, who light their parents' funeral pyres and so ensure their safe passage to their next lives (126). Sons also usually remain in their parents' homes, whereas daughters move into their husbands' homes. It is therefore almost always one or more sons (and/or their wives), not daughters, who take care of elderly parents.

Besides this "ideology of the patriline," an ideology that emphasizes the importance of having sons, there is another set of attitudes and practices germane to gender both in Junigau and in Narikot, the village where Bennett conducted her fieldwork. Bennett calls this set of attitudes and practices the "filiafocal" model, in contrast to the just described "patrifocal" model, because it sanctifies virginal daughters (1983:142–44). Although these two models generate contradictory valuations and tensions in everyday interactions, they are also integrally connected. It is the sacredness of virginal daughters that makes them valuable "gifts" in *kanyādān* (gift of a virgin) arranged marriages.[1] Thus, in Junigau at arranged marriage ceremonies all of a woman's natal relatives, with the exception of females junior to her, wash her feet in deference to her higher ritual status (145). Once the Brahman priest has completed the marriage ceremony, however, the bride's status undergoes an abrupt reversal, both literally, when she is moved from the groom's right to his left, and figuratively, in terms of the application of red powder to the (symbolically vaginal) part of her hair as a ritual defloration (83–87). Even in capture marriages and elopements in Junigau, the red powder marks the irrevocable loss of virginity. Before the groom applies it, the woman is a virgin, confident that she can rely on the warmth and protection of her natal home; afterward, however, she "belongs" to her husband's family. In Junigau, therefore, a woman's life is sharply divided between her premarital years in her natal home (*māita*) and her postmarital residence in her husband's home (*ghar*) (cf. Raheja 1994:27–29). Ananda Kumari, a woman who eloped in the early 1990s, characterizes the distinction as follows:

As long as a woman stays with her mother and father, they'll look after her. But after going to someone else's home, how much suffering there is! Right? She has to do whatever is left to do. She has to eat whatever is left to eat. She has to wear whatever is left to wear. She has to go places she's never gone to before. How much suffering there is, oh, after becoming a daughter-in-law! There will be suffering. Until a woman gets married, whatever she does is easy, right?

Junigau residents—women and men alike—stress that, no matter what kind of wedding a woman has, once she is married and living with her husband's family her fate will be the same as that of all other daughters-in-law.[2] Moreover, she should consider her husband a god, according to the dominant gender ideology, washing his feet and drinking the water off them every morning, praying that she might die before he does, and addressing him with an honorific form of *you* (*tapaĩ*) while she herself is addressed by her husband using the most demeaning form of *you* (*tā*).

On the ground, however, in everyday interactions between women and men in Junigau, what occurs is far more complex than the dominant discourse would lead one to believe. For one thing, a woman's position in her marital family improves as she moves up in the hierarchy among women in the household, reaching its pinnacle when the woman becomes a mother-in-law herself after her sons marry. These different roles and positions in the hierarchy are expressed in many ways, verbally and nonverbally, in Junigau. In the introduction to the volume she edited with Ann Grodzins Gold on women's speech genres in North India, Gloria Goodwin Raheja recognizes this multivocality of women's lives: "There is no single South Asian female voice, no single female consciousness, that unequivocally rejects or accepts prevailing North Indian ideologies of gender and kinship" (Raheja 1994:29).

So, for example, during the festival of Tij, Junigau women sing songs about their lives that intertwine acceptance and resistance, complaint and complicity.[3] Furthermore, daily interactions between women and men display far more fluidity and flexibility than the rigidity of the dominant discourses on gender would suggest. Thus, after many years of marriage a Junigau woman may no longer address her husband with the honorific form of *you* and may stop washing his feet in the morning. I agree with Raheja, therefore, that, "Far from speaking only in a language dominated by males, the women we have come to know imaginatively scrutinize and critique the social world they experience" (1994:26). Nevertheless, I would caution against taking too romanticized a view regarding the potential for substantial, rapid transformations of gender relations in Junigau and elsewhere in South Asia. While it is true that spaces set aside for ineffectual resistance can sometimes be converted by women into avenues for effecting significant change, evidence from Junigau, at least, indicates that hegemonic discourses regarding gender remain quite influential, even as practices are changing dramatically. As some new structures of feeling in the village emerge, causing villagers to reconceptualize gender and agency, other ideologies endure, continuing to reinforce how Junigau residents think about gender roles and the hierarchical relationship between husbands and wives.

In addition to symbolic and ideological constructions of gender that place women in inferior positions in Junigau, economic practices achieve the same results, though perhaps with even greater efficacy. According to Nepali law, women may not inherit their fathers' property unless they remain unmarried until the age of thirty-five (Gilbert 1992:746–77), and even then most women choose not to split their shares from those of their brothers. In Junigau, the only women who own property are widows, and even they are viewed as holding the property in trust for their eventual male heirs. In a village that relies on land and men's army remittances for subsistence, women, who are barred from owning property and cannot join the military, must rely on men to support them financially.

This depiction is a bit one-sided, however, as there are some women in Junigau who enjoy considerable economic independence. When men in the village leave to serve in the military, women are left behind to run the households. Older women in particular often control decisions about household resources in the absence of the household's males, and even once the men return home on pension their wives and mothers frequently exert substantial influence in economic matters. In addition, although most Junigau women (indeed, most villagers in general) have no way to earn money while living in the village, a few women have recently acquired special skills that have enabled them to leave Junigau and gain employment elsewhere in Nepal as, for example, a primary school teacher or a worker in a textile factory. These cases are very rare, however.

Changing gender ideologies in Junigau have affected not only attitudes toward, and options for, women; new structures of feeling are also emerging concerning appropriate forms of masculinity. What it meant to be a man in Junigau in the 1980s and 1990s differed sometimes subtly and sometimes substantially from earlier conceptions of suitable behavior for men. In previous generations, when high school degrees were unnecessary for enlisting in the British, Indian, or Nepali armies, the few young men in Junigau who continued in school were often ridiculed as being less manly than those who dropped out and joined the military as soon as they were old enough.[4] Notions of caste and ethnicity merged with gender here as well, for such studious boys were likened to high-caste Brahman and Chhetri boys, who, despite their higher ritual (and often economic) status, were seen as weaklings who, unlike "real" Magar men, would not or could not fight. In contrast, Magar men in generations past took pride in their reputation as brave soldiers. When in the 1980s first the British and then the Indian Army began requiring recruits to finish high school before enlisting, attitudes regarding masculinity, ethnicity, and education shifted. While it is still very unusual for Junigau men not to join the military, the few young men in recent years who have chosen to pursue other professions after finishing high school are much less stigmatized than they would have been in the past, when nonsoldiers were derisively labeled ḍhākare—those who spent all day carrying loads in their baskets, or ḍhākar.

Villagers' expectations for the kinds of relationships they will have with their spouses after marriage are also changing. While most, if not all, husbands and wives in the village still refer to each other using asymmetric forms of *you* and demonstrate other outward signs of inequality, throughout the 1990s, as elopements rose, young villagers of both sexes expressed a desire to find a "life friend" who would enable them to have a companionate marriage. As will be seen in the narratives of marriage excerpted in the following chapter, a common theme echoed by both women and men nowadays is that women should *consent* to their marriages. The extent to which consent is intermingled with coercion in all types of marriage will be explored further.

Plate 11   Jiba Kumari Rana carrying a load of firewood and fodder

Plate 12   Shiva Kumari Lamtari cooking rice

Sexuality in Junigau

Sex is not a frequent topic of explicit conversation in Junigau. The situation Bennett describes for high-caste women in Narikot resembles Junigau women's attitudes toward sex:

> Most women professed that they themselves did not really enjoy sex, and they were, I noticed, uncomfortable talking seriously about their own physical and emotional responses. On the other hand, there was a great deal of vigorous sexual joking carried on among the women—sometimes even

within earshot of the men. . . . However, though some women did confess to having enjoyed sex when they were "young and healthy," and all seemed to enjoy joking about it, my impression was that even those women who did have good sexual relationships felt it somehow improper to admit their own sexual pleasure. (Bennett 1983:176–77)

While double entendres are common in everyday conversations, only my closest female friends spoke openly with me about their sexual practices. Partly this was because I was unmarried for most of my fieldwork, and an outsider, but even the women who were my closest friends did not discuss the subject seriously without embarrassment—with one another or with me. Nevertheless, there are many occasions, both informal and ritually defined, such as the *jyutī* songfests I describe elsewhere (Ahearn 1998), when sexual joking occurs, either among women or between women and men. And over the years, especially once I returned as a married woman, I gained enough knowledge about sexual practices in Junigau to provide an overview of changing sexual practices and attitudes toward sex in the village.[5]

Premarital sex is relatively uncommon in Junigau, despite high-caste stereotypes that portray Magars and other Tibeto-Burman groups as sexually promiscuous. I know of only one case of premarital pregnancy in Junigau (that of Rita Sara, whose story will be told later), and that occurred many years ago. Of course, this could mean that people are successful in hiding their affairs and/or successful in preventing premarital pregnancies, but opportunities for people of the opposite sex to be alone together in the village are extremely rare and birth control has only recently become available.[6] For young villagers who are studying at, and often living near, the college campus in the Tansen (such as Sarita and Bir Bahadur, who were mentioned in the first chapter and whose courtship will be the subject of chapter 9), however, such opportunities to meet unchaperoned are becoming more common.

Extramarital affairs are equally rare in Junigau, though these were rumored to be slightly more prevalent than premarital affairs. Some rumors were particularly scandalous, such as when a father-in-law was reportedly sleeping with one of his daughters-in-law or when one of the schoolteachers was supposedly having an affair with his landlady. The lack of privacy in the village made it extremely difficult, however, for anyone to do anything without everyone else knowing about it. Moreover, any woman caught in the act of cheating on her husband would be unceremoniously kicked out of her marital home. This occurred in one case that I heard about, in which the wife had an affair while her husband was away in the Indian army. When the family learned of the affair, without even notifying their son they forcibly removed their daughter-in-law from their house and deposited her at the home of the man with whom she was having an affair. Luckily for her, that family took her in. If they had not done so, she probably would have had to resort to menial labor or even prostitution in Tansen, for her natal family most likely would not have taken her back. Women from other villages to whom this occurred were reported to have committed suicide rather than live with the shame of their situation.[7]

Many Junigau women, especially the older ones, have told me that they do not enjoy sex with their husbands at all, some saying that they go to great lengths to avoid having to sleep with them. One woman, Lomi Kumari, successfully avoided having sex with her husband for three years after their marriage because he was often away in the Nepali army and during his infrequent home leaves she hid in the cowshed or out in the fields until he fell asleep. Many older women also report having stopped having sex with their husbands once the women's childbearing years were over, relieved to be free of this "duty." Love marriages have largely changed women's aversion to sex, although several young women who had eloped told me that they had viewed their first nights alone with their husbands with extreme trepidation. According to childbirth statistics and narratives I have been collecting for a new research project, Junigau couples who eloped in the 1980s and 1990s started sleeping together almost immediately after getting married, which often resulted in the birth of a child within a year or two of marriage. This contrasts to the much later dates for the birth of a first child for Junigau couples who married in earlier periods. In the old days, even when the woman did not go to the extremes that Lomi Kumari did to avoid having sex with her husband, the husband himself was commonly extremely shy and the two were often as young as twelve or thirteen.

Sex between spouses, which usually occurs in the presence of other sleeping family members, is often perfunctory and lacking in foreplay, Junigau women told me. One woman laughed uncontrollably when I asked what she considered ignorant questions about sexual practices; of course, the man is always on top, she explained, and as to whether people take off their clothes— why ever would they? (Most women wear no underpants, sleeping in a petticoat, *lungī* (sarong), and blouse, whereas men usually wear shorts and an undershirt to bed.) The lack of foreplay seems to be changing somewhat, as young villagers report learning about kissing (a practice many villagers find repulsive) from Hindi films and a few couples have set up their own residences apart from the man's extended family, thereby gaining more privacy. Younger women are still reluctant to admit that they enjoy sex, but that is not surprising in a society that considers such admissions to be extremely immodest. I have even heard a young man whose arranged marriage was imminent express a similar disinterest in sex. When he was teased that he would soon have a wife to have sex with, he replied that he had no interest in engaging in such activities with her. This answer was viewed by villagers as indicative of his unhappiness at having to get married when his parents demanded that he do so and of his desire to be seen as "proper."

One time I was asking Didi and Bhauju some questions about sex, one of which was whether it hurt the women the first time she had intercourse. No, both assured me, it did not hurt unless the woman was really young, which did not happen any more now that child marriage had been discontinued. It could also hurt, Didi added, if the woman was really old the first time she had sex— and then she looked at me, still unmarried in my thirties, and hastened to add that even then it probably didn't hurt *that* much.

When I returned to Junigau for the first time as a married woman in 1998, my close female friends teased me about my husband, and one older woman took my earlier questioning of her about her sex life as permission to question me explicitly about mine. "Remember how you asked me what it was like?" she said. "Well, now you know, right? So, is it as I said?" And she reminded me of the saying she said she had found to be true: *"naso pasyo, māyā basyo"* ('the vein/hose [i.e., penis] entered, and love followed'). (In other words, a woman would come to love her husband after having sex with him.) So, she asked— did I now agree with the saying? Did I find that I loved my husband after having sex with him? I responded diplomatically, if somewhat evasively, that I loved him very much.

Trends in Junigau Marriage Practices

What kinds of marriage took place in Junigau in the past? How did marriage practices change during the 1990s? In this section, I present survey results as a quantitative overview. In the following chapter, I will supplement these numbers with narratives of each type of marriage in order to demonstrate the various meanings and values villagers associate with each kind of marriage.

Categorizing marriage types in Junigau was not easy. At one point during my fieldwork, I had eleven different categories, depending on three separate criteria: (1) what type of ceremony took place—*ghurung ghurung* (accompanied by a band, a Brahman priest, and feasts) or *lurung lurung* (a Brahman priest but no band and only small feasts); (2) whether there was a matchmaker involved or not; and (3) who initiated the marriage (the groom, the bride, parents, other relatives, or someone else). While only arranged marriages could be *ghurung ghurung,* not all arranged marriages were so festively marked. And, while matchmakers, who were usually related to the bride and/or groom, were most commonly employed to negotiate arranged marriages, they also were called upon at times to help organize a capture marriage or negotiate with the bride and groom directly in the case of an elopement. Because of the complexity of marriage practices, I eventually settled on the three categories that Junigau residents themselves use: arranged (*āmā bāle dieko,* "mother and father gave"), capture (*jabarjastī chhopeko,* "forcibly/violently taken"), and elopement (*āphai gaeko,* "gone by themselves"). Since the marriages within these categories varied from one another, however, I also asked in my survey, interviews, and informal conversations about who initiated the marriage, what the ceremony was like, and what involvement the various parties had in the negotiations.

I administered a comprehensive survey to all 161 ever-married people in Junigau's central ward in 1993 and updated it in 1998 by interviewing the 33 people who had married since my first survey. All the tables contain information about first marriages only. The vast majority of Junigau's central ward residents (90 percent of women and 75 percent of men) had only married once. Men were more likely to marry a second or third time than were women, but only four villagers of the central ward (three men and one woman) had married three times. No one had married four or more times. Widow remarriage occurred in Junigau but only rarely.

When divorce took place in Junigau, it was almost always the wife who initiated it (although she may have been coerced into doing so by her husband or his relatives).[8] Men who were unhappy in their marriages had the (technically illegal) option to marry a second or even third wife, residing with all of them together or setting them up in separate households. Of all eighty-nine ever-married men in Junigau's central ward, eight (about 9 percent) had polygamous marriages. When second and third marriages did take place, they were overwhelmingly elopements.

Of the three main types of marriage—arranged, capture, and elopement— arranged was the most common overall in the village, accounting for over half of all first marriages. Among the remainder of all marriages, capture marriage occurred 13 percent of the time, while elopement occurred 33 percent of the time (see fig. 1).

When we look at changes in marriage practices over time, some interesting patterns appear.[9] There is an unmistakable increase in elopements and a concomitant decrease in arranged and capture marriages. The number of elopements almost quadrupled in the period between 1983 and 1998 compared to either of the earlier periods and comprised more than half of all first marriages during this time period (see fig. 2).

Arranged marriages peaked in the 1960–82 period, most likely because that is when villagers were recovering from a famine in the 1950s, and were using some of their newly gained prosperity to throw lavish wedding feasts. In addition, many more Junigau men were successful in enlisting in the lucrative Indian and British (or British ex-colonial) military, bringing in more cash to spend on weddings. The figures indicate that capture marriages, on the other

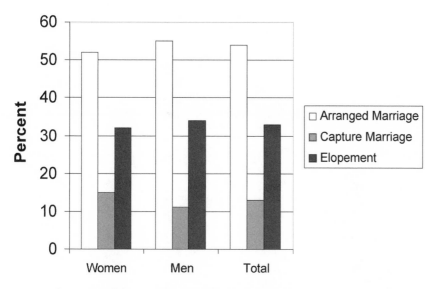

Fig. 1. Overall first marriage types by sex in Junigau's central ward ($N = 194$)

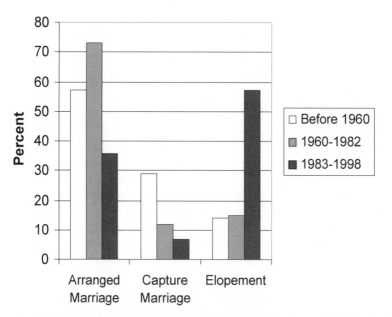

Fig. 2. Women's first marriage types over time in Junigau's central ward ($N = 105$).
Only women's marriages are presented here, as the men's figures are almost identical.
These time periods reflect locally significant shifts in the availability of various forms
of schooling, indicating periods of social change more generally.

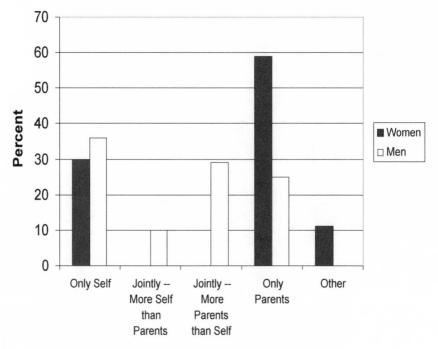

Fig. 3.   Overall first marriage decisions by sex (N = 194)

hand, became extremely rare. Furthermore, in the five years between 1993 and 1998, sixteen of the eighteen marriages (89 percent) that occurred in Junigau were elopements, whereas only two (11 percent) were arranged matches and not one was a capture marriage. The trend toward elopement, therefore, accelerated quite rapidly during the 1990s.

The survey contained a separate question about who made the decision that the marriage should take place. The primary decision makers for the various types of marriages were not predictable simply from knowing whether the marriage was arranged, a capture, or an elopement. The five possible responses to the question about who made the decision to marry were: only the individual her/himself, jointly but more the individual than the parents, jointly but more the parents than the individual, only the parents, and someone else altogether. Included in the last category of "other" would be, for example, when a woman was captured, in which case her future husband and/or his parents would have initiated the marriage. Also included in the last category of "other" are official or unofficial matchmakers, called *kalyāhā* in Junigau.[10] In all three kinds of marriages, matchmakers or intermediaries were sometimes involved. When they became the primary decision makers, they are listed in the "other" category. (See fig. 3.)

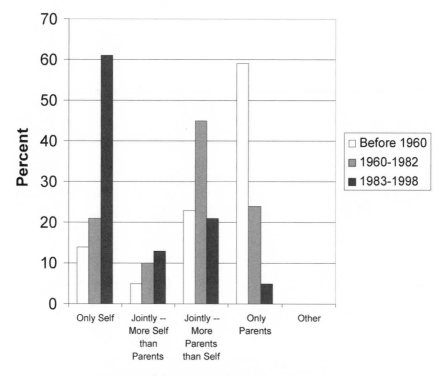

Fig. 4   Men's first marriage decisions over time (*N* = 89)

Clearly, the primary decision maker differed quite distinctively in women's and men's first marriages. Of all ever-married women in the central ward, fewer than one in three decided to marry on their own initiative. In over half of the cases, women's parents were the sole decision makers in their daughters' first marriages. It is important to note that in not a single case did a woman report that she and her parents jointly decided on her marriage.

In the case of Junigau men, just over one-third of them were the sole decision makers in their first marriages, approximately the same rate as for women. In only a quarter of men's first marriages, however—less than half the rate for women—were parents the sole decision makers. In the remainder of first marriages, men and their parents jointly decided on the timing of their weddings and the identity of their wives. Sometimes this consisted of parents saying something like, "Son, we've decided you should marry. How about X as a wife?"—to which a dutiful son was expected to agree. In most recent cases of arranged marriage, however, the son, who is often bringing home a sizable salary from his Gurkha military service, has had more say than the parents as

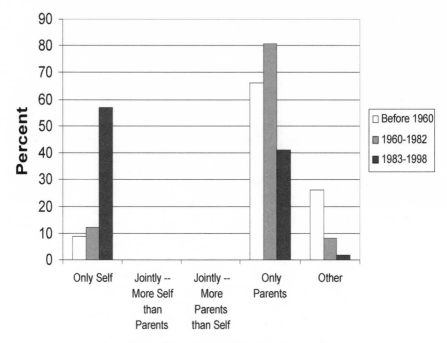

Fig. 5.   Women's first marriage decisions over time (*N* = 105)

to whom he will marry. Indeed, in a couple of recent arranged marriages the son has had total say in the arrangement of his wedding.

When we look at trends in decision making over time, first-marriage decisions have increasingly been made by young women and men themselves. As is clear in figures 4 and 5, parents were the sole decision makers in fewer and fewer first marriages in the village, especially in their sons' marriages, where the rate of sole parental decision making dropped from almost two-thirds before 1960 to only one in twenty in the 1983–98 time period.

Young women, who were rarely if ever even informed by their parents during the arrangement of their first marriages, were by the 1990s more and more frequently deciding to marry without consulting their parents at all; indeed, the rate of sole decision making for women more than quadrupled over the years.

To summarize, marriage practices in Junigau changed dramatically during the last decades of the twentieth century. Although over half of all first marriages in the village were arranged, by the 1990s elopements had become far more common than arranged marriages and capture marriages had virtually disappeared. Parents were consulting their sons (but not their daughters) in arranged marriages. Similarly, whereas parents continued to wield a great deal

Plate 13   Indra Bahadur Rana and Lali Rana shortly after their elopement

Plate 14   Harkha Bahadur Thapa and Maya Thapa, another couple who eloped

of influence in marriage decision-making processes, by the 1990s more and more young women and men were the sole decision makers in their own marriages, choosing to elope rather than participate in an arranged marriage.

Cross-Cousin Marriage in Junigau

One important result of the rapidly accelerating trend toward elopement in Junigau has been a shaking up of the village's kinship system. Unlike the Brahmans, Chhetris, and most other castes and ethnic groups that live nearby, the Magars of Junigau practice what anthropologists call "preferential matrilateral cross-cousin marriage." In other words, most villagers consider a man's ideal marriage partner to be his mother's brother's daughter (MBD) and, conversely, a woman's ideal partner to be her father's sister's son (FZS).[11] In an effort to avoid the male-biased term *matrilateral cross-cousin marriage,* I therefore call these matches "MBD/FZS marriages." In anthropological parlance, a descent group in a society that practices this type of marriage will either be "wife givers" or "wife takers" in reference to any other group. As grating as this terminology may be to those who recognize yet further male bias in anthropology's analysis of kinship, on the level of structural and normative "rules" such labels make some sense in Junigau and are reflected in local linguistic practices. Because Junigau is a patrilocal as well as patrilineal society, women almost always become members of their husbands' households, indeed, nominally of their lineages as well.[12] Since Junigau men remain in their natal homes after marriage, whereas women leave theirs to join their husbands', it is possible to speak (again, in theory at least) of the unidirectional movement of women from one patriline to another.

One of the resulting structural implications of this MBD/FZS model is that the distinction between "wife givers" and "wife takers" introduces an asymmetry that creates hierarchies in the village. Unlike the situation in many Indian societies, however, in Junigau "wife givers" are ritually and socially somewhat superior to "wife takers." On an everyday basis, there is not much difference between the two groups—indeed, Junigau Magars claim that all Magars are equal—but "wife takers" must be the first to greet their ritually superior in-laws.

MBD/FZS marriage forms the basis for kinship relations in Junigau. Village residents have a saying: "Magar kinship terms are like the teeth on a chicken's comb" (*magarko sāino, kukhurāko kāīyo*)—in other words, they are both numerous and varied. Almost everyone in the village is addressed using kinship terms. As I mentioned in chapter 2, merely assigning two people the terms for MBD/FZS cross-cousins (*sālī* for a woman, *bhenā* for a man) is enough to initiate a flirtation, if only a joking one, even when the individuals involved are mismatched in age and marriage status and even when the kinship relation is only a "village kinship relation" or a "speaking kinship relation" (*gaule saino* or *bolne saino*) between unrelated strangers. Dumont remarks that such categories of kinship are tinged with affinity (1983; cf. Trautmann 1981:173).

Thus, Junigau's kinship terms carefully distinguish among the various types of cross-cousins, depending on their marriageability. A Junigau man's preferred spouse is his *sālī*, that is, a daughter of his mother's brother. His forbidden marriage partner would be his *bhānjī*, that is, a daughter of his father's sister. For a Junigau woman, on the other hand, her preferred spouse is her *bhenā* (father's sister's son) and her forbidden partner would be her *māmā* (mother's brother's son). Junigau residents therefore call preferred cross-cousin matches *sāli-bhenā* marriages, while taboo cross-cousin marriages are called *māmā-bhānjī* matches.

When a woman and a man marry in Junigau, they actually *become* MBD/FZS cross-cousins if they were not already related that way before marriage, and so they address their in-laws accordingly. Trawick writes of the Tamils, "If you marry a stranger, that stranger *becomes* your cross-cousin" (1990:151; emphasis in the original). For this reason, a term like *pusai* means both "father's younger sister's husband" *and* "husband's father." When the marriage is an actual MBD/FZS match—what villagers call *sākhai sāli-bhenā*—these two terms will refer to one and the same person. Otherwise, a woman's husband's father becomes, for the purposes of address, her father's sister's husband. Similarly, to take another example, a man's wife's father might not be his "real" (*sākhai*) mother's brother, but upon marriage he will be expected to address him as such. "Structure, which demands cross cousin marriage, interprets history as if cross cousin marriage had occurred, and prevails," Trautmann concludes (1981:225).

Moving away now from kinship as relations among categories of individuals, let us consider to what extent actual Junigau villagers follow the "rules" and practice MBD/FZS marriage. Although MBD/FZS kinship terminology and marriage rules definitely act as ordering principles for behavior in Junigau, by no means does every marriage accord with these principles. As can be seen in table 2, which shows the premarital kinship relation in Junigau first marriages up through 1993, only 9 percent of marriages were with actual (*sākhai sāli-bhenā*) matrilateral cross-cousins and all of these were arranged matches.[13] The two marriages that took place between "extremely inappropriate cross-cousins" (*sākhai māmā-bhānji*) were both elopements.[14]

It was only in the 1980s that actual "wrong" cross-cousin (*sākhai māmā-bhānji*) marriages began to occur in Junigau (see table 3). More distantly related *māmā-bhānjī* matches have taken place for a long time in the village, although the incidence of such marriages has never been high. Until the 1980s, most

TABLE 2.   **Premarital Kinship Relations According to Women's First Marriage Types (in percentages)**

	Arranged (n = 53)	Capture (n = 16)	Elopement (n = 18)	All Marriages (N = 87)
Actual MBD/FZS cross-cousins	15%	0%	0%	9%
Classificatory MBD/FZS cross-cousins	34	38	28	33
Distantly appropriate	13	6	11	12
Distantly inappropriate	0	13	6	3
Extremely inappropriate (MBS/FZD)	0	0	11	2
No previous relation	38	44	44	40

Note: Figures may not add up to 100% because of rounding.

marriages were with either an appropriate actual (*sākhai*) cross-cousin, an appropriate classificatory cross-cousin, or a nonrelative. Villagers married extremely distantly related MBD/FZS cross-cousins with far more frequency than they married closely or distantly related "wrong" FZD/MBS cross-cousins. In fact, "wrong" FZD/MBS marriages greatly disturb most Junigau residents, and when asked to explain why they invariably describe how such marriages create confusion, sometimes unreconcilable, in kinship relations. When someone marries the "wrong" kind of cousin in Junigau, kinship terms and subtle yet important hierarchies are turned on their heads, and kinship in general is said to be "confused," "mixed up," "broken," "lost," or "ruined."[15] People no longer know how to address one another, and as a result sometimes they stop talking to cer-

TABLE 3.   **Premarital Kinship Relations in Women's First Marriages over Time (N = 86, in percentages)**

	Before 1960 (n = 34)	1960–82 (n = 26)	1983–93 (n = 26)
Actual MBD/FZS cross-cousins	12%	12%	4%
Classificatory MBD/FZS cross-cousins	35	46	19
Distantly appropriate	9	12	12
Distantly inappropriate	6	4	0
Extremely inappropriate (MBS/FZD)	0	0	8
No previous relation	38	27	58

Note: One case is missing because the exact date of marriage could not be determined.

tain individuals altogether out of awkwardness. The partial, and possibly eventually total, breakdown of the kinship system in Junigau is one of the most significant results of the increase in elopements. The ramifications of this breakdown are many, since kinship organizes everything in Junigau, from labor exchanges to household composition to affectionate friendship.

What happens when a villager marries the "wrong" spouse? In Junigau, the answer is that there is both a highly formalized adjustment technique for reconciling conflicting kinship terms after a "wrong" marriage and some "makeshift" individual choices (cf. Trautmann 1981:228). As part of almost every marriage ceremony in Junigau, whether the marriage is arranged or the result of an abduction or elopement, there is a ritual called the ḍhobheṭ. In the case of arranged marriages, it takes place the morning after the all-night "gift of a virgin" (kanyādān) ceremony; in capture marriages or elopements, the ḍhobheṭ occurs only after the bride's parents decide to grant it. The essence of the ḍhobheṭ is the presentation of the groom to each of his new in-laws in turn. Before he greets each one with the correct hand gestures indicating the appropriate amount of respect, he places a coin on top of a yogurt container on the ground in front of him. The in-laws whom he greets then return the coin and the greeting, sometimes adding some money of their own if they are particularly generous or pleased with the match.[16] Only the bride's sisters may keep the money. Sometimes they, like the bride's mother and grandmothers, are offered some cloth as a present from the groom, which they may either keep or return.

These ḍhobheṭ ceremonies resolve most dilemmas caused by marriages that are not with actual MBD/FZS cross-cousins in Junigau. Problems have arisen in recent years, however, as more and more elopements have been occurring with actual FZD/MBS cross-cousins (the "really wrong" kind of marriage). So many of these forbidden marriages have occurred in recent years in Junigau that many villagers bemoan the "loss of kinship" in the village. In one Junigau marriage, a woman eloped with her brother's wife's brother, who was already a distantly related MBS cross-cousin before her brother's marriage and became an even more closely related one afterward. Her parents were so upset at this "tit-for-tat" (sātai sāt) marriage (or direct sibling exchange) that they refused to grant a ḍhobheṭ ceremony for over five years, claiming that to do so would be ludicrous, for who would be willing to turn kinship relations on their head like that, making formerly junior kin senior and vice versa? As a result, the woman was prevented from visiting her natal home for all those years and was not supposed to talk to any of her natal relatives (although she did so secretly with the women in her natal family). Finally, her parents gave in and invited the couple back for a perfunctory ḍhobheṭ ceremony in 1994. No one outside the immediate family was invited, and kinship terms were adjusted only for the closest relatives.

In a similar case that occurred four years ago, a Junigau woman eloped with

Plate 15   A *ḍhobheṭ* ritual in which Hema Kumari Rana's parents host a feast to bless
her elopement with Vikram Saru

her mother's father's brother's son's son—an extremely close and extremely
"wrong" form of cousin marriage. When her husband brought her home to his
parents' house, his father refused to admit her as a daughter-in-law; instead, he
sent his son out of the village and ordered the woman back to her natal home.
Realizing that her natal family would not accept her back, as she was "polluted"
(*bitulo*), the woman stubbornly remained in her husband's family's cowshed,
begging food to eat from sympathetic relatives. After a few weeks, her husband's father relented, admitting her to the household and calling back his son.
It was not until five months later that the woman's family granted the couple a
ḍhobheṭ ceremony, and even then it was a perfunctory occasion at which kinship terms were changed only for the closest kin. The elopement eventually
precipitated a breakup of the man's family, with the property and wealth being
divided among all the sons so as to prevent the necessity of living in one large
household under uncomfortable circumstances (cf. March 1991).

The ultimate "wrong" kind of marriage, that is, marriage with a non-
Magar, has only happened a few times in all four wards of Junigau, but it appears to be on the rise with the increase in elopements. In the 1980s, one
woman became pregnant by a Newari man, possibly after a rape, and was sent
to live with him in Tansen. One Junigau family moved to the Terai around the

same time, and their eldest daughter married a Gurung man there. Another Junigau man was rumored to have married a Chhetri woman in the early 1990s in another district at Nepal, but he returned to the village without her and subsequently married a Magar woman. In the late 1990s, there was a man from the central part of the village who met and married a Thakali woman while working as a police officer in another part of Nepal. Conflicts arose when he brought her home to Junigau, so the two have settled in Kathmandu. In another Magar village in Palpa District, a family that is related to a family in Junigau experienced the unprecedented "tragedy" of having first a daughter and then a son elope with members of the untouchable Kami caste. In all these cases, even with the relatively "high caste" Chhetri wife, the non-Magar spouse was considered by Junigau residents to be of lower caste status than they themselves were. (On the other hand, members of all these other groups, except for the Kamis, would almost certainly consider the Magars to be of lower status.) This perceived lower status has implications for who will live with the non-Magar spouse, who will eat food that the non-Magar cooked, and other issues involving ritual purity. For this reason, in none of these few cases of marriage with a non-Magar does the couple live in Junigau. Even among those villagers who most vigorously advocate the right to choose one's own spouse, the thought of marrying a non-Magar is anathema, for it results in losing one's status as a Magar and as a member of one's own family.

As elopements become more common in Junigau, the incidence of "wrong" kinds of marriages is increasing, both with non-Magars and "wrong" kinds of cousins. It is unclear whether "terminological adjustments" via the *dhobhet* ceremony will enable Junigau to remain a kinship-based MBD/FZS cross-cousin marriage society and whether marrying non-Magars will ever be accepted enough to have the couple live in the village. What we are witnessing is the emergence of new structures of feeling that value individual choice and romantic love over family obligations and "appropriate" kinship relations between spouses, but long-standing village values surrounding kinship and Magar identity are still in evidence and may remain so indefinitely.

In the following chapter, I draw on Junigau residents' narratives of marriage in order to bring to life this quantitative overview of marriage trends and to demonstrate how villagers themselves describe how they got married.

CHAPTER FIVE

Narratives of Marriage

Arranged Marriage

When asked to list the various types of marriage that occur in Junigau, villagers almost always begin by identifying formal, arranged-marriage ceremonies sanctioned by both sets of parents (āmā bāle dieko—"[bride's] mother and father gave"). Even as recently as the 1990s, arranged marriages have continued to represent the ideologically (though not numerically) dominant form of marriage in the village. While some arranged matches are celebrated in a perfunctory manner, most are marked by songfests, extravagant feasts, and lengthy rituals led by a Brahman priest. Elaborate, time-consuming, and expensive, such ceremonies serve as the hegemonic model against which all other marriages in the community are judged. Even villagers who enter into or express a preference for other types of marriage take as their point of departure the Hindu "gift of a virgin" (kanyādān) rituals that have been adopted by Junigau Magars in their arranged-marriage ceremonies.

All arranged marriages are negotiated by the bride and groom's senior male relatives. Senior female relatives may have a say in the negotiations, but they are not officially involved. What typically happens is that a young man's parents decide it is time for him to marry—either he has achieved a respectable status by successfully enlisting in one of the armies, the family desperately needs the labor of a daughter-in-law, or the son has reached his mid-twenties without being able to enlist in the military and the family decides he should marry before he gets too old. Young men almost always resist attempts by their parents to convince them to marry. More recently, many have told me that they would prefer to marry a woman of their own choosing, but even older men who married at a time when arranged marriages were more common expressed a desire to remain unencumbered by the responsibilities of a wife and (eventually) children. In addition, it is a truism in Junigau that no one—man or woman—   ·

would ever admit to wanting to get married; such an admission would be considered by many villagers to be too immodest.

Once the decision has been made that it is time for a son to marry, the family considers who might be an appropriate match. People told me that the couple should ideally be similar in all respects: Magar identity, wealth, education, beauty, skin color, height, age, temperament, and so on. They also must either be related to each other appropriately or be completely unrelated to each other. Sometimes families use the services of a matchmaker (*kalyāhā*)—there are several older men in the village known for their matchmaking skills—but more often families simply ask around and use their own connections to learn about suitable brides for their sons. When a young woman is identified as an appropriate match, the son may or may not be consulted concerning his feelings about her. (As the survey results reported in the previous chapter indicate, young men are increasingly being consulted in this way.) The young man may even visit the young woman's home, either openly as a suitor or surreptitiously in the guise of other business in order to take a closer look at his prospective bride.

Once the groom's family decides, with or without the groom's input, that a young woman is an appropriate candidate, they send a small party out to request (*māgne*) permission from her senior male relatives for the young man to marry her. This party might consist of a matchmaker, if one is involved, or, if not, it will usually consist of men who are related to the groom's family through the family's women (*chelibeṭī*). Thus, a groom's sister's husband or a groom's mother's brother would be appropriate for this task. The groom himself does not accompany the group. The groom's representatives bring along a bottle of rice alcohol (*raksī*) as a gift (*māgne pāur*), and if the bride's senior male representatives agree to the marriage they all drink the *raksī* to seal their pact.

The negotiations that take place before the agreement do not include demands by the groom's family for a dowry. While this practice is common in India and increasingly prevalent in Kathmandu and even Tansen, in Junigau both families give gifts and there are no demands ahead of time that will make or break a match. In the 1990s, a bride's family members would typically give gifts of plates and pots, the type and amount of which were standardized depending on the closeness of the relation, while a groom's family would provide the bride with three sets of clothing (usually two saris and a *lungi*, plus blouses, shawls, shoes, and other accessories) and expensive gold jewelry. The amount of jewelry would vary depending on the wealth of the groom's family, but they would ordinarily do their best, often going deeply into debt.

A few weeks before the actual wedding ceremony a preceremony takes place. The groom's representatives again travel to the bride's house and present a container full of yogurt, which is then fed to the bride's senior male relatives (the *thekī khuwāune* ritual). At this meeting, precise dates are set for the various parts of the wedding ceremony—which day the groom and his male relatives will travel to the bride's house for a nightlong ceremony with a Brahman priest in attendance, which day the couple will travel back to the bride's house for a feast, and which day the couple will return to the groom's home for more feasts (and to live for good). It is often at this *thekī khuwāune* ritual that the bride first learns about her impending marriage. Before this, her family tries to keep the marriage negotiations secret, both to spare her the pain of knowing for a longer period of time that her departure from her natal family is imminent and to try to prevent her from eloping with another man, thereby dishonoring her family. This latter occurrence is extremely rare in Junigau, but if it occurs after the *thekī khuwāune* ritual has taken place the bride's family is obligated to provide another suitable young woman for the groom to marry and there is a great loss of face for everyone involved.

The actual wedding ceremony takes place at the bride's home. The groom and his male relatives (the *jantī*) travel to her home, with the groom carried in a litter by untouchables. Once at the bride's home, the groom takes part in an all-night worship ceremony (*pujā*) officiated by a Brahman priest from a nearby village. Most of the hundreds of wedding guests ignore the *pujā*, instead enjoying the feast and the dancing. Throughout the *pujā*, the bride wails audibly and refuses to make offerings with her own hand, requiring her attendant to make them for her. While the groom and his male relatives are away from his home, the groom's female relatives take the opportunity to sing and dance bawdily (*jyutī nāchne*).[1] The following morning, the groom and his party accompany the bride and a few of her attendants back to the groom's house.

Along the way, the bridal party stops to conduct the pounded rice ritual, which beautifully demonstrates some of the intersections between language and culture and shows the importance of analyzing language as a form of social action. In a typical Junigau arranged marriage (but *not* in a capture marriage or elopement), after the ceremonies at the bride's house are completed the bride is carried in a litter or sedan chair to her husband's (and now her own) home. At a convenient place on the path to the groom's house, everyone stops to rest and conduct a ritual that symbolically constructs through language the hierarchical relationship between the new husband and wife. Taking out a leaf plate full of pounded rice, a popular snack, the bridal attendant places it in the bride's lap. The bride herself is still fully veiled and sobbing audibly. Coached by his senior male kin, the groom begins by asking his wife quite formally for the pounded rice snack:

lyāunus,	dulai,	chiurā;	tapaīko	hāmro	jantī	bhokāyo
bring (high honorific)	*Wife*	*pounded rice*	*your (high honorific)*	*our*	*wedding party*	*was hungered*

Rough translation:
[Please] bring the pounded rice, Wife; our wedding party has gotten hungry.

At this formal request, in which the groom asks his wife for the pounded rice using an honorific form of *you*, the bride (or rather the bridal attendant, who moves the bride's hands to make the appropriate gesture) pours a little of the pounded rice into the handkerchief the groom is holding out. Upon further coaching, the groom asks a second time for the rice, this time in an informal manner using forms appropriate for close relatives and/or familiar equals:

lyāu	dulai,	chiurā;	timro	hāmro	jantī	bhokāyo
bring (middle familiar)	*Wife*	*pounded rice*	*your (middle familiar)*	*our*	*wedding party*	*was hungered*

Rough translation:
Bring the pounded rice, Wife; our wedding party has gotten hungry.

Again, the bridal attendant helps the bride pour a few kernels of pounded rice into the groom's waiting handerchief. One last time the groom's senior male kin instruct him to ask for the rice—but this time using the lowest form of *you*, that most commonly used in Junigau to address young children, animals, and wives:

le,	dulai,	chiurā;	tero	hāmro	jantī	bhokāyo
bring (lowest familiar)	*Wife*	*pounded rice*	*your (lowest familiar)*	*our*	*wedding party*	*was hungered*

Rough translation:
Bring the pounded rice, Wife! Our wedding party has gotten hungry!

Hearing this peremptory command, the bride and her attendant finally proceed obediently to dump all the remaining rice into the groom's handkerchief, after which he hands out portions of the snack to all the members of the wedding party. As difficult as the shifts in linguistic form are to translate, what should be clear here is the progressive movement downward in status for the bride after marriage. Just as she is moved to her husband's left after the groom places red powder in her hair, so once she is his wife must she be addressed by

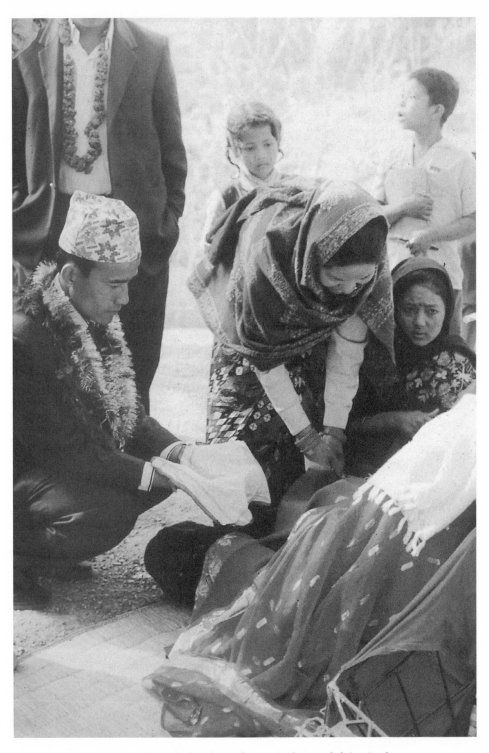

Plate 16   Chet Bahadur Thapa takes part in the pounded rice ritual

him using the lowest form of *you*. Her symbolic loss of virginity and defiled status make her ineligible to be addressed honorifically by her husband.[2] Given the three "attempts" necessary before the groom manages to succeed in addressing his new wife properly, it is evident that he needs to be socialized, at least symbolically, into treating his wife as lower than himself in the hierarchical order. Not only do the groom's senior kinsmen assist him in this regard, but the bride, too (aided by her attendant), rewards him when he finally addresses her in an appropriately contemptuous manner. What we see in this ritual, then, is the establishment through linguistic practices of a hierarchical relationship between the newly married spouses and the (at least partial) acceptance by both the bride and the groom of their places in that hierarchy.

As ideologically dominant as the institution of arranged marriage remains in Junigau, the meanings, values, and actions to which it gives rise allow for the expression of emergent, potentially oppositional structures of feeling. Individuals associated with arranged marriages in Junigau not only create, reflect, and reinforce relationships of domination but also sometimes challenge them. Using case studies and narratives of marriage from Junigau, I examine here the ways in which villagers, particularly women, physically enact and discursively express their culturally constrained, but never totally negated, agency. I argue two main points: first, that resistance and accommodation are always interwoven—there is no such thing as pure resistance—and; second, that these "accommodating protests," to borrow Arlene MacLeod's important concept (1992), may open up other spaces for the expression of more explicitly, efficaciously resistant actions on the part of both women and men. Thus, the spaces available to women in arranged marriage ceremonies for the expression of intentionally ineffectual resistance can be reconfigured at specific historical moments—such as the 1990s—to allow for the emergence of actions that have the potential to transform practice and meaning not only within marriage ceremonies but also across the community as a whole.

Let me illustrate what I mean by such spaces with reference to the case of Pancha Maya, who behaved during her wedding ceremony in a way that has always been quite typical of Junigau arranged marriage brides.

Pancha Maya's Repositioning

Although I had attended many weddings as a Peace Corps volunteer, Pancha Maya and Shyam Bahadur's wedding, which took place in the fall of 1992, was the first I attended as an anthropologist. I was both fascinated and troubled by the details I observed during the all-night worship ceremony led by *hāmro bāun* (our Brahman), the Brahman priest from a neighboring village who leads all of Junigau's life cycle rituals. All night long Pancha Maya sat cross-legged to the right of the groom, Shyam Bahadur. Completely covered with layers of

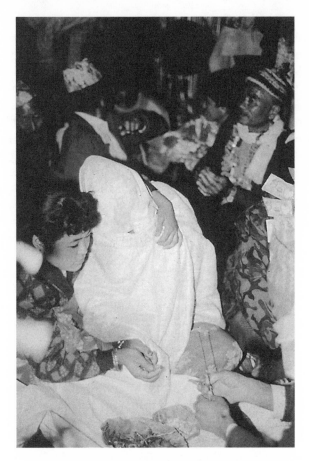

Plate 17   A bridal attendant, Hema Kumari Saru, makes
offerings on the bride's behalf

shawls and leaning heavily on her bridal attendant, an older married woman
she hardly knew, she wailed heartrendingly hour after hour. Whenever the
Brahman priest directed the couple to make an offering, Pancha Maya's bridal
attendant lifted the bride's limp hand and performed the ritual for her. Toward
dawn, the priest announced the start of the final and most crucial part of the
Hindu wedding ceremony as practiced in Junigau: the groom's placement of
red powder (*sindur*) in the part of the bride's hair, an act that symbolizes the
consummation of the marriage and therefore the ritual defloration of the
bride. As Pancha Maya began to wail more loudly, the priest ushered her natal
kin out of the courtyard and into the house, explaining that they should not
have to witness the event because it would surely disturb them.

Shyam Bahadur and his father unfolded a long, narrow, white cloth and wrapped it around a tall vaselike container. As the groom attempted to stretch the cloth all the way to Pancha Maya's forehead, she desperately tried to remain covered by her shawls and thus protected from his thrusting hand. During the next several minutes, Pancha Maya struggled to hold her shawls tightly closed while her attendant and Shyam Bahadur fought to pry the shawls far enough apart for him to thrust the red powder down the long, narrow, white cloth and rub it into the part of her hair. Three times Shyam Bahadur traced the red powder along the cloth and down Pancha Maya's part. Only after the third application of the powder did Pancha Maya finally go limp.

As soon as the ritual was finished, the Brahman priest told Shyam Bahadur to wash his "polluted" hands. The priest then directed him to move Pancha Maya from his right, where she had been sitting up until that point, to his left. Pancha Maya resisted this symbolic reduction in status, and Shyam Bahadur needed help in order to drag her struggling, sobbing body to the other side of the mat. Once Pancha Maya had been repositioned, the marriage ceremony was complete.

How can we best interpret Pancha Maya's actions when she was in the process of becoming a married woman? For the purposes of this analysis, let us limit our examination to the meanings surrounding the application of the red powder. As skeptical as I initially was of claims in the anthropological literature that this part of the Hindu wedding ceremony serves as a ritual defloration of the bride, once I witnessed the event myself at various weddings and talked to villagers about it I became convinced of this interpretation. Notice the event's iconic imagery, such as the phallic vase used, the bloodlike red of the vermilion powder, the thrusting of the groom's fingers down the "vaginal" part of the bride's hair, and the "pollution" that results. It is not only this imagery that leads me to point to this part of the wedding ceremony as a ritual defloration, however, for Junigau residents themselves readily identify the moment of application of the red powder with the bride's loss of virginity. As an example of how villagers elucidate the significance of this event, I will quote from a conversation I had with a village woman named Juni Kumari.

> *JK:* We're no longer virgins, see? After the application of that red powder, with that person we have to =
> *LMA:* = Even without sleeping with your husband...? =
> *JK:* = Uh huh, even without sleeping, without staying, without speaking with him, after the application of the red powder, we are HIS...No one else will have us. Until that red powder is applied, see, we can go anywhere—we're virgins, see? But after the red powder is applied we can't walk around like that.

Plate 18   The red powder (*sindur hālne*) ritual

So, the application of the red powder signifies the loss of a woman's virginity. What, then, does apparent resistance to the application of the red powder signify? The answers to this question are complex and contradictory. On one level, a woman who struggles and wails during the application of the red powder might be expressing a strong fear of impending sexual intercourse. Furthermore, she might also be exhibiting a reluctance to become sexually active, for "good" women are not supposed to display any kind of eagerness in relation to sex. Thus, on this level, a bride's so-called resistance reinforces the prevailing gender ideology and might better be termed accommodation. On another level, a struggling bride can be said to be opposing the reduction in her status from a daughter to a daughter-in-law. A bride's resistance may never jeopardize the performance of the wedding ceremony, but we can in some cases view it as an implicit awareness of and commentary upon the difficulties and reduced status that most Nepali women face after marriage. A bride may also be expressing her anger at the degrading symbolic defloration she is experiencing at the hands of her soon-to-be husband *and* her own bridal attendant. (Note that another woman is intimately involved in forcing the bride to succumb to her own defloration.)

On a third level, a bride's struggles during the application of red powder and her refusal to make offerings with her own hand can be considered to occupy a space that is securely situated within the constraining frame of the arranged marriage ceremony itself, one in which it is possible for the bride to express, albeit ineffectually, her resentment at not having been consulted before her marriage was arranged. It is just this space that Pema Kumari, whose actions were described in a previous chapter, occupied when she wrote the letter to her father complaining about his having arranged her marriage without her knowledge or consent. So, within the frame of the arranged marriage ceremony, struggling brides might also be viewed as objecting to the way the match was arranged. As Nita Kumar remarks in her introduction to the volume *Women as Subjects: South Asian Histories,* "Even when the terms of the discourse seem unchanged, the slight displacement of a symbol from its conventional positioning is enough to codify completely different, opposing meanings for the subject" (1994:21).

The specific historical configuration of Junigau in the 1980s and 1990s and the accompanying social, political, and economic changes mentioned in earlier chapters have allowed this latter interpretation to arise. Because of the changing social context, sentiments and actions are emerging that have the potential to challenge the practice of arranged marriage in the village in a way that the struggles of arranged marriage brides themselves cannot. The following example demonstrates how arranged marriage participants are reinterpreting village marriage practices.

Khim Prasad's Consternation

Khim Prasad, a young man who was a student of mine in the early 1980s, got married in 1993 while I was conducting my dissertation fieldwork. Khim Prasad's family arranged his marriage, to which he consented only reluctantly. When Khim Prasad's bride struggled during his application of red powder to the part of her hair, what was in its own context an act of ineffectual resistance took on other meanings for Khim Prasad that have implications for marriage practices in general in the village. Describing his discomfort during the struggles of the red powder ritual, Khim Prasad stated:

> I…felt very troubled. Yes, boys and girls who do that kind of marriage…Let them do a "love marriage" instead! LET NO ONE, AT NO TIME do that kind of arranged marriage! I mean, in my heart/mind[3] I felt enormous suffering. This is the emotion that came to me.

Thus, in this particular historical and social moment conditions are allowing for the emergence of new structures of feeling that are contributing to the shift in marriage practices currently under way in Junigau. Another instance of these new patterns can be seen in the instructions Khim Prasad first gave to the male elders who were about to request permission on his behalf for him to marry his future wife. Listen to this excerpt from his narrative:

> I said, "When going to request permission to marry the girl…that is to say, does that girl's consent exist or not?" It's not all right for there only to be the boy's consent, you know. I told them to ask, but they gave me no answer. I said, "Does the girl consent…or not?" Silent! They said nothing! The biggest, the "main" thing of all, now, in this day and age is for the girl to consent totally and freely when it comes to the boy.

In the cases of Pema Kumari and Khim Prasad, Junigau residents can be seen as agents acting within the structural constraints placed upon them by arranged marriage practices. At particular historical moments, such as the one I argue opened up in Junigau during the 1990s, a space that was once only wide enough for a woman to express her disapproval of an arranged marriage in ways that did not threaten the performance of the wedding ceremony was reconfigured to allow for a different kind of expression. Furthermore, actions that in the past always served to reproduce a system of inequalities became at a very different juncture ways to transform it or to change the meanings and values associated with it. As Raheja and Gold note, "The active rebellion that may at one moment be impractical or impossible may at another moment become plausible precisely because the idea of social transformation has been nourished in proverbs, folk songs, jokes, rituals, legends, and language" (1994:26).

The actions and narratives of marriage of Khim Prasad and Pancha Maya exemplify an important alteration in Junigau's structures of feeling. The new emphasis on the importance of consent points to a shift in the ways in which marriage is being conceptualized in Junigau. Far from being a rigid, timeless institution, marriage is a set of lived experiences configured by and reconfiguring of social structures, historical circumstance, and oppositional agency.

Capture Marriage

In Junigau, the term villagers use to refer to capture marriages is *jabarjastī chhopeko*—"forcibly/violently grabbed." Unlike in some other societies, these abductions are not faked; they involve real force. Only rarely do the bride and groom even know each other beforehand. As reported in the previous chapter, capture marriage comprises 13 percent of the first marriages of all ever-married women in Junigau's central ward. Of these abductions, almost two-thirds took place before 1960, and none occurred in the final five years of the survey (1993–98). The two main types of capture marriage that villagers identify are: (1) those in which the woman's parents gave permission for their daughter to be abducted by the groom and/or his male relatives, and (2) those in which the woman's parents were not consulted and the abduction was carried out by the groom and his friends. Within the first category are also those marriages that are arranged by the two sets of parents without the knowledge of either the bride or groom, such as the marriage of Shom Kumari and Arjun Bahadur, described later. The following case studies and narratives of marriage convey some of the contradictory and rapidly changing structures of feeling villagers associate with the practice of capture marriage.

Anita Kumari and Ram Bahadur Disagree

In the midmorning stillness of late autumn, the large courtyard was empty, and at first I thought no one was home. The door to the separate cooking house was open, however, and after calling out my greetings I heard the friendly voice of Anita Kumari, the household's senior woman. Once she had invited me inside and offered me tea, we caught up on the news in our respective families and I explained the purpose of my visit: to fill out a survey form for all ever-married residents of Junigau's central ward. Well, Anita Kumari remarked hesitantly, I had come at a bad time, since she was the only one home. Her sons were in India, her daughters-in-law were off working in the fields, and her husband was seeing to some land they owned in a distant village. I replied that I would not mind returning at another time to question the rest of the married members of her household, concentrating for the moment only on Anita Kumari's own marital history.

Over the course of an hour or so, Anita Kumari told me the story of her capture marriage. She was abducted as a young teenager by her husband and his male kin while she was returning from working in the fields. In vivid terms, Anita Kumari told of struggling furiously but unsuccessfully as men grabbed her arms and legs, yanking them in different directions. The men took her back to her husband's house, where they confined her until the Brahman priest arrived. He performed an abbreviated wedding ceremony, and once the red powder was applied to the part of her hair Anita Kumari stopped resisting, she said, knowing that she was "his" whether she wanted to be or not. Anita Kumari ended her story by describing how she eventually came to love the man who had abducted her.[4] After all, she commented, it is perfectly natural to learn to love the father of one's children.

A couple of days later I returned to Anita Kumari's household to question her husband and daughters-in-law. Once again, her daughters-in-law were off working in the fields, but this time I did catch Anita Kumari's husband, Ram Bahadur, at home. A stern, powerful man in his fifties, Ram Bahadur answered all my questions readily. When we came to the part of the survey that asked the respondent to characterize his or her wedding, however, I inadvertently discovered that Ram Bahadur was sensitive about his marriage. "So, yours was a capture marriage?" I asked. Turning to glare at his wife, who had just walked into the room, Ram Bahadur answered indignantly: "No! We married properly! It wasn't a violent capture! We had an arranged marriage that was quite proper!" Feeling terrible about my blunder and fearing that there would be negative repercussions for Anita Kumari, I quickly apologized and moved on to the next question. Anita Kumari, however, just laughed from the doorway, scolding her husband: "Why did you lie? You know it was a violent [capture] marriage!" Not wanting to get caught in the middle of a marital dispute I myself had initiated, I hurriedly completed Ram Bahadur's survey, thanked him, and rose to leave. On my way out, Ram Bahadur asked me what I had recorded on my survey sheet for their type of marriage. When I replied only half-jokingly that I had written down "arranged marriage" for Ram Bahadur and "capture marriage" for Anita Kumari, they both found this quite humorous and we parted on good terms.[5]

How can we understand Ram Bahadur's reluctance to admit that his marriage was by abduction?[6] As the vignette about Ram Bahadur and Anita Kumari demonstrates, capture marriage can be a sensitive topic to some Junigau inhabitants, especially those concerned with what others (such as an anthropologist) might think of them. Ram Bahadur, a particularly proud and somewhat pompous man, was eager to have me believe that his marriage had been a "proper" one, despite the fact that he must have known that all his relatives (not to mention his wife) would dispute his story. Such reluctance to admit that one's own marriage was by abduction is rare in Junigau, but I believe that a shift in the structures of feeling in the village makes Ram Bahadur's attitude toward his own marriage more understandable.

Why do capture marriages evoke such a complex reaction in Junigau and elsewhere? Indeed, in the process of my research I have discovered that it is not just in the village that the practice is viewed with ambivalence. In the anthropological literature as well, capture marriage, observed by scholars and travelers as far back as Herodotus, occupies an uneasy place.[7] Inextricably intertwined with anthropology's evolutionary theories about the developmental stages of society, marriage by abduction became tainted by this association with the discipline's early (and now discredited) debates. Consequently, the practice has received very little in-depth study by anthropologists since the turn of the century.

In the following two sections, I present excerpts from Junigau residents' narratives of capture marriage in order to facilitate a more complete understanding of the practice as it occurred in the village up through 1993 and to suggest some reasons for the decline in, and possible disappearance of, abductions in recent years. The narratives present a detailed picture of a marriage practice often overlooked by anthropologists.

Arjun Bahadur and Shom Kumari Are Surprised

Unlike Ram Bahadur, most villagers were quite willing to discuss capture marriage with me, even in reference to their own weddings. Arjun Bahadur and Shom Kumari, both now deceased, were married in a capture marriage that their parents arranged with the complicity of Shom Kumari's friends. Although they reported being so shy when they were first married that it was years before they talked to each other at all, in their later years they displayed more affection toward each other than do most other married couples in the village. In the following excerpts they jointly tell the story of their wedding, patiently explaining the events until it became obvious to me that neither of them had had any knowledge of their imminent marriage. (This was the first I had heard of such marriages.) On the day they were married, they had walked down with separate groups of friends and relatives to Ranighat on the Kali Gandaki River to celebrate a holy day. Shom Kumari was approximately fourteen years old at the time, while Arjun Bahadur was approximately eighteen.[8] Shom Kumari's companions, who were complicit in the abduction, made sure she stopped in with them at Arjun Bahadur's house on the way home.

From this point in the narrative, Shom Kumari goes on to relate how vehemently she resisted her abduction once she realized it was taking place. Like many other Junigau women of all marriage types, Shom Kumari depicts herself as someone who possessed the agency to resist, even though she considered her marriage inevitable, while Arjun Bahadur portrays himself as having been so embarrassed that he hid while Shom Kumari was being abducted.

SK: Then later, first my friends said, "All right, we'll have some liquor here, then we'll go," you know, then they sat there and had liquor, you know. =

AB: = And then, at that time they had already gone to get the Brahman priest, it seems.

SK: My friends began to drink the liquor, you see; and I, well…like this, "When will we leave? Let's go quickly, let's go quickly!" I kept saying. Then outside, outside on the veranda, *HWISHA, HWISHA, HWISHA* [whispering sound effect], I heard them talking secretly. "Oh…I see that they're planning to capture me!" I said to myself, and creeping outside, I tried to run away at first, but then they grabbed hold of me and took me back inside, then… =

LMA: Who grabbed hold of you?

AB: The oldest son from one of the other houses.

SK: Then, well, "We're going to keep you here today," said [inaudible]. "Sure, you'll keep me, you whore/widow!"[9]—saying which, I punched her with my fist! Then all the women fell over, you see—*GHETRENG!* [sound effect] I bit some women's hands—*KARĀK!* [sound effect]. Then a man said, "What's happening here?" and I ran away, you see, then later, well, I struck them, later. That one there [i.e., Arjun Bahadur]—who knows where he was? They say he was intoxicated. Well, it happened like that; Mother and Father violently… =

AB: = I was so shy/embarrassed [*lāj lāgyo*], I was hiding! [laughing] I thought I'd die [inaudible]!

Shom Kumari poignantly describes her goal in life before she was abducted: to remain unmarried and to take care of her aging parents.

SK: I had said to myself, "Now, I'm just going to stay up here on the hill and take care of my father and mother"—I said; I was so single-minded. But according to my *karma,* it was written that I would end up here in this valley! They yanked me here, dragged me here—they closed the door, captured me, kept me!

In her narrative, therefore, Shom Kumari ultimately attributes her marriage to fate (karma). She does not blame her parents, who knew about and approved of the abduction because they had no money for an arranged marriage feast, or her friends, who were in a similar position to that of bridal attendants, whose job it is to ensure that the bride takes part, however unwillingly, in the various parts of the wedding ceremony. Here we see that there is no simple dichotomy of female is to male as victimized is to victimizer. The configurations of resistance, accommodation, complicity, and power are complex in any situation; Junigau capture marriages are no exception.

Juni Kumari and Bhum Bahadur Have "The Worst Kind of Wedding"

Juni Kumari and Bhum Bahadur, both in their early thirties at the time and married for twelve years when I conducted a series of interviews with them in 1993, appeared to have developed a close, affectionate relationship. The first interview, with Juni Kumari alone, took place while her husband was still in Kathmandu, where he had been working for two years. When Bhum Bahadur could finally afford to return to the village, he ended up staying indefinitely and was teased by many that he could not bear to leave his wife again. When Bhum Bahadur and I talked about six months after I had first interviewed his wife, his cocky mannerisms were offset by his frequent appeals to his wife for information or corroboration. Juni Kumari herself, an articulate, extremely intelligent (though barely literate) woman, managed the household finances and labor and made many of the decisions regarding the whole family, although she always consulted with her husband and mother-in-law.

Off and on for years before her marriage, Juni Kumari had been living with her father's sister in Junigau to help her out, and it was while she was living with her aunt, whose house was quite close to Bhum Bahadur's, that Juni Kumari was captured. I heard numerous stories like Juni Kumari's of Junigau women being abducted when they could be perceived by men as being somehow weak or lacking in male protection, such as when they happened to belong to female-headed households (usually after their fathers had died and their brothers were in one of the armies). In Juni Kumari's case, however, she portrays herself in most of her narrative as someone who was deceived but who nevertheless did her best to regain her freedom at the time of her abduction.

On the question of how they met and why he captured her, Juni Kumari and Bhum Bahadur tell similar but not identical stories. After reluctantly admitting that she knew Bhum Bahadur before their marriage, Juni Kumari speculates that he abducted her because he liked her. Bhum Bahadur tells a slightly more complicated story. With no sisters and his two younger brothers having just died, he had to quit school to help with work around the house and in the fields. Although his parents kept pressuring him to allow them to arrange a marriage for him (which would supply the household with a working daughter-in-law), Bhum Bahadur repeatedly resisted. It seems, from his own sheepish admissions, from his wife's statements, and from the remarks of other villagers, that Bhum Bahadur had taken a strong liking to Juni Kumari and stubbornly refused to marry anyone else. On the question of possible complicity between the two in planning the abduction, both Bhum Bahadur and Juni Kumari adamantly insist that there had been "no courting" (*mileko chhaina*), by which they mean they had not spoken or met other than in public at the water tap. Some villagers claim otherwise, however, stating that the two had been seen "laughing and talking" (*hāsne bolne*, i.e., flirting) before the abduction. In cases such as this, issues of agency, consent, and complicity become extremely difficult to disentangle. And yet no villager I ever asked told me that women stage their abductions. Indeed, the response to my question was invariably something like, "Why would a woman want to do that? Why wouldn't she just elope?" For as long as the oldest Junigau residents can remember, elopement has been an option at least as viable and attractive as abduction—in recent times, in fact, much less stigmatized. Still, there may have been cases in Junigau in which the woman was not displeased to be marrying a particular man, as resistant as she might have been to the type of timing of the marriage. The level of complicity or collusion on the part of the woman is therefore almost impossible to determine, even, perhaps, by the participants themselves. Nevertheless, in all the cases of capture marriage with which I am familiar in the village, I find no evidence to support Jan Brukman's observation about the Koya of South India that, "One need hardly point out that collusion at some level is practically a requirement in cases of abduction" (1974:308) or Charles McDougal's remark about the Kulunge Rai of eastern Nepal that "the principals usually reach an agreement between themselves before the 'capture' is carried out" (1979:107).

In cases in which capture marriages are effected in Junigau without the knowledge of the woman's parents, the groom is the primary agent. Indeed, he may not even inform his own parents that he intends to bring home a bride. In years past, it used to be widowers who would resort most often to such abductions in order to obtain a wife, but in a few recent instances of capture marriage without the consent of the woman's parents the man has been young, never married, and particularly willful—like Bhum Bahadur.

In the following passage, Juni Kumari labels capture marriage the worst way to get married, offering as a reason that a woman who is abducted without her parents' knowledge or consent will not be able to unload her suffering onto them and expect them to take responsibility for her since they did not arrange the marriage. For woman, therefore, a capture marriage, like an elopement, can result in the forfeiting of support from their natal families—a potentially devastating loss if the husband or his family turns out to be abusive.

LMA: What's the worst kind of wedding?
JK: To take after capturing, just like that [inaudible]—without letting the woman's parents know. To take after capturing is no good, see? Isn't it?...Who knows why? Maybe because that's how I was taken. What it's

like is—there's suffering, see? Later, after going to Mother and Father, one can't say, "I've experienced this kind of suffering, it's like this for me." We can't cry with our parents like that—it's not possible to endure the suffering, see, right? We can't show them suffering, see, we can't, right? Mother and Father say, "They didn't let me know; we didn't give you away. You went on your own, they captured you." For us, see—for us there's nothing that can be done [inaudible]—there will be suffering, won't there?

As the narratives of capture marriages demonstrate, marriage by abduction has until recently been very much a part of Junigau's marriage system. Far from being an exotic, perhaps only imagined, practice figuring in nineteenth-century ethnologists' theories of cultural evolution, marriage by abduction was until the early 1990s an ordinary, if not everyday, event in Junigau. Indeed, despite growing sentiments against capture marriage in Junigau, there is nothing to prevent it from recurring. In order to understand its persistence through the early 1990s as well as its subsequent decline, we must answer three questions: (1) what structural forces enabled capture marriage to endure among Junigau's Magars? (2) why have there been no capture marriages since 1993? and (3) what does this trend tell us about shifting structures of feeling in the village?

First, the survey results reported in the previous chapter remind us that the capture marriage rate fell precipitously after 1960. The most obvious reason for this decline is the increase in employment of Junigau men in the lucrative Indian and British armies that occurred after World War II. Before that time, only a minority of village men served in the military, and most of those were in the Nepali Army, which paid very little at the time. The decrease in capture marriages can therefore be tied directly to the rise in arranged marriages that was made possible by the remittances soldiers were bringing back from overseas. Lavish wedding feasts soon became the norm, and parents stopped facilitating their daughters' abductions.

Nevertheless, while economics helps to explain the decrease in capture marriages in Junigau, an equally important reason relates to the shift in structures of feeling that has stigmatized abductions. Although remittances from sons working abroad have increased, so have the costs associated with lavish wedding feasts. Indeed, many families go into debt in order to throw such feasts. Given the economic strain that accompanies arranged marriage wedding feasts, one would think that as their costs increased so would capture marriage. And yet we see an increase not in capture marriage but in elopements. This trend can be attributed to the shift in attitudes and expectations surrounding agency, consent, and marriage.

Attitudes toward capture marriage in Junigau have changed considerably.

Largely because of significant economic, educational, and social changes in Junigau, villagers are beginning to conceive of their own and others' (especially
women's) agency differently. Younger people especially tend to consider the
"consent" (*mañjur*) of both parties to a marriage at least desirable, if not essential. Whereas older Junigau inhabitants often explain their objections to
capture marriage by saying, "It's as if the girl had no one to protect her,"
younger villagers tend to criticize any marriage to which both parties do not
"consent." Even many of the older villagers are aware of the change in the way
agency is being conceived, some commenting ruefully that nowadays young
people want to choose their own mates, unlike in their day.

Still, capture marriage persisted in Junigau into the 1990s, albeit at an extremely low level. Why? The reasons for the persistence of capture marriage,
even at a low rate, have more to do with gender relations than economics.
Those capture marriages that occurred in Junigau after 1960 were the result of
strong-willed young men who decided to abduct a bride either because they
themselves were somehow "unmarriageable" due to their financial situation or
personality traits or because they became so infatuated with a woman that they
insisted on capturing her. The symbolic loss of virginity that occurs when red
powder is applied to the part of a woman's hair during all types of wedding ceremonies renders a woman's options minimal because at that point she is said
to "belong" to the man who put it there. Thus, a man in Junigau does not even
have to rape a woman in order to deprive her of her virginity—or, rather, he
rapes her symbolically with the red powder.

Even though parents no longer arrange their daughters' abductions, and
even though no abductions occurred during the final five years of my research
period, men whose desires are strong and who are unscrupulous enough will
probably continue to consider capture marriage an option. I would not be
surprised if men were to succeed occasionally in capturing women in Junigau
as long as community sentiment holds that a woman is better off staying with
her captor once he has put red powder in her hair. Her other options—
attempting to return to her natal home, where her parents are unlikely to wel-
come her back, or eloping with another man (assuming one is willing)—are
unattractive, for they are said to reflect poorly on the honor of the woman and
her family and hold little possibility of an economically and emotionally stable
life. Without the means to achieve an independent livelihood, Junigau women
will remain dependent on their fathers, brothers, husbands, and sons.

Why were Junigau parents once so willing to allow their daughters to be abducted? As heartless as this act may seem to those of us from a different culture, many parents who facilitated their daughters' capture marriages were
only doing so in order to fulfill their (Hindu) duty to ensure that their children
do not remain unmarried. Indeed, although a capture marriage has not been

arranged by Junigau parents without either participant's knowledge since the 1960s, the prevalence of the practice in the past demonstrates that young men used to have little say in their marriages, conforming themselves instead to the wishes of their parents. Many villagers considered it justifiable to force children into matches that were at the time mainly expected to be economic and pro-creative rather than affective in character.

Thus, returning to the vignette that opened this section of the chapter, Ram Bahadur's reluctance to admit to his own capture marriage can be seen as the act of a man who is extremely anxious to appear above criticism. Fearing that I might judge him harshly, as either a high-caste Brahman or a young, Western-influenced Magar might, he told me that his marriage had been a "proper" one, not an abduction. As past practices become reinterpreted in this manner, future practices will be reconfigured.

Elopement

Although elopement has been practiced in Junigau for generations, the nature of courtship changed dramatically in the 1980s and 1990s. Previously, elope-ments would be preceded by an extremely brief or nonexistent courtship. Such abbreviated courtship still occurs, though less commonly than before. Couples might, for example, meet at a songfest and then elope a few hours later or a matchmaker might arrange an elopement between two people who have never met each other. Villagers also report that in the past some matchmakers used to cast spells on women in order to make them willing to elope.

Nowadays, most courtships are longer and include expressions of roman-tic love, usually in the form of love letters. Young people in Junigau do not "date" openly in the way that Americans do. They might try to meet secretly in the district center to view a Hindi or Nepali film (usually a variation on the theme of star-crossed lovers) or they might look for a place where they can meet in private. But because most parents do not approve of their children, es-pecially their daughters, carrying on even a light flirtation, courtships in Juni-gau are never public, even when, thanks to village rumor, everyone knows what is going on. The inability of young couples to meet in private, or even at all, used to lead quickly to either elopement or dissolution of the relationship. Since the 1980s, however, as most of the young women in the village have be-come literate, the exchange of love letters has emerged as an alternative form of courtship. Couples might see each other every day while working in the fields or attending school, but because opportunities to meet are so rare many have resorted to writing love letters as a way of carrying the courtship forward.

When Junigau residents speak of people who have eloped, they use one of several phrases. The most common is *āphai gaeko*—"went on their own"—which can be modified depending on whether the couple arranged the elopement themselves, used a matchmaker, had a spell cast on the woman, or married as the result of a premarital pregnancy. The term *āphai gaeko* contrasts semantically with *āmā bāle dieko,* the phrase used to describe arranged marriages that literally means "mother and father gave [the woman away]." Another common way of referring to particular elopements, those that are preceded by courtships presumed to involve romantic feelings on both sides, is to use the English phrase "love marriage" (*lav merej*). It is my sense that "love marriage" is of relatively recent usage, dating back only to the 1980s at the earliest, for it is used more frequently by younger villagers than older ones and refers most often to a type of elopement that involves the exchange of love letters. An older term, *poīlo gaeko* (went to a husband), derives from a slang word for husband (*poī*) and describes in a somewhat derogatory manner women who elope. "Elopement" itself is an inexact translation of these types of marriage, and "love marriage" is even worse because both terms conjure up images for most Western readers that do not pertain to most older *āphai gaeko* marriages in Junigau. I considered calling these matches "self-initiated marriages," but, as will become clear, such a label is also inappropriate in many cases. In the end, I settled on "elopement" because it connotes a hasty, surreptitious marriage involving a minimum of ceremony, which describes most Junigau elopements.

With the exception of the English phrase "love marriage," all of the Nepali terms for elopement seem to have been in use in Junigau for as long as people can remember, which is not surprising given that the practice goes back at least that long as well. Indeed, Junigau residents who have traveled to Magar villages in the far eastern part of the district, where only the Magar language is spoken and distinctively Magar dress and rituals are practiced to a greater degree than they are in Junigau, report that virtually all marriages in those Magar areas are either elopements or abductions.[10] It therefore seems reasonable to suggest that when Junigau Magars adopted the Hindu *kanyādān* marriage customs of their high-caste neighbors they not only continued some of their own practices, such as a preference for MBD/FZS cross-cousins as marriage partners, but retained elopement and abduction as alternative forms of marriage.

As noted earlier, abduction has become much less acceptable in Junigau as a form of marriage, and even in cases of arranged marriage villagers are increasingly voicing the opinion that a woman should be given a chance to consent to or reject her own marriage. In this section, I present four narratives of elopement that raise the question of how villagers define *consent* in reference to elopement. Many women—and even some men—who eloped reported at least some coercion on the part of their suitors or the matchmaker. According to villagers, whereas marriages termed "abductions" in Junigau do not often involve the complicity of the woman, marriages termed "elopements" generally do involve some of the same kinds of coercion used in abductions. Women in particular, but sometimes men also, depict themselves in their narratives of marriage as having resisted coercion before consenting to elope, even when they had been carrying on an intense courtship for months or years with their eventual spouse. Obtaining a woman's consent in an elopement therefore almost always requires "persuasion" of some sort (*phakāunu*, "to persuade, coax, flatter, seduce"). Thus, consent and coercion go hand in hand in narratives of elopement.

Because chapters 6 and 9 relate in detail two courtships involving love letters, in the remainder of this section I present the stories of four couples who did not exchange love letters before eloping, two of whom married in the 1960s and two of whom married in the 1990s.

Ramila Is Enchanted

Ramila, a widow in her fifties at the time I recorded her narrative of elopement, was typical of many Junigau residents, especially older women, in that she eschewed agency when talking about how her marriage transpired. Instead, in Ramila's narrative of marriage we find an example of a woman claiming that her elopement was caused by a spell having been cast on her. Ramila portrays herself as resisting a matchmaker's enticements and threats but being unable to withstand the power of his magic. Ramila had met the man the matchmaker was trying to convince her to marry, but he was much older than she and they had never courted or even talked together aside from brief greetings. Note the coercion from the matchmaker that Ramila reports having endured:

> And when I said that [i.e., when I refused to elope], the matchmaker said, "Don't you talk like that! Don't doubt my word!" "Yeah, I don't believe a word you say!" I said. When I said, "I don't believe you at all"—he slapped me! And from then on, it was like, what's happened to me? What's happened? I want to see the old man [i.e., my future husband], I want to talk to him. If I met other people and talked the way we're talking now, I didn't feel like talking. If I didn't see him, I wanted to ask, "Where has he gone today?" It was like that.

Later in her narrative, Ramila provides another version of how she eloped. She states that the spell was cast on her not through a slap but through a sip of alcohol, which Ramila adamantly tried to reject because, like cigarettes, alcohol used to be considered improper for women to consume. In the excerpt that follows, Ramila describes how the matchmaker, a distant relative, calls her to a neighbor's house under false pretenses and convinces her to taste some of the distilled liquor:

> The matchmaker said to me, "Hey, make some chutney!" I made some chutney with mint and tomatoes. "Okay, drink some liquor!" the match-maker said. I replied, "I NEVER drink!" They said, "Drink some liquor!" And I said, "I NEVER drink!" The matchmaker said, "No, you must drink." But I said, "I won't drink it." "No, you must drink some, see, even if it's only THIS much—drink it!" the matchmaker scolded. I drank just a little bit of liquor, and from then on I wanted to see the old man [i.e., my future husband] so much! While I was drinking liquor over there, I just wanted to come here [to my future husband's home]. I loved him![11]

Ramila then tells how the spell wore off when she had some more alcohol as she was in the process of running away with her husband to India, where they would subsequently get married and live for several years:

> I felt like crying. The old man [i.e., my future husband] had given me more liquor to drink. "You must drink some, you must drink just a little bit [in-audible], you must drink some," he said. I said, "I won't drink any; I'm not feeling well." Then, while drinking it, I felt like crying and wanted to come back here. I started thinking of my father and mother. When I said I wanted to turn around and go home, he said that my honor was already lost. I had gotten that far; how could I return?

Concluding her narrative without any further details about the elopement, Ramila repeats the saying about people's fates being written invisibly on their foreheads. She attributes to her fate, or karma, both her elopement and the fact that her difficult marriage lasted so long. Almost as an afterthought, however, she states that a woman must remember her honor and stay in her marriage no matter how difficult it might be:

> We didn't dislike each other enough to break up. This is my fate, I said, see? If not, well, "What fate has written on one's forehead is covered up by skin," they say, you know, right? There's that saying here, right?…Who knows what one's own karma will be like? No one has seen it, right? What has fate written for me? Well, for myself it was written that I would marry; if it hadn't been, I would have left him, see?…A woman must remember her honor and stay in her marriage.

Ramila's elopement, which occurred in the mid-1960s, was the most recent elopement involving accusations of magic that I heard in Junigau. Younger women attribute their elopements to other factors besides spells, mainly blaming either fate or relentless attempts at persuasion on the part of the suitor or matchmaker. Most still refrain from claiming primary responsibility for their marriages, as such an appearance of eagerness to marry continues to be viewed with disapproval by other villagers. Even those who advocate obtaining the woman's consent before any type of marriage would probably be shocked if a woman spoke "shamelessly" (*lāj nalāgdai*) of having initiated her own elopement. This is not to say, however, that Junigau women never orchestrate their own marriages; some do, if only indirectly, but would never admit it. When describing their actions afterward, these women always emphasize that they consented only under duress.

Rita Sara: "To Touch Him Was to Love Him!"

In her youth during the 1960s, Rita Sara was a young woman in her teens known for her beauty and vivacity. In those days, the young unmarried people of Junigau used to gather regularly at a widow's home to drink and hold all-night songfests. Sometimes they would be joined by married village men who were home on leave from one of the armies. It was in this setting that Rita Sara met her future husband, a married man ten years her senior who was so good-looking, she exclaims, that, "To touch him was to love him!" Rita Sara's narrative is unusual in that she readily admits to having been infatuated with her husband-to-be at the time and to being relatively happy throughout her marriage, even though she married a man who already had a wife and children.

The way Rita Sara was married—with no formal ceremony (i.e., no Brahman priest, no red powder ritual), having become pregnant before her marriage—is very uncommon in Junigau. Nevertheless, it is described by villagers as one type of elopement, albeit usually a disgraceful one: *āphai gaeko borī bokāera* (went on their own after he filled her womb). In the rare instances when it does occur, as soon as the pregnancy is discovered, the woman's male relatives call a meeting and demand to know from her who the father of her child is. After confirming with that man to make sure he will take responsibility for her and the baby, they unceremoniously deliver her to his doorstep, and, if she is lucky, his family will take her in, for the marriage is considered to have occurred already, as evidenced by her pregnancy.[12] If the man denies that he fathered the baby, or if the two are related in a way that precludes marriage, the two families will negotiate, and one family or the other will pay the family of a poor man to take the pregnant woman as his wife.

I am aware of very few other cases of premarital pregnancy having occurred in Junigau. No one mentioned pregnancy as a common reason for having to elope; the only woman in the central ward who admitted to having married because she was pregnant was Rita Sara, and I heard rumors of very few others having done so. Surprisingly, Rita Sara spoke of the conditions under which she married quite matter-of-factly and had no objections to my presenting her narrative here. She seemed unconcerned about the social stigma villagers often attach to premarital pregnancy, perhaps because her own elopement was long ago and her status as favored wife of her husband was well established.

In her narrative of elopement, Rita Sara describes how she ended up married after "laughing and talking" (*hāsne bolne*) with her future husband—an idiom referring to flirtation and courtship. Rita Sara and her future husband began to court on one of his leaves from the Indian Army, but it was not until a later leave that she became pregnant. Claiming that both her family and his, with the exception of his first wife, were very understanding when they learned of her pregnancy, Rita Sara perceptively notes that wives who remain in their husbands' favor seldom have trouble with their in-laws or other villagers. Indeed, Rita Sara is not ostracized in any way I have been able to detect by her neighbors or kin.

In the following excerpt from her narrative, Rita Sara presents herself as having rejected the option of becoming her lover's second wife and yet also having wanted to accompany him to India when he suggested she do so. In the end, when she becomes pregnant, Rita Sara speaks of how the village elders, not she, decided her fate:

> Now, I didn't consent, I didn't. I used to say, see—Well, I DIDN'T say: "I'll do a double marriage [i.e., become someone's second wife]," right? That's not something that should be done; in the end I didn't say—well, we spent time together like that; what to do? While talking and spending time together, that condition [i.e., pregnancy] occurred. Now, at first, when that hadn't happened yet, first, the first times we would laugh and talk, he would say, "Later I'll come back to get you, I'll take you away, I'll come back to get you," see? "I'll go with that one," I would say to myself, see? I would say that, see, and then when he came back again on another leave, while laughing and talking, THAT, [i.e., the pregnancy] happened. That happened, and then, he did, he went away back to India, you see, and after he left, well, they sent a letter from here; from his home they sent a letter. The elders from around here said, "This, this is what should be done, do it like this, what should be done..." and then they wrote a letter and sent it, see? They sent it there. "It's definitely mine," said your mother's brother.[13] "It's mine, it's mine. Bring her home and take her in," he said.

Interestingly, the preceding passage contains a reference to letter writing, but Rita Sara, who is illiterate, did not take part in it. Instead, the (male) village

elders used their literacy skills to write to the man who impregnated Rita Sara
to ascertain whether he would take responsibility for her and the baby.

In the conclusion of her narrative, Rita Sara, like many other older Junigau
women, blames her elopement on fate. When speaking of the predestined nature of her marriage, however, Rita Sara's otherwise fluidly flowing narrative
becomes halting:

> We…didn't court for very long…It was probably our, umm…right? Wasn't
> it?…It was probably written [i.e., fated], you know! Now, just seeing
> something isn't enough to obtain it, you know; it has to be written [i.e.,
> fated], they say, right? When others tried to convince me to elope with
> them, and I refused them, I guess it just wasn't written [i.e., fated]. Well,
> in the end, here…[long pause]—I mean, umm, I HAD to come to this
> person, right?

Perhaps because she was struggling to explain the reasons for her premarital pregnancy and subsequent marriage in a manner that would make what she
did seem socially acceptable (i.e., not her fault), Rita Sara resorts to attributing
it to fate: one cannot be judged and found wanting for having done what one's
karma prescribed. Her dysfluency in doing so, however, indicates at least some
awareness of the part her own actions played in determining her fate.

The remaining two narratives of elopement, both of which occurred after
1990, suggest some different reasons for eloping besides those listed by their
predecessors. In addition to parental pressure, for example, for sons to choose
a wife or have one chosen for them by their parents, many young men also report the goal of finding a "life friend"—a category quite new to the village, as
companionate marriage has never before been a widely expressed expectation
or desire. Some young women also claim that they are searching for a life friend
as a marriage partner, but more often than not I heard them emphasizing different goals such as finding a husband who had regular employment and who
did not drink. Increasingly, young women are also adding to their list of desired traits in a prospective mate the young man's ability to ensure that the
newly married couple does not have to live with his parents in a joint household. Realizing that obtaining the husband of her choice does not change much
in the daily life of a daughter-in-law if she is still at the mercy of her mother-
and father-in-law, young women in Junigau are seeking men who can avoid pa-
trilocality. Furthermore, they are seeking to acquire skills of their own that will
make them economically independent. The two women whose stories appear
here are among the few in Junigau who have managed to do so.

Despite these differences in recent courtship practices and attitudes, however, some familiar themes reemerge in the narratives of elopements from the

1990s. Although the young women and men often depict themselves as agents weighing their various options, many still attribute their elopements to coercion or fate. In the narrative below, for example, Pabi Sara describes how she was persuaded through "violent talk" to marry Kul Bir, and Kul Bir identifies the social pressures that convinced him to marry Pabi Sara.

Pabi Sara and Kul Bir "End Up Married"

In her mid-twenties when she eloped in 1993, Pabi Sara was fast approaching the age when she would be considered unmarriageable to all but widowers or otherwise undesirable men. Outwardly, however, Pabi Sara did not seem much concerned with the effect her age would have on her marriage prospects. Instead, she concentrated on using her weaving skills to earn enough money to enable her to continue to live with her younger sister in Tansen, away from the more arduous agricultural work she would have to do if she lived with her parents in Junigau. In early 1993, however, Pabi Sara met Kul Bir at a wedding she attended in his village, an hour's walk from Tansen.[14] She barely recalls having been introduced to him, but Kul Bir was so taken by her that he sent her a letter a few days later with the single cryptic sentence: "Is it your wish to, or not?" Not knowing who the sender was or what he meant by this question, Pabi Sara tore up the letter. A few days after throwing the letter away, Pabi Sara received word that the author wanted to meet with her in person. After asking around about Kul Bir's character, she agreed to meet with him in the presence of several of her friends and two of his companions. In the following excerpt from her narrative, Pabi Sara describes how she ended up eloping with Kul Bir:

> PS: Actually, I never said I was going to get married…I didn't know that my wedding was about to happen…On that day, on the day we met to talk, that person married me. It happened like that. On the day we met, we married.
>
> LMA: What did you do in that case? While talking and talking in that room…?
>
> PS: While talking and talking, I said, "I won't do it, I won't do it!" [inaudible] He says, "Do it!"; his talk was violent. His talk became raised up, while mine got lower…He made his own opinions and desires win, see? He made them win. There was a big discussion, see? As for me, I didn't like him that much. I said, "I won't marry now. My younger brother hasn't even married yet." "Your younger brother's marriage will happen later, it'll happen later," he said. Oh—what to do? While I kept saying, "I won't," I realized that this was my karma; I realized that this was probably my karma, right? And then how I felt! And then we left late at

night…How quickly! When I remember what I said to a person I'd only seen once before, I really feel like laughing! I didn't even know this person whom I'd only seen once before. It was as if we had never met, and then afterward I thought, "Oh, well, what to do? I'm married to this person!" I never said, "I'll do it." Even though I kept saying, "I won't do it, I won't do it," I ended up married.

Despite the attribution to fate, Pabi Sara articulately describes the thought processes she went through in trying to decide whether to elope with Kul Bir. Top among her concerns was a desire to continue her weaving and a need to assure herself of Kul Bir's praiseworthy character. In the following excerpt, Pabi Sara narrates how she debated within herself the likelihood of finding someone better than Kul Bir. She also expresses awareness of what might await her if she were to remain unmarried. Indirectly, then, Pabi Sara expresses her own agency even as she denies it.

PS: I was so angry, see! I said, "I won't do it," and then while I kept saying that, he said something or other, see, to me. Right?

LMA: Like, what did he say?

PS: "People will honor you because you'll be the wife of the eldest son. I'll see that you stay at home and don't have to go off to cut fodder. I won't make you suffer in that way…" Who knows what he said, see? I said, "I want to keep doing this kind of weaving work," see? Then I think to myself one time, "Will I be able to find this kind of person elsewhere, or not?" I think to myself again. As a person, he's not good-looking, but inside his heart/mind things seemed to be in agreement. And then I thought again to myself, "Will I be able to find other people like this one, or not? Well, as far as finding someone goes, I'll probably be able to find one. But then again, it'll probably be someone bad-looking and acting," I thought. "Oh, all right," I started to think at the end. And so I got married.

LMA: And actually you didn't come to like him in just one minute =

PS: = No, I didn't. After a while, I came to understand more and more, and to think more and more—see? Oh, what all I thought about! Afterward, this brain of mine couldn't think anymore. "Oh, I won't think too much—let it be!" I started to think. And so I got married…Now, that kind of person—umm, see? Like, for instance, an old woman… Well, let's say we've reached a certain age. Then other people will say about a woman who's gotten really old, "So-and-so's daughter has gotten so old, hasn't she? How old she's gotten! Now no one will take [i.e., marry] that one! Even dogs will kick her, see? Even dogs will touch her with their feet as they walk by." That's what people will do. So, I thought, and then—I thought a lot—then later, what to do? I was going to get married. Actually, I said, "I won't do it," see? Then he—while listening to him talk, I started to like him. He's not a good-looking person. But what he says is good. And I find that his habits and behavior are good…Who knows? I said, "I won't do it." I probably just had to marry him. Then I think, my fate—[inaudible mumbling]—there are probably no others I was meant to marry. It was meant to be this person, I think.

Like Pabi Sara, Kul Bir attributes their marriage mainly to fate, but he also emphasizes how he had been searching for a woman such as Pabi Sara, one who had a skill that could earn money for the two of them, thus enabling them to live apart from his parents. Although Kul Bir had been working in a factory in India before meeting Pabi Sara, shortly after their marriage he quit his job and returned to Tansen, where he and Pabi Sara still live in a neolocal residence along with their two young daughters. Once Pabi Sara taught Kul Bir how to weave bags and shawls, the two of them began working together out of their rented room to earn a living. A kind, shy, deferential young man, Kul Bir spoke to me only briefly of his marriage. His parents had been pressuring him to marry, he said, but he refused to do so unless he could choose his own wife. In the following excerpt from his narrative, Kul Bir mentions another kind of social pressure as well:

It's like this, see—I thought it possible that if I didn't marry, the other villagers would laugh. I had that idea. It's like this—if I didn't marry, people would say, "He walks around the village, he walks here and there" [i.e., he flirts with women]. I thought they would talk. So, for that reason I said to Father and Mother, "All right, then, if I find a girl who's like what I've said, I'll marry." And in the end, I found just that kind of girl, didn't I?

Both Kul Bir and Pabi Sara, therefore, claimed that they were at least partially coerced into eloping.

Dimi Is "Developed"

Dimi attended the same weaving classes as Pabi Sara did and for several years wove bags at her parents' home. A proud, intelligent young woman, Dimi used to make frequent comments about Junigau's need for "development" (*bikās*). At the time, some villagers considered her conceited because of her dismissive remarks about what she termed the backwardness and ignorance of Junigau's residents. In the early 1990s, Dimi used her weaving skills to obtain a job in a garment factory in a town on the Indian border. While living there, she became reacquainted with another factory worker from near Junigau, Chandra Kumar, a young man whom she had first met at the village school. They did not court or exchange love letters, she says. Instead, he sent his representatives to ask her parents for permission to marry her, but twice they refused him. Abandoning his hopes for a formally arranged match, Chandra Kumar enlisted the aid of his sister in persuading Dimi to elope with him, and eventually Dimi agreed. In the excerpt that follows, note how Dimi constructs herself as an agent:

> LMA: How did you decide to get married?
> D: To get married, well, he asked me, "Are you going to get married to me or not? Now, do you have a wish to do so, or not?" you know, right? "Well, I do wish to, but, you know, I'll marry only if there's some work I can do afterward; if not, I won't marry," I said. I said that, see? Then he said, "All right. If you have a wish to do that, then do it. And if you don't wish to, then just stay at home! You can just stay at home after the 'marriage.'" After we eloped, he then said, "Now, don't work." He said that, see? But I replied, "No, I will work because, you know, not that many daughters-in-law in this village, see, have worked after getting married. For that reason, if we show what we're doing by example to others, then others will also be able to do it. The old people at home—the mothers- and fathers-in-law, the fathers and mothers—will allow women to go." So, that's why I work, see?

Unlike many other Junigau women (and some Junigau men), Dimi is not reluctant to assert that her own actions resulted in her marriage, although she clearly states that it was only after Chandra Kumar and his sister persuaded her. It is in Dimi's regular conversations and her narrative of elopement that I see the strongest evidence of a shift in how villagers are conceiving of their own agency, a shift that will be explored further in the following chapters. Explicitly and consciously echoing the development rhetoric that she has heard on the radio and in her trainings, Dimi frequently mentions the importance of taking action to improve one's situation. She believes that she and her husband set good examples in this regard, and she does not hesitate to urge her friends and relatives to discard "backward" beliefs and take responsibility for improving their lots in life by attending literacy classes or skills trainings. Dimi also views the change in marriage practices in Junigau as evidence of progress and development, as can be seen in this excerpt from her narrative:

> D: The more people understand, the more they'll marry someone they like. They've started to think this way already, see, even the older men and women.
> LMA: Customs keep changing.

D: Yes, it's finally becoming developed; well, there's still a ways to go before it becomes developed here. People here [in Junigau] don't understand, see. They just don't understand. The more they come to understand about development, the better it will be. Then young men and women will be able to do their own work and support themselves.

Dimi's words echo the development discourse so omnipresent in Junigau, a discourse that conveys ideological messages about "good" and "bad" behavior, "developed" and "backward" subjectivities. On the backward side Dimi places capture and arranged marriages, extended family households, and fatalistic attitudes toward one's actions. On the developed side, she places marrying a person of one's own choice, working for money rather than for one's family, and, above all, education. Indeed, Dimi attended the female literacy classes and learned to read from the textbook analyzed in chapter 7.

Ironically, although this ethnography takes what Street (1984) calls the "ideological" approach to literacy, many Junigau residents such as Dimi adhere to the "autonomous" model of literacy, believing that literacy in and of itself as an autonomous technology brings about dramatic cognitive, social, and political transformations. "If literacy is tied to logic, development and progress," Baynham writes, "its opposite, 'illiteracy,' is tied to illogical thinking, backwardness, underdevelopment, both at the individual and social levels" (1995:48). Most inhabitants of Junigau would agree with this ideology, at least on some level. Nevertheless, as Stacy Pigg reminds us, Nepali villagers do not merely assimilate such Western models; social categories like "illiteracy" and "development" are not simply imposed from outside but become renegotiated and reconfigured at the local level (1992; cf. Escobar 1995:48–49). Teasing out these various factors as they appear in the love letters of two Junigau residents is the task of the next chapter.

CHAPTER SIX

Meeting by Way of a Letter
Shila Devi and Vajra Bahadur's Courtship

There really wasn't anything to write about, except to meet by way of a letter. While saying to myself, "Should I write a letter, or not?" I wrote this. Again, you'll say, "Why was it necessary to write if you didn't feel like it?" Right? But it's not like that. I'm writing this because I feel like doing so.
—Letter from Shila Devi to Vajra Bahadur, 2047/12/3

Meeting "by way of a letter" means many different things to Junigau correspondents. To a couple I call Shila Devi and Vajra Bahadur, it offered the opportunity to create new identities; to negotiate power and agency in their relationship; to establish intimacy and trust; to share views on life, love, and letter writing; and to express emotions that they could not express verbally. In this chapter, I focus on the sixty-six letters that comprise the correspondence of Shila and Vajra in order to illustrate some of the meanings and values Junigau residents associate with the new courtship practice of love letter writing.[1] In addition to shedding light on the reasons why many young villagers are turning to love letters as a form of courtship, this set of letters also facilitates a discussion of some of the potential pitfalls involved in writing such intense love letters. Not every correspondence ends in marriage. This chapter shows how the courtship of Shila and Vajra both benefited and suffered from the intensity of their correspondence. Before tracing both the micropolitics of their letters and some of the broader implications of their correspondence, however, I provide some background on the relationship between Shila and Vajra.

Like Oil and Water?

I met Shila on the very first day I arrived in Junigau in 1982. At that time, she was a lively, skinny, mischievous little girl of twelve or so who had long since been pulled out of school in order to help her widowed mother. From time to time, Shila would attend evening female literacy classes, but often she was kept busy at home or in the fields. I met Vajra a few days after my arrival in Junigau when I started teaching at the village school. He was one of my brightest students in seventh grade English, and he eventually went on to study at the campus in Tansen. In those years, I never imagined that the studious, painfully shy Vajra and the vivacious, popular Shila would ever be attracted to each other. Nevertheless, by the summer of 1990, when they were both in their early twenties, it was clear to everyone who attended Tij songfests that year, including me, that they were courting.

Vajra and Shila had known each other all their lives, but both say that it was only after they worked together on the construction of a youth club building in 1990 that they began to notice each other. In a December 1992 interview, Vajra described how afraid he used to be of girls and women; if one accidentally brushed against him, he said, he felt a current (*karant*) of electricity. Eventually, however, as his parents increased their pressure on him to marry, Vajra started thinking about what kind of person he would like his life friend (*lāiph phrend*) to be. In explaining how his courtship with Shila got started, however, Vajra eschewed agency, instead claiming that love "just happens" to people. In the same conversation, Vajra then went on to describe a phenomenon I have heard echoed in many villagers' accounts of how they started their courtships. Infatuation starts with a *dekhā dekh*—an exchange of glances. No one has to do anything. Thus, the village agentive theory regarding romantic love is that it is something that happens to people rather than something for which they themselves are responsible. Love, like other types of emotion, "befalls" or "is felt by" people (*lāgyo*). In the following account of the picnic at which Shila and Vajra first exchanged glances, note the use of intransitive verbs and impersonal phrasings as Vajra describes how their courtship progressed:

> *VB:* We went on a picnic there, and on the way to the picnic, at that time our courtship started, let's say, you know! [laughs] A little bit, umm, what should I say, now? At that time our courtship had its "start."
> *LMA:* Did you talk?
> *VB:* No, we didn't talk. There was just an exchange of glances, one to the other, the other back—like that, see? Then later, well, well, it didn't become unbounded in any kind of direct manner. Umm, slowly, slowly, little by little, writing one or two words to each other, like that—yes, like that. I'd come and meet her, and doing so, it happened like that.
> *LMA:* And you exchanged letters?
> *VB:* Yes, gradually we began to exchange letters, little by little. Later on it became extremely profound, it became very deep. [laughs briefly]

From such descriptions, one would think that their courtship was tame and low key, at least in public. But by the end of summer in 1990, there were many public occasions, such as Tij songfests and family feasts, at which Shila and Vajra were quite evidently exchanging more than glances. Shila was usually the aggressor at these events, mercilessly teasing Vajra when he declined to dance or was too shy to even look at her. This teasing became an issue in their love letters, as we shall see. On other occasions, too, Shila seemed anything but tentative in her attentions to Vajra, such as during one special dinner Shila's family hosted. Vajra and I were among the guests, and all evening long Shila performed what was almost a parody of appropriate hosting behavior as she and her sister-cousin forced upon Vajra more and more food and alcohol with less and less hostesslike courtesy. During the meal, Vajra was politely shy about eating. Shila and her sister-cousin urged him on—"*khānu,*" they said, using the infinitive of "to eat" as a polite command. There was much joking, however, and soon Shila turned *khānu* into *khā!*—the lowest form of the imperative, which in Junigau is usually reserved for small children, animals, and wives.

Such relentless teasing characterized most of the interactions between Shila and Vajra that I witnessed during that summer. At times, Vajra attempted to tease Shila back, but most of the time he endured her jibes silently. One exception was a Tij songfest that occurred on 20 August 1990, at which Shila and Vajra engaged in what is known as *juwārī khelne*—a type of song contest long practiced by Magars and other ethnic groups in Nepal in which a young man and woman take turns composing lyrics to a melody. Backed up by other members of their own sex, Vajra and Shila sang in a jokingly antagonistic manner, as is usual in many such interactions between the sexes in Junigau. The loser of a *juwārī khelne* contest is the person who fails to come up with lyrics (either composed on the spot or borrowed from other folk songs) when it is his or her turn to sing a verse.

In the lyrics of the *juwārī khelne* contest that follow, Vajra tried to persuade Shila to elope with him. Everyone in attendance was quite aware of, and amused by, their increasingly acrimonious exchange. At first, the lyrics contained formulaic protestations of love, taken from old Nepali folk songs, but then when Vajra urged, "Let's go [elope]," the song's lyrics became more personalized. Shila answered that she wanted to go "across the hill"—that is, if she were to elope she would want to leave the village so that she would not have to live with Vajra's parents and siblings in a joint household. When Vajra assured her that they could move to a village "below Tansen," Shila struck back with a barb that implied she did not believe he could find a job there. After that, the song became an exchange of hurtful remarks, all in jest but with a serious core.

The entire text of the song follows. The first line of every couplet is generally a standard phrase from Nepali folk song lyrics, chosen for its ability to rhyme with the more specific and personally relevant second line. Each couplet is followed by the chorus, which everybody sings.

Chorus:	I haven't received any news
	Return home, my lord [husband]
Shila:	What did his appearance do to me?
	Suffering never leaves me.
Vajra:	I'm crying, crying
	Sometimes I cry, sometimes my heart/mind is happy
Shila:	I walk down the steep hill, knitting
	How will I be able to do this while going uphill?
Vajra:	Finally, finally, we meet today
	Today is the day we will meet
Shila:	[misses turn]
Vajra:	At the *chaupārī*,[2] I sit eating and eating figs
	My life has passed by as I wait for my love
Shila:	I was on the other side
	The *bar-pipal*[3] trees in between us blocked me from your view
Vajra:	Let's go [elope], all right?
	Won't it make my heart/mind cry to leave you and go away?
Shila:	Dare to love
	If we're going to go [elope], let's go across the hill
Vajra:	If you're going to eat, ask for what you want and eat it
	If we're going to go [elope], let's run away and go
Shila:	In the corners, sequins
	While running away will you take up with another?
Vajra:	Sequins in the corners of the handkerchief
	Let's go—walk!—I won't take up with another
Shila:	Ripened fruit
	If you'll take it, I'll get ready and go
Vajra:	My love, if you're going to love, then love nearby
	It's not far to go to just below Tansen
Shila:	Love, on your head is a hat
	Where is there a job for you below Tansen?
Vajra:	The black cow went up into the hills
	It is my fate to take care of you
Shila:	I cut grass, but I didn't stretch out a rope
	I don't agree with what you have said
Vajra:	If you're going to sing, then sing [nicely] like before
	I can find another just like you, you know!
Shila:	The sound of drums
	Hey, I can find hundreds of thousands like you!
Vajra:	Sing another song; this one has made my heart rot
	To take you would be useless for me

At this point, the song ended, and Vajra soon left for home in a huff. I remember wondering how to interpret Vajra's reaction to the lyrics. Looking at the corpus of Shila and Vajra's extant letters, we find that Vajra wrote Shila a letter just after the songfest. In it, he claims not to be angry. Instead he asks Shila whether it was because he had left the Tij songfest early that she appeared angry and refused to speak to him when they both turned up at the tea shop in the village at the same time.

shree, shree, shree

Date: 047/5/4[4]

"May Pashupatibaba ensure our well-being for always."

Dear, so dearly beloved......[5] [Shila] Father's Sister's Daughter,[6] many, many remembrances and continual love-within-love from your beloved. I remain well and hope that you are also well.

There was no real reason to write this letter. I find that you are very angry with me. I'm not angry. Perhaps it's because I didn't stay at the Tij dance the other day?! You alone know, perhaps. Please forgive me. Now I'll agree to anything you say. I'll do whatever you say.

I felt particularly bad this morning. If I had gone by way of the upper path by the front of the shop this morning, I wouldn't have said anything to you. But as soon as you saw me—maybe because you thought you'd have to speak with me—you went by way of the lower path. That's okay. If you don't want to speak because you're angry with me, then I can't......[do anything about it]. I say again that at some point you will certainly understand whatever I have done to anger you and you'll forgive me. What to do? Sometimes it [i.e., life] even goes like that.

In reckoning a person's life, what is there, after all? Sometimes there's this, sometimes that. Sometimes sunshine, sometimes shadows.

Why should I write many things? There are probably many mistakes here; may I obtain forgiveness for them. Finally, having arrived here, I would like permission to stop this racing pen. I'll write about other things in another letter. Okay, I bid you farewell.

Your crazy lover
Always loving you
"Bye-bye"—love—love—love—love—love
I'll be waiting here for your letter.

Clearly, Shila's teasing, the song lyrics, and Vajra's angry departure created a rift in their relationship, but the letters that follow immediately after this one make it evident that the rift was not serious. The anger that is present in this letter, however, emerges again and again throughout the correspondence of Shila and Vajra. I return to the beginning of their courtship, therefore, to trace the various expressions of anger and other emotions in their letters.

Angry as a Black Hornet

> I get angry as a black hornet; now, do you......?
> > —Letter from Shila Devi to Vajra Bahadur, 047/8/13

> Sometimes how angry we both are, right?
> > —Letter from Vajra Bahadur to Shila Devi, 047/8/17

Aside from love, anger is the most prominent emotion expressed in the correspondence of Shila and Vajra Bahadur. It is mentioned at least once in over two-thirds of their sixty-six extant letters. In some cases, they use the words *anger, angry, angrily,* or *angrier* up to sixteen times in a single letter. Why does anger figure so prominently in these love letters? What does anger mean to Shila and Vajra Bahadur, and how is the word used in their letters?

In their first letters, anger is often mentioned speculatively or hypothetically, as in the following letter, written by Shila.[7] I present the entire letter here, as it sets the tone for much of the rest of the correspondence.

> 2046/10/19) Dear......[Vajra] Mother's Brother's Son, greetings with re-
> membrances and also......[love] from miserable......[Shila]. Mother's
> Brother's Son, I'm in good health. I wish you good health, too. Today
> it's only after many days, or shall I say many months, that I find myself
> writing a few words to you. Perhaps I'll give this to you. Perhaps you'll
> get angry. As angry as you get, as many mistakes as there are in these
> few words written by this miserable one, I request that you unfold all
> the folds and read this.
> > Mother's Brother's Son, why did you beg forgiveness from me? What
> have we done wrong? If you beg forgiveness from me, I can't give you
> forgiveness. If you want to beg forgiveness, beg me to my face. I won't
> agree to read the begging for forgiveness on paper.
> > And again, you said you wouldn't speak to me from now on at the
> water tap, right? That's okay. But even if, like an elephant, you don't
> speak, still, if you're going to beg forgiveness, then......you'll have no
> other choice but to......
> > Mother's Brother's Son, there's one thing, what should I say? The day
> before yesterday on the way back from Tansen you said, "You're prob-
> ably annoyed," right? Again, while you were taking me home you also

said, "You're probably annoyed," right? Now, what ever was the error that would have made me or the others annoyed?

Mother's Brother's Son, you said, "Above all, I pray to Sri Pashupatinath that you may spend your life in success and happiness/ease [*sukha*]," right? (Is that right?) Hoping with great enthusiasm that I, this miserable outsider, will live in happiness/ease, I have written these two or four words happily/easily. (I had no idea.) Again, you said, "If there's any suffering, I don't want to attach myself to anyone's name," right? Whether you attach yourself or not, I myself will......[attach myself to you]. Okay, Mother's Brother's Son.

I want to say goodbye and end this letter here. Forgive my mistakes or not, but you have to write back. You probably don't want to, right......? If you do want to, then......[write back].

("bye-bye")
Shila

In letters such as this one, Shila combines self-effacement with assertiveness in very interesting ways. Speculating that Vajra Bahadur might be angry upon receipt of her tardy letter, she nonetheless tells him that no matter how angry he gets, and no matter how many mistakes she makes in the letter, he should unfold it and read it anyway.

Another common trait in these letters (especially Shila's) is the use of ellipses, which often appear when letter writers want to avoid stating outright what might be too embarrassing for them to admit or too compromising if the letter were intercepted, which is what happened to Jiri, whose story was related in chapter 3. In her letter, Shila uses ellipses at the beginning in place of her own name and that of Vajra Bahadur. She also uses them when she doesn't want to complete a thought that might seem too bold or threatening if stated explicitly. The sentence, "Whether you attach yourself or not, I myself will......" requires Vajra Bahadur to connect the dots, as it were, and assume that Shila intends to attach herself to him no matter what. Thus, the ellipses in Shila's letters entail not only the coconstruction of meaning (which is involved in all communication) but also the same interesting combination on Shila's part of assertiveness and hesitation. Ellipses help her to be both bold and circumspect, direct and indirect, in her assertions. In a 1998 conversation with Vajra Bahadur, he recognized how the ambiguity and multifunctionality of ellipses could benefit the writer: "Any meaning can emerge [from the ellipses]. One often wants to say all different kinds of meanings, but if one chooses one of them and writes it down, only one meaning will emerge."

Vajra Bahadur's earliest—and no longer extant—letters also seem to combine self-effacement with assertiveness, at least as far as we can determine from

Shila's early responses to these letters. In the letter just quoted, for example, it seems that Vajra Bahadur had begged Shila to forgive him for having "annoyed" her and the others. In Shila's second (extant) letter, she once again suggests that Vajra Bahadur might become angry after reading her assessment that he is in a hurry to marry:

> (046/11/3) Why are you in such a hurry to marry? Then again, when I say that you're in a hurry to marry, will you get angry......? Well, if you get angry, you get angry.

Their letters show that in these early stages of their courtship Shila and Vajra Bahadur were trying to forestall misunderstandings and anger by speculating that the other person might actually be angry or annoyed. Because they could only rarely meet and talk freely in person, they had to rely on the written word to convey subtle emotional nuances, and neither Shila nor Vajra evinced much confidence in their letters that their correspondence would be capable of doing so successfully. Strikingly, when anger is mentioned in these letters, it is almost always in reference to the recipient, not the sender. Both Shila and Vajra continually asked for reassurances that the other was not angry, upset, or annoyed, and both asked for forgiveness for actual or imagined transgressions. Here, for example, is the third (extant) letter that Shila wrote to Vajra:

> (046/12/23) Dear, so very dear Mother's Brother's Son, many, many remembrances from this miserable one. *Namaskār*[8] from this miserable one. You look very angry now. If I opposed you [*hajur*][9] or somehow caused opposition to you [*hajur*] by saying *namaskār,* then I'd like to be forgiven. Why do you look so......different to me than before......? Why is this? I can't understand anything. Why, why, why do memories of you......keep coming to me? [along left margin] If you have memories of this ascetic [*bairāgī*] one, then please accept this letter, or else what will I......[do]? [diagonally upside down across bottom, mostly illegible] Why are you angry? Perhaps by saying *namaskār* and by means of calling you names I caused an injury to your heart. I'm sad about that. Okay, farewell. Bye-bye.

This letter can be read several ways, and as such it provides a reminder of the indeterminacy of meanings that emerge from any text or discursive event. A practice theory of meaning constraint allows us to rule out many unlikely interpretations, however, leaving us with a narrow range of more likely meanings the letter writers might have taken away from the exchange. On the one hand, it could have been written by a deeply apologetic Shila who was begging for forgiveness for "causing an injury to [Vajra's] heart" by teasing him or "by means of calling him names." On the other hand, one might read a hint of mockery into the letter in the form of Shila's apology merely for having greeted Vajra Bahadur respectfully. Of course, both interpretations are simultaneously possible, especially in the absence of further evidence (such as Vajra's reply to the letter, which no longer exists) or recollections by the two correspondents. Neither remembers the incident to which this letter refers, but both told me in 1998 that the frequently expressed anger in their letters only made them want to see each other more. In this excerpt from Shila's next letter, we can see some of this tension between anger and love:

(047/1/1) Except for letters, I can't give you anything. Rather, my thousands of words have angered you, right......? What, after all, can I bring you [*hajur*] to make you happy, right......? When I opened your letter and looked at it, you said, "I'm not angry; rather, you seem angry at me"—you said, right......?

   In that case, if neither of us is angry, and if both of our heart/minds are fine, then why do we act angrily toward each other, right? In that case, I......[love] you. And what do you say? Is there......[love in you for me]? Or what?

As the courtship between Shila and Vajra Bahadur progressed, the anger expressed or alluded to in letters seems to have become more substantive and serious. Several letters make it sound like the relationship was close to ending. (Indeed, they destroyed the first few letters of their correspondence after an early breakup.) In the following letter, written in the spring of 1990, Vajra Bahadur admits to "walking angrily" and making mistakes, but he claims not to have shown tokens of their love (i.e., letters, photos, a handerchief, etc.) to others, although he admits that someone may have found some things that he had hidden. He also mentions having laughed and joked with a sister-cousin of Shila's, which evidently made Shila quite jealous and angry. Still, he maintains that he loves only Shila:

(047/2/14) I'm feeling very bad that you saw me walking so angrily. As long as your heart/mind is suffering, my heart/mind also continues to suffer. It could be that I've given you such injury and suffering! First of all, I feel so miserable about all the mistakes I've made and all the injuries you've suffered. Whether I committed those mistakes wittingly or unwittingly, to God [*iswar*] they'll still be mistakes. We humans are only God's servants or pupils; why wouldn't we make mistakes? But not to repeat mistakes we've already made is our main duty. In an extended complaint you said that I showed tokens of our love to others, right? You can believe me or not, but I've never shown any of those sorts of things to anyone and will never show them to anyone except you. It could be that someone found some hidden things; for that, who is at fault? Probably I am. I'll try not to make this mistake again.

Another issue: you're angry because you saw me laughing and speaking with your sister-cousin. But when you saw evidence of this the other evening, you said without getting angry, "May your life be successful." No matter how much you dislike me, up through today I still love none other than you. The day before yesterday (Saturday) on the way to the river I certainly made you very angry. It was as if salt and red peppers were rubbed into your wound. I shouldn't have gone there. I made a big mistake in going. Now, because you're angry with me, you've told me never to talk to you again and you say you will also from now on (maybe for your entire life?) never speak to miserable me. Okay, don't speak to this miserable one. But I could never do that because no matter how angry I get I like to laugh and talk. My heart/mind won't allow me to just walk without talking. This miserable one finds that it is written [i.e., fated] for him to receive this treatment. I'll live all alone, having extinguished my heart/mind, gathering up two teardrops as an offering.

Vajra Bahadur then goes on in the same letter to write about the importance of knowing how to get beyond one's anger, expressing a sense of his own agency that contrasts with the fatalism he has just expressed:

Human beings are such that everyone gets angry from time to time. However one gets angry, one also has to know how to get rid of that anger. In a moment's anger if you place such a big punishment on me (the punishment of never speaking again), that's okay. My love is only for you. But your love......[seems not to be just for me]. Again, you'll probably get angry reading this letter. Whenever I see you, you're always angry. Why, oh why, when I see you walking, looking angry, does my heart get cut into slices?

How can I explain to you, how can I change your anger into happiness if, when I come near you, some sort of opposition is caused? If you'll be happy away from me, then I'll stay far away from you. I only want to see you happy forever.

Shila answered this letter with a heart-wrenching denial in which she claimed not to be jealous of Vajra Bahadur's conversations with her sister-cousin or to have been angry on the way to the river:

(047/2/14 or 15?) I'll say one thing—and if you get angry, you get angry. You said I got angry when you talked with my sister-cousin—that could never happen. Did I say, "May you be successful in that life"? Did I really say, "May you be successful with her"......? That's okay—if you feel desire for my sister-cousin, then be successful with her. Why do you always say, "If you want happiness from me, I'll stay far, far away from you?" . . .

On the way to the river you said I wasn't talking because I was angry. Did you say that in anger, or what? They said that I said, "From now on I'll talk to nobody." But when did *you* talk to *me*? All day long I was angry, you said, but on the way home, instead of walking ahead, not one......[word] did you speak to me. "I'm not going to speak to anyone; I won't speak," they said I said, right? Saying that, it felt like a big penalty to you. Well, whatever happened at the river, happened. Let's leave off talking about the river issue.

The inability of Shila and Vajra Bahadur to speak freely to each other with enough regularity was taking its toll on the relationship; mistrust and misunderstandings were growing on each side. Moreover, since both had invested deeply in the relationship in terms of emotional commitment, the stakes were high enough that any sign of displeasure was interpreted (or misinterpreted) as anger and a desire to end the courtship. Take, for example, this excerpt from a letter written by Vajra Bahadur in the summer of 1990 after an incident that occurred at the water tap:

(047/3) It makes me feel really bad to see you walking along so angrily. The day before yesterday at the water tap when the water was splashing, I didn't speak to you with an unpleasant attitude. I only said as much as I did because when it was time to put your jug under the tap, I thought you might get splashed, but you interpreted my words backward and immediately left angrily. The next day on my way home a happy heart/mind didn't show itself on your face. How awful I felt to see you looking at me with big, angry eyes! You can't really be angry at me without a reason—there must be some reason, right? But I haven't been able to learn it.

Anger also emerged when arrangements to meet clandestinely fell through. Vajra and Shila told me that they used to meet whenever possible, either at Shila's house, out in the fields as they were cutting grass (i.e., fodder) or taking their families' cattle out to graze, or at the district center. Many times, however, these meetings were far from private. Still, both looked forward to them and showed disappointment when they couldn't occur, as this letter from Vajra Bahadur describes:

(047/4/2) The day before yesterday I wasn't able to come to your house—you had invited me to apply henna. That was my mistake; actually, I should have come. But there was a reason I couldn't come, and for that I'm very sad. Because of this I find that you're very angry with me. What to do? Sometimes, who knows why, something happens. I really wanted to come so much. What can I say? If I come by day after day, what will your mother and the others say? That's the only reason why I couldn't come. Because you got angry over this little thing, you won't even talk to me, and when you come to get water at the tap, you move far away to talk, and you won't even look at me. Such is my heart/mind because of this!

In hopes of meeting you, I went off to cut grass instead of harvesting the jute. Even though the others were going, I wouldn't listen and headed in another direction to cut grass. For an hour I waited for you without cutting any grass, but you didn't come. I felt extremely sad. Are you so angry at me that you won't even meet me or talk to me from now on, or what? When we met in the evening, our conversation didn't go very well—how very, very bad I feel! When you show me so much hatred, how bad that makes me feel!

In answer to this letter, Shila responded as follows, showing disappointment bordering on total despair at not having been able to meet:

(047/4/8) Mother's Brother's Son, what were you talking about? I'm not angry with you. Again, it's hard to meet these days! What to do......? Because of conditions at home and having heard the talk of the villagers, who says we can meet? I feel like saying goodbye and leaving this world.

Another cause of the anger and misunderstandings between Shila and Vajra was Shila's propensity for teasing and joking, especially around Vajra Bahadur. Her letters show that she was well aware of this tendency, but in the following letter, also from the summer of 1990, she claims that she cannot control it. She both takes the blame for having treated Vajra Bahadur "meanly" and eschews responsibility for having acted that way, stating instead that perhaps it's because she's "extremely unlucky" that Vajra Bahadur's name just pops out of her mouth when she doesn't intend it to.

(047/3/26) Maybe it's because I'm extremely unlucky, I don't know—why is it that really bad things always come to me? Even when I do something well, it turns out badly. If I speak well, it comes out wrong. And to you I speak extremely badly, don't I? You might say that it doesn't seem so to you. But how meanly I have treated you! And while speaking to you, how I have spit upon you! How meanly I have treated you and spoken to you, you probably thought, haven't you......?

But don't think that way, okay? No, then again, for whatever reason when I say to myself that I won't say it, then just like that, from my mind and mouth......'s [i.e., your] name comes out. Why is it that when I say I won't say something, it comes out of this mouth of mine anyway? It probably has made you extremely angry, right?

Again, in a later letter, Shila realizes that her joking around has gone too far, and she confesses to putting on an angry demeanor on the outside while continuing to love Vajra Bahadur on the inside. These letters thus allow Shila and Vajra to contemplate issues of personhood that involve internal and external states or personas, as in the following letter written by Shila:

(047/8/13) It seems that it's become "bitter" to you because of my joking, right? I joked to make you......?, but it became bitter to you [*hajur*]. That's okay. Then again, who knows why, when I see you I feel like laughing and joking. As angry as I might be on the outside, in my heart, continuous love and respect for you keep afflicting me. In my external manner, I like to laugh and kid around with you. Get angry or laugh if you want—I laughed and joked as a lover, but you didn't like it, did you? That's okay. If you don't like me, look for a beautiful......[woman]. Go ahead—speak with those other women; what......[difference] does it make to me?

Vajra Bahadur also tried on occasion to joke with Shila, but misunderstandings resulted from some of these attempts as well, as can be seen in these excerpts from two of his letters:

(047/5/7) And another thing—you got very angry when I was speaking meanly. But just as you made a "joke," I, too, was doing just that. But you got angry. You just get angry at little, little things.

(047/8/12) You say things about others, but others are not allowed to say anything about you—you'll get angry for sure.

As the months passed, references to anger in the letters that Shila and Vajra Bahadur wrote to each other increasingly involved other villagers. Late in the summer of 1990, Shila heard a rumor that Vajra Bahadur's father had gotten angry with him because of his relationship with Shila. In the following letter, Vajra Bahadur tells her in no uncertain terms that the rumor is false—merely the talk of "those who are angry at our love":

(047/4/25) My father has neither scolded nor said anything at all about the subject of you and me. Whatever you heard is entirely false. That can only be the talk of those who are angry at our love. It seems to me that that's just the behavior of enemies who want to see us separated. One must listen to talk, but not all talk can be true. Here if one listened to all the talk, it wouldn't take long until one became crazy. What—does a forest bird talk? No, it doesn't. It's necessary for us to write letters according to the road of truth. Yes, I agree that my father sometimes gets angry. He scolds me, but not about the subject of us. To this day, I still have no knowledge of his ever having scolded me about the subject of us. If I have lied, may it be considered a huge sin.

In the fall of 1990, Shila heard another rumor about Vajra and his father, and in the letter below she urges Vajra Bahadur to tell her without getting angry whether it is true or not:

(047/7/15) Somewhere or other I've heard that you're going to marry someone else. Even if you do, that's okay......? I don't say this because my heart/mind lies; my mother said it. She said, "Vajra is going to get married, it is said. I heard it while I was on my way to another part of the village, Vajra and his father had a big argument, it is said. Vajra's father said, it is said, 'You *must* marry the girl we, your mother and father, like,' he said, it is said," my mother said. Is it true or not? If it's not, please laugh and send a response without getting angry.

In his next letter, Vajra Bahadur declares vociferously that the rumors Shila has had are untrue, that they are merely the products of those whose who wish to do them harm. In a conversation with me in 1998, however (a conversation at which Shila was also present), he admitted that he and his father had indeed been fighting regularly about marriage at the time. Every Friday, when he would return to the village from studying in Tansen, his parents would pressure him about marriage. Still, Vajra Bahadur did not want Shila to know about these arguments, and so he answered her letter in the following manner:

(047/7/17) What did you say—"Somewhere or other I heard that you're going to marry someone else." And that I had an argument with my father. All that talk is a lie. If I'm lying to you, may it be considered a big sin for me—Pashupatibaba is my witness. My life might end, but I'll only die after having fulfilled my oath, my promise. You must be my companion. Look, Shila, ever since our enemies became jealous of our love, they have sought to throw it into disarray by doing bad things to distance us from each other. Shila, no

matter what people say, we must keep this foremost in our thoughts: I am
your companion, and you are mine.

Another issue that emerged in the latter stages of their correspondence was
the secrecy of their relationship. At different times, Shila and Vajra Bahadur
each accused the other of talking about their relationship to or in front of others. By this point, most villagers knew about the courtship, but Shila and Vajra
still wanted to maintain the illusion of secrecy. The following letter refers to an
incident at the large fair, *dasaī purniyā*, associated with the full moon after the
Dashain festival. Vajra had told Shila he was going home, but then she saw him
sitting with his friends, and, it seemed to her, Vajra was telling them things she
had told him in confidence. This made Shila livid. In the following letter, Vajra
Bahadur claims that he did not discuss their relationship with his friends;
rather, he says, his friends were merely teasing him.

(047/6/23) The other day at *dasaī purniyā*, you really were angry with me.
That's why you said to my younger brother that you wouldn't speak any
more to my older sister. Why are you angry with me? I was about to head
home, but—what to do?—I had to stay there because I couldn't avoid my
friends' scolding. And you saw that. I was only sitting in the corner, providing company to my friends. What—could I ever......[share] your misfortunes with others? I certainly could not. What—don't I know all about us?
Those boys were just teasing me about us. Because I sat with them, you're
so angry that you're not talking to me any more. Upon hearing that, I felt
so sad! What my heart is like!

On another occasion, Shila evidently mentioned their relationship in front
of others, including her mother, just because she was upset with Vajra Bahadur,
and in his next letter he scolds her for it:

(047/8/17) Shila, whatever talk occurred yesterday evening was only between you and me. You shouldn't have opened up the talk about the two of
us in front of everyone. Sure, everyone gets angry, but you shouldn't have
done that just because you were angry. What did your mother think, perhaps? She probably said some things. Oh, how I am feeling!

Toward the end of 1990, Shila and Vajra Bahadur faced the most serious crisis of their courtship when Vajra Bahadur heard rumors that Shila had been, or
might still be, involved with another man. During conversations in 1998, Shila
explained that she had merely struck up a conversation with a young Newar
man in Tansen one day around this time, and he had asked her whether she

would be his fictive sister during the Bhai Tika festival.[10] She felt it would be impolite to refuse, so she answered noncommittally. Before she knew it, the young man and several of his friends showed up in Junigau asking for Shila. She and her mother served them food, then Shila told the young man she could not be his fictive sister. They never saw each other again, Shila said. Still, rumors circulated throughout Junigau about a possible relationship between Shila and the young man, a relationship that would have been all the more scandalous because the young man was a non-Magar. In the following anguished letter, Vajra Bahadur beseeches Shila to tell him the truth about the rumors and not to get angry with him for believing them:

(047/9/4) Please understand—I heard the talk; I didn't make it up in my heart/mind. Again, you'll get angry at me for believing things that may or may not be true. Don't get angry with me. Why, oh why, do I keep wanting to discuss these things with you? If you want to know who said them, where, when, what all was said, then I'll tell you openly, openly. [inserted later with a caret: In my own writing.] You must also tell me everything without hiding anything. If you hide things, I'll get extremely angry at you. Perhaps I won't speak to you for my <u>entire life.</u> And our love will be broken forever. Shila, there could never be sin in my heart/mind; whatever I've heard, I say. Even though I can't give you anything else, I've given you a true, pure love. My oath to you: if you don't hide anything from me, I won't get angry with you. Only after hearing everything from you will I be your companion, <u>but don't leave me in darkness</u>, or <u>you</u> will commit <u>a great sin</u>.

Before he received a reply from Shila, Vajra Bahadur wrote her another letter on the subject of the rumors he had heard. Again, he urged her not to be angry with him:

(047/9/5) You're angry with me, aren't you? What—have I broken off my love for you? Haven't I agreed with you? Have I forgotten our promises?
   I only told you things I had heard, but you're angry with <u>me</u>. That's okay. Shila, look, above us is God [īswar]; God alone exercises judgment. People raise others up and knock them down a lot. Perhaps people also walk along talking about us. If something happens, then they tease us even more. Everyone, being human, will get angry a lot or a little. When one is angry, anything might be written, anything might be said. Throughout this heart, love is hidden. Whatever and however much happens, my love and respect for you won't die.

Shila responded at first with cynicism and anger to Vajra Bahadur's questions about her relations with other men:

(047/9/5) Tomorrow, while I'm in Tansen, your very best friends will say so many, many bad things about me—that I fooled around, put it [i.e., someone's penis] in, took it out, slept with other men, had my photo taken, and many more things. Whatever they say, that's what you should consider to be true—never forget that, okay?

Eventually, however, after several more letters and, most likely, a few more secret meetings, Shila and Vajra Bahadur managed to get beyond issues of anger and turned to planning their elopement.

Wedding Plans

As is the case in most Junigau love letter exchanges, from the very start of their correspondence, Shila and Vajra Bahadur wrote often of marriage. Also from early on it was Vajra Bahadur who urged that they marry quickly. Shila, on the other hand, argued right up to her last letter for postponing the wedding, at least partly because of their (in her opinion) inappropriate kinship relationship. Their mothers called each other "older sister/younger sister" even though they were only distantly related, and they themselves had since childhood used with each other the terms *māmā* (mother's brother's son) and *bhānjī* (father's sister's daughter). According to Magar kinship ideologies, these kinds of cousins are not supposed to marry. Thus, although Shila and Vajra Bahadur had no close "blood" ties to each other, their *bolne sāino* (speaking/fictive kinship) was not suited to marriage. In her second (extant) letter, written in the early spring of 1990, Shila is already indicating concern about their kinship relationship and the villagers' possible reactions to it:

(046/11/3) I say this: I was in favor of waiting about one and a half to two years to get married, but today as I read your letter about getting married I felt so......Why, oh why, do I feel so......today after reading your letter? You and I, after courting, will certainly get married, but what will the other villagers who see it and hear about it say? Of course, there's nothing to fear once both our hearts have agreed—but what to do? Our kinship relationship makes it extremely difficult. You said to me, "You're afraid to love," but what to do? In response to that, I say you also have to fear the community a little bit. Then again, if you don't......

Vajra Bahadur responded to these concerns of Shila's about their kinship relationship by reminding her of how distantly they were related and of how common such "inappropriate" marriages had become in Junigau. As elopements began to outnumber arranged marriages in the late 1980s, many young people in Junigau were choosing the "wrong" kind of cousin to marry, which resulted in shifting alliances in the village and complete reconfigurations (or sometimes erasures) of kinship relations. In the following letter, Vajra Bahadur clearly states his opinion on this matter of kinship:

> (047/4/15) Another thing: you asked how to change our mothers' kinship relationship. Well, it's not that close a relationship—it's just for the purpose of speaking to each other [*bolne sāino*]. Is our kinship relationship really that close a one? If you look at kinship relationships, from one perspective they're one thing and from another, another thing. A kinship relationship is only for the purposes of speaking. In whatever manner, if the small leaves of a tree die, there are always new ones again. Village kinship relationships are like that. You, I, our mothers, and the villagers have all already changed kinship relationships. Oh, what has already happened around here! What—now that we love each other, can there really be separation? Certainly not, it seems to me.

Vajra Bahadur was also very aware of the power of community rumor and disapproval, but he frequently referred to it as yet another reason to get married quickly in order to stop people from talking about their courtship. Take, for example, this letter written by Vajra Bahadur in the fall of 1990:

> (047/6/23) If we don't see each other for even one day, how unpleasant it is! Your likeness comes before my eyes—what to do? If we do meet and speak, the villagers will certainly......[talk]. Therefore, I say that we should join quickly with each other in a relationship of life friendship, and then no one will be able to say anything. Why should we keep giving the villagers more things to talk about?
> Shila, you probably know the saying, "The more talk there is, the more misery there will be." How long a time our love has already lasted! . . .
> . . . Shila, if our union can't be, how much more they will laugh! Therefore, let's promise to make a union whatever conditions arise; let's not allow anyone to laugh, okay? If we move the time of our union further and further forward, then our lives will get more and more difficult.

Time and time again in their letters, Vajra Bahadur takes on the role of persuader, while Shila attempts to delay their marriage. In several letters, such as the following one, written at the end of October 1990, he presents an ultimatum:

> (047/7/12) I can't understand your talk. When I said, "Let's do it in Mangsir [mid-November to mid-December 1990], okay?" you said all right. Was it

out of coercion, or what? I know this much: I have loved with you, and we have loved each other. You yourself know what I'm talking about. If your heart/mind is otherwise, then that's it. If it's the same, if you love truly, then before Mangsir 4th, your and my, or, rather, our, union will occur. Beyond that, I don't know what will happen.

Aside from the issue of coercion, which appeared frequently in the narratives of elopement presented in the previous chapter, and which will be discussed further later, in this excerpt there is also a hint of desperation because by this time (late fall of 1990) Vajra Bahadur was under enormous pressure from his parents to marry so that there would be a daughter-in-law in the household to help with the work. Repeatedly, Vajra threatened to break off the relationship if they did not get married by a certain date. Each time, however, Shila called his bluff and made him postpone their wedding plans. On this subject also, her tone combined malleability with assertiveness. In response to Vajra's letter above, for example, Shila wrote:

(047/7/15) You say, "I find that you are thinking of marrying and spending your life with a foreign soldier," you said. My thoughts haven't gone in that direction at all. If you say that, then I......? (What—if I married a foreign soldier, would you......[find] another life friend or love?) That's okay. It's your choice. What can I say, after all? Now you forget the promise that we made. If you don't forget I am ready, or, rather, consent to marry you. I consent, consent, consent! Except that you say the 4th of this Mangsir, you said, but that soon I......I'd be ready whenever you say, but I......That is to say, I am such a poor match. I'm an......[orphan—a fatherless daughter]. I'm such a poor [i.e., not wealthy] daughter, which you probably already know. "Let's get married," you[11] say; a woman must relinquish her family. I will relinquish my family, but my home's afflicted state makes me a very poor match. . . .
. . . Yes, we made a promise. What—have I already forgotten the promise and left your company......? Really, you wrote, "Before the 4th of Mangsir your and my, or, rather, our, union will already have occurred. Beyond that what will happen I don't know." What—if our marriage doesn't happen by Mangsir 4th, are you ready to marry someone else? That's okay. If you want, marry another much prettier, very educated girl that you like ever so much.

Although early on in their courtship Shila and Vajra Bahadur discussed the possibility of an arranged marriage, they both agreed that their complicated kinship relationship made it extremely unlikely that Shila's mother would agree to an arranged match. Still, Shila was reluctant to agree to an elopement because she knew it would be painful to her mother for her to get married in this less prestigious way. Nevertheless, she was willing to "consent" to an elopement by late 1990; she just wanted to delay it as long as possible.

In the spring of 1991 a sister-cousin of Shila's got married to a brother-cousin of Vajra's, thereby "opening the door" for their own match because this new, much closer (and appropriate for marriage) kinship relationship superseded their previous distantly inappropriate one. Vajra Bahadur urged Shila to use this excuse to elope immediately, but she still wanted to wait at least a month. In the following letter, written in mid-March 1991, Shila bemoans her fate and yet also takes the initiative to suggest a wedding date the following month:

> (047/12/3) The main thing—what should I say?—is that my younger sister-cousin's wedding was just the other day, and yet you say we should get married before a month has passed. But why do it in the same month, I say? My idea is, rather, that we do it in Baisakh [next month]. Because I've said that, you'll probably get angry......Why......? So, people will say, "One month hasn't even passed since the sister-cousin's wedding, and they've gotten married!" Oh, what more will people say......? Oh, what an unlucky one I am! The village, the home—they all hate me. I had hoped to find the company of someone in this world, but today it feels like that hope is gone. But who knows what will happen. I can't figure anything out. Even if I did figure things out, what should I do? After luck/fate [*bhāgya*], or should I say time, plays around with mysteries, what is left, after all?

The last three letters in the courtship correspondence are important enough to warrant close analysis of them here. In mid-April (the third day of the Nepali month of Baisakh), Vajra Bahadur wrote Shila a long letter urging her to "think for herself" and elope with him within a week (before the tenth of Baisakh). Vajra Bahadur is also clearly "thinking for himself" here, not only about marriage but also about the life of a Gurkha soldier. Although such a life is ordinarily highly valued in Junigau, Vajra Bahadur deplores it. Notice the implicit theory of agency Vajra is espousing in this letter: he believes that both he and Shila have the power to act in ways that will have an impact on their lives. Vajra is urging Shila to believe in this ability to create through her actions the kind of life she wants. Here are some excerpts of this desperate-sounding letter:

> (048/1/3) Shila, I've already written many words and explained a lot to you. Now I have no more of those kinds of words. Think for yourself why you love. Are you going to conduct your whole life like that, and are you going

to spend your whole life with your mother, or with your life friend? Shila, let's not have regrets later on. If a breakup occurs, it would be as if something like a loss of honor had occurred. Instead, since we live in a world like this, it would be better to......[get married]. Why are you afraid of your mother? It's your life, not your mother's, you know. One's marriage will be with the person one desires; one wears the flower that one likes and eats the things that one likes. Marriage can never be because of others' violent coercion. We only live for two days. If one can't spend such a short life with the person one likes, then what kind of life is that? That life is loathesome.

Your mother's wish is to give you in an arranged marriage to a soldier, but I'm no soldier. I don't even like that. A soldier's life is the life of an animal. There's no difference between an animal's life and a soldier's life. Why must anyone have to live for even one day as an animal, right? Whatever one's life is like, may one be able to survive. What—can one only survive if one is a soldier, otherwise not? Let's leave off this talk. You say you won't elope, right? If we could have had such an arranged marriage, that would have been best. Everyone feels like, "Let's do it the best way." Don't I, too, want us to do it the best way possible? But what to do once it [i.e., the situation, the kinship relationship] is like that? It's necessary to elope. There are ten kinds of marriage types.[12] Whatever the circumstances require, that's what must be done, in my opinion. To what extent are you able to think? You must think for yourself. I'm going to be watching how your mind works, how well you can think. . . .

. . . That's okay, Shila. Today our love, all those promises, have all gone to waste, haven't they? The villagers are really laughing, aren't they? It's your opinion, isn't it, that only you have honor, not I. That's okay. I don't want to hurt your heart/mind. Go marry the boy your mother gives you to, whether you like him or not because after not having married the boy you like, that's what must happen. I was sure I would have your company, but......[now I'm not sure]. I want to give you one suggestion: don't love anyone any more, or else you'll......[betray them] just as you did me in the end. If you can't extinguish your love, then why love in vain? To love someone, then to......[marry] someone else is a curse. Rather, instead of that, it's better not to love at all. Only betrayal [rest of sentence crossed out].

Shila, I am not to blame at all in this. I have not sinned. Whatever I did, I did so as if you were my own. But you have a different opinion. Shila, it's not possible for you to blame me. May you not cry later on from regret, Shila. One must listen to what everyone says, but people will say this, and people will say that. But one must make up one's mind oneself. One must straighten out one's own world. Shila, I've coerced you a lot on the subject of getting married, haven't I? From now on, for the rest of my life, I won't say anything. Why, oh why, did my heart/mind suffer when you wouldn't do what I said? My heart/mind has begun to fly away. I feel like my heart is about to break. If this heart breaks, it will never again come to life for you. Shila, to walk around making things smell is a curse. Will you really pass your life well with another boy?

Shila, our union must occur before the 10th of this Baisakh [i.e., within a week]. Shila, say whatever you want—if it can't occur by then, then think: it can't occur your whole life. If it can't occur, then let people say whatever they want, and let whatever happens, happen—I'll make up my own mind. Just as a bone can't be put back together again once it has been broken, so, too, once a heart has been broken, or a heart/mind broken, it can also not be put back together again. Write a letter stating clearly what to do and when to do it on the 10th, and that's how we'll do it. [next sentence inserted between the lines:] Shila, this is my final decision. Forgive my mistakes. We'll meet again in another letter. Your friend who awaits your letter, "V.B."

Shila replied to this letter four days later (on the seventh of Baisakh). In her response, she resists Vajra's assertion that he will be watching how her mind works. She writes that she cannot compete with his mind because she is "illiterate" and uneducated. But if he wants to compete "socially" then she is ready to marry him before the tenth of Baisakh (a mere three days hence), she says. This letter was the last Shila wrote during her courtship with Vajra Bahadur. Here it is in its entirety:

(048/1/7) Dear, dear......friend, best wishes for the new year 2048, and with love I am coming to you by way of these notebook pages. I am well and hope that your health is also good. From your dear......[life] friend, hundreds of thousands of remembrances, hundreds of thousands of smiles, hundreds of thousands of desires for affection......

There might be thousands of mistakes in this letter; for them I beg forgiveness......First, I'm sad that I couldn't answer your letters quickly. Since reading your letters I've been so, so......Don't I carry the same number of burdens that you do? Aren't I as full of injuries as you are? But what to do? No matter how many injuries there are, on the outside one must give......[the appearance] of laughter.

Friend, my mother might want to give me in marriage to a soldier or to whomever, but it's <u>my</u> wish, [i.e., my marriage is up to me]. I have the desire and wish to marry my own beloved, but you[13] have started to talk about various methods. Have I said I wouldn't marry you? That's okay. You want to watch my mind, right? But I can't compete against you with my mind. I'm just an illiterate......[woman], a person who hasn't had an education. How can I compete with my mind against you, a person who has had that kind of......[education]. I'm just a......[woman]. If you're seeking to compete with our minds, then you can do so with someone else who has......[education]. But that's okay. If you want to do so or think so socially [i.e., instead of intellectually], then I am ready to be yours before the 10th, just as you said. But if you start talking about minds, soldiers, or old women, then I'll......[get angry] with you. You wanted to say to me, "How many, many women there are who are younger than you who have already gotten married, but you've already become an old woman!" You wanted to say this, right? "You also have to think about the future......Shila, may you not have regrets later," you said, right......? But that's okay. Even if I were a youngster, I would probably know my own......opinions. I also know that one must think ahead of time for the future......You don't have to explain things to me so much; I'm not a little nursing child! What do you have to keep explaining to me? I'm already an extremely old woman!

Again, you say, "Your mother is thinking of giving you in marriage to some soldier." Don't you consider it difficult to enter my mother's heart/ mind......? I don't like soldiers. If I were going to be married to a soldier, I probably would have married one already, but why didn't it happen? You know why. Who is the soldier, and where he is from—you know that, too. You have full knowledge. But why didn't a marriage occur with him? Did I not want him, or did he not want me? That I don't want to explain. But let people say what they will—aside from you, I have no others who are mine. Whatever—after we get married, it won't be possible to say this and that carelessly to me in various manners.

Okay, why should I keep writing so many things? Forgive this old woman's mistakes.

Your love who has no mind
You, a very mind-ful person
Farewell farewell farewell farewell
"O.K. By By"

Vajra replied to this letter two days later, on the ninth of Baisakh. Here is the complete text of this response, his final courtship letter to Shila:

(048/1/9) Dear Shila, my life friend, heartfelt, auspicious good wishes for the new year 2048, and hundreds of thousands of remembrances and hundreds of thousands of kisses and hundreds of thousands of tokens of affection.

Being well, I also hope for your good health.

Shila, what to do? I find that life is a mixture of sorrow and joy. As sad as you are—that's how sad I am, too. I have spilled out my own sorrows to you in letters. Don't you ever consider that oppressive. Shila, I'm not cruel. How many troubles you probably have—we both know how many. In life, each person has his/her own stories—that's the law of the world. Shila, you can say anything to me without bashfulness. It's not all right to act as you do forever [i.e., to stay unmarried]. If I hurt your heart/mind with too many words, because of that I'm very miserable. I never want to deliver suffering to you.

I also never want to deliver any suffering to you in the future. I don't want to make your heart/mind miserable. But will you do those sorts of things to me? Shila, is it all right for two life friends to do things that make each other's heart/mind miserable? It's certainly not all right. Both must understand this when they act. "Life friend" means to share each other's joy and sorrow. You must be wise, and I must be wise. Shila, we'll talk of various joys and sorrows when we meet.

Instead, let's head for the main thing. Shila, as easy as it is to talk about something, it will be more difficult to put it into action. Shila, I said that our wedding must occur before the 10th. Now there's just tomorrow left for us of that time. If it doesn't occur today, it must occur tomorrow. That's what it seems like to me. Let's make our life's joyful union today, okay, because there's so little time. Today would also be very appropriate because you'll certainly go to do work or carry water at your sister-cousin's wedding feast, right? My brother-cousin and I will come to eat at the wedding feast in the evening, and we'll meet you there. We'll have a conversation. Shila, let it not happen differently. Okay, Shila, we'll talk about other things when we meet. I beg forgiveness for my mistakes. Shila, let's meet this evening. Okay, farewell.

Your miserable L[ife] Friend,
V. B. [Last Name]

Just as Vajra Bahadur has written, he and a cousin of his went to the wedding feast of a cousin of Shila's (not the same cousin who had married the previous month). Vajra sent his cousin to meet Shila and bring her back to him so that they could go together to his house, where they would then call in his relatives to acknowledge their marriage. In an interview in 1992, when she was still a new wife and daughter-in-law adjusting to her change in life circumstances, Shila seemed to have lost a lot of her earlier spunk. She described the events of that day as follows, both eschewing responsibility for her actions and scolding herself for them in a manner that echoes the complicated and rapidly changing conceptions villagers have of their own agency:

LMA: Tell me about your own wedding.

SD: Oh, what happened, what happened? I have no idea.

LMA: You have no idea? You know about your own wedding, don't you?

SD: Oh, who knows how it happened, how—my wedding, oh—I had NO idea. I never thought that my wedding would be like that. It was sudden, see, like that.

LMA: Really?

SD: Yes. I really didn't want to have my wedding like that, see?

LMA: Really? What was it like? Why?

SD: Of course, it wasn't a violent wedding, right? We had been courting for a long time, see? . . . Later on, he wrote in a letter, "Let's get married." But I kept saying, "I'm uneducated. You should marry an educated woman," I kept saying, see? [inaudible] I said, "No," you see; that's what I wrote. Then after going on like this for a long time—suddenly we got married. . . .

LMA: What was your wedding day like?

SD: On the day I got married, I had no idea; I never said to myself, "Today will be my wedding, perhaps."

LMA: Really?

SD: He had said something, see? He had written it in letters, twice he had [proposed a marriage date] in letters—umm, he wrote, "On a certain day, umm, like this we'll get married." But I didn't consent. Then I, like that: I REALLY hadn't decided to say, "All right," see? Until the very last moment, I kept saying to him, "For yourself you should—there are others. There are so many others! The others, umm, with you—you should marry someone as educated as yourself!" I also kept saying that our kinship relationship wouldn't work; I always said that in letters, see? I never said, "All right." And then in a letter he wrote, "Let's elope tomorrow or the next day. Let's get married on a certain day." I said, "Umm, I really don't know," said I. And even then he sent another letter saying the same thing. I didn't send a reply. Then I went to my sister-cousin's wedding. [laughs] I went there, and I had NO idea! All day I carried water with my friends. Carrying water, serving food, see? Then after I worked there all day, he [i.e., Vajra Bahadur] and [Vajra Bahadur's cousin-brother] came to my sister-cousin's wedding feast in the evening to eat. In the evening, to eat— and [Vajra's cousin-brother] said, see, "Go meet my older cousin-brother [i.e., Vajra Bahadur]." Then I, I was startled—finally I remembered what

Vajra Bahadur had said in the letter! I became so startled! My heart started trembling, see! I hadn't thought I'd marry like that. I finally remembered that he'd said that, see? Then I went to meet him. Vajra said, "I said today; what happened?" "I don't know!" "Oh." Then, umm, he said, "Today you have to give me a final answer." "I gave you one days ago," I replied. "In that case, you consent, right?" And then Vajra's brother-cousin and he—they were friends, and I was alone. And then, he said, "Today we MUST get married!"—just like that—I have no idea what happened!

LMA: Then, there, there—it was nighttime?

SD: Yes, it was nighttime. Just like that, then, who knows what it was?

LMA: Then together…?

SD: We went.

LMA: To Vajra Bahadur's home, or…?

SD: Yes, we went together. Oh, what happened? Remembering my wedding, the day of my wedding, I get angry with myself!

LMA: [we both laugh] With whom?

SD: With myself!

LMA: Now, why would you get angry?

SD: Because—I didn't want to get married that way; what happened? I, now, they didn't even take me violently. They didn't even pull me along. In the end, I came on my own. I wasn't crazy. I didn't lose consciousness. "What happened?" I ask myself….[While waiting for the brief wedding ceremony to be performed, I] just kept sitting there, yes. This heart of mine, it went chilingpaṭa, chiling, chiling [sound effect of a churning heart]—should I run away? What should I do? Should I run away? What should I do?…It happened like that. Well, it was my lot in life; if it's written [fated], then that's what one has to endure, I say now, sometimes. I scold myself alone, and then again, no, it was written like this, I say.

In a 1992 interview, Vajra Bahadur's summation of the courtship focused not on the actual day of the elopement but on the entire courtship. He, too, however, combined fatalism with a sense of individual agency in his final statement:

VB: In a way, I say sometimes that this was probably written to be my fate. In actuality, we do it ourselves, but it's like that, see? Our fates are written.

Epilogue: Seven Years Later

Once Shila accompanied Vajra Bahadur to his house on that night of the tenth of Baisakh in 2048 (the end of April in 1991), their families rapidly accepted their union. Shila's mother was upset initially, having wanted to marry her daughter off in a large, arranged marriage ceremony to a high-ranking, high-earning soldier from a distant village. Very soon, however, she realized that Shila's marriage to Vajra Bahadur enabled her to stay in the same village and visit her mother often, helping out with work in the fields.

In the years since they eloped, it seems to me from talking to them, observing them, and listening to what other villagers say, Shila and Vajra Bahadur have had a very close but extremely volatile marriage. There have been several times when they would argue to the point where Shila would go and stay with her mother for a few days. But to date they have always made up. A year after their elopement, Shila gave birth to a son, and in the early years of her marriage she seemed to have transformed herself into a traditionally meek daughter-in-law who lived with her husband's extended family. In 1996, however, Shila and Vajra Bahadur opened up their own tea shop in the village, and since then not only has Shila's old assertiveness and infectious laughter reappeared but Vajra Bahadur, too, has taken on a more central leadership role in the village. The two of them talk often about business matters and share what appears to me to be a pretty equal distribution of labor. In this, they are atypical for Junigau but not unique.

While many factors may have contributed to the relationship Shila and Vajra Bahadur have had since they married, it is clear to me that it is largely attributable to the type of epistolary courtship they had. Letters enabled Shila and Vajra to express deeply felt emotions, including anger, fear, and love, that would not have been easily expressible aloud. Indeed, in 1998 Shila told me that there are things she said to Vajra Bahadur in her letters (mainly protestations of love) that she had never said to him aloud in over seven years of marriage. And both of them told me that they still use letters to communicate on occasion during arguments or misunderstandings. One of them will leave a letter for the other in a certain place in the store, and the other will read it and respond in kind. Unfortunately, they have never kept these postmarital letters.

In the courtship of Shila and Vajra Bahadur can be seen all the elements discussed in previous chapters relating to changing conceptions of agency, gender relations, and social dynamics more generally. Their correspondence thus serves as an excellent case study both of the unintended consequences of female literacy and the ways in which broader social transformations are both reflected in and shaped by village love letters.

PART THREE

Love, Literacy, & Development

CHAPTER SEVEN

Developing Love

Sources of Development Discourse in
Nepali Love Letters

In the summer of 1990, Vajra Bahadur wrote the following words to Shila Devi, with whom he had been corresponding at that point for about six months:

> There's nothing special [to write about], except that memories of you keep torturing me so much that I'm scratching a few words onto this page in order to give my heart some peace . . . Come today, and let's create an understanding that will make our love successful and that will make us never be separated.

In this letter and in many of the other two hundred or more love letters I have collected from the residents of Junigau, young correspondents construct romantic love in a culturally specific way. Love happens *to* Junigau villagers; it afflicts and torments them, catches them in a web, makes them feel like they're going crazy. Yet it also empowers them, giving them a sense of agency in other realms of their lives, thereby connecting them up with "development discourse" (cf. Escobar 1995; Grillo and Stirrat 1997; Pigg 1992) and Western, commodified notions of "success." This conception of romantic love differs significantly from older conceptions of love in Junigau and from mainstream U.S. formulations of romantic love (cf. Jankowiak 1995; McCollum 1998; Quinn 1982, 1996).

What are the sources influencing villagers' conceptions of romantic love? How have the practices surrounding reading and writing shaped the discourse found in Junigau love letters? What kinds of materials are Junigau young people reading? This chapter is divided into two parts. In the first, I describe the meanings Junigau residents came to associate with romantic love in the 1990s. In the second, I analyze the written materials Junigau young people read and discuss the ways in which these materials promote new ideas about selfhood, emotion, development, and agency.

What Love Means to Junigau Villagers

As elopements have become increasingly popular in Junigau, many young villagers have told me that they are searching for a "life friend" (often using this phrase in English). The ideal of passionate romantic love, followed by a warm companionate marriage has taken strong hold in Junigau. People such as Dimi, whose elopement was described in an earlier chapter, explicitly label arranged marriage and especially capture marriage as "backward" (*pichhyāḍī*) practices, while elopement is labelled as "developed" (*bikāsī*).

In the hundreds of love letters I have collected from generous Junigau residents, romantic love is often associated not only with development but with success and autonomy in decision-making ability. Paradoxically, however, while love empowers lovers in non-romantic realms, people do not have any control over love itself. Vajra Bahadur explained this to me in 1996:

> There's a song in Hindi, see? What it says is in relation to "love," see, is '*pyār nahī kiyā jātā; pyār ho jātā hai*' [Hindi: Love is not created; love just is]. This means that affection, love, can't be created. Love can't be created, see? It happens by itself, it is said. In an "automatic" way, love settles in, one to the other. Now, really, that's how it happened with me.

This concept of love as happening uncontrollably is not new in Junigau. When I asked older people if they loved their spouses, they would often answer with a shrug and a sheepish smile that, yes, they did. Even in cases where a husband might gamble, be verbally abusive, or take another wife, the first wife would frequently tell me that she couldn't help it; she still loved him. There is a difference, however, between this older idea of love befalling someone and more recent conceptions of the emotion. In the 1990s, Junigau young people came to view romantic love as empowering them in other realms of their lives—an emotion of which to be proud, for it was associated with development and success. In earlier times, villagers had viewed romantic love with a good deal of shame or at least embarrassment. Love had no positive aspects to it; in fact, it primarily brought pain and trouble. Several older women shared a saying with me that conveyed their philosophy of love: *naso pasyo, māyā basyo*—"The vein/hose [i.e., penis] entered and love followed." One would come to love one's husband, in other words, after having sex with him. This saying is interesting not only because of the causal theory for love it espouses but also because it was almost always said to me in the context of a woman explaining why she stayed with a husband who treated her poorly. This kind of love was far from the empowering kind of love in which Junigau villagers in the

1990s came to believe; this kind of love was to be avoided, disavowed, or, if all else failed, reluctantly tolerated.

The love letter correspondences featured in this ethnography powerfully illustrate the more recent understanding of romantic love as being out of one's control and yet also somehow empowering. In Bir Bahadur's first letter to his eventual wife, Sarita, for example, he wrote:

> In the whole "world" there must be few individuals who do not bow down to love. . . . In which case, Sarita, I'll let you know by a "short cut" what I want to say: Love is the union of two souls. The "main" meaning of love is "life success."

Along the same lines, in two later letters, Bir Bahadur writes,

> When love and affection have become steady, one will certainly be able to obtain the things one has thought and worried about. . . .
> . . . May our love reach a place where we can in our lives overthrow any difficulties that arrive and obtain success.

Thus, love in the 1990s is considered empowering even as it makes people "bow down." Junigau love letter writers believe that love enables them to achieve "life success," which they define as carving out lives for themselves that mirror the images they see and hear about in a diverse array of media, from textbooks and magazines to Hindi and Nepali films to Radio Nepal development programs. These images promote a lifestyle based on formal education, knowledge of English, lucrative employment, the consumption of commodities, and a sense of self founded on individualism. So popular is this notion of success that one Junigau couple recently discarded "Mohan," the name given to their son by a Brahman priest in favor of "Saphal" ("Success"). Furthermore, when "success" is mentioned in reference to romantic love, Junigau letter writers reveal their assumption, or at least hope, that "successful" romantic love will result in marriage and that marriage will be idyllic in nature. Even as romantic love is portrayed as being beyond letter writers' control, therefore, it nevertheless is linked with a sense of agency in other realms of their lives. The same paradoxical qualities of love can be seen in these excerpts from a letter written by Vajra Bahadur to Shila Devi:

> What on earth is this thing called love? Once one falls into its web, one is ready to do anything at the invitation of one's beloved. Why, oh why, is it that what you say, memories of you, and affection for you are always tormenting me?

And yet a few paragraphs later he writes, "These days nothing is impossible in this world. A person can do anything." Shila Devi responded with the following:

> Mother's Brother's Son, what is there left [to write about]? . . . May we be successful, I say. What is your wish......? Of course, even when there are wishes and desires, no one knows anything about the time and circumstances under which they will be fulfilled.
> Some people say that if it's their lot in life, [whatever it is] they'll do it. But it seems to me that it's up to each person's own wishes...... Even without my telling you this, you would be knowledgeable about it.

Thus, love is increasingly associated with being "developed" and successful, and it is more and more associated with independence and the ability to overcome all obstacles in life. Love has become the agent, and it has made Junigau villagers feel like agents in all realms of their lives but one: love.

Written Sources of Development Discourse

Where do these new ideas about love, success, agency, and personhood come from? By the 1990s, development discourse was ubiquitous in Junigau in textbooks, magazines and novels, Radio Nepal development programs and soap operas, Hindi movies in Tansen, love letter guidebooks, and everyday conversations. In the remainder of this chapter, I focus on the written sources of development discourse and new ideas about agency. In the next chapter, I turn to actual literacy practices surrounding reading and writing, as well as the viewing of films, and explore how literacy practices in Junigau have changed over time.

Textbooks

The National Curriculum: Teaching Nationalism, Hierarchy, and Hinduism

All government schools in Nepal, including Sarvodaya High School, use the same set of textbooks published by the Ministry of Education and Culture. When I taught English and math in the early 1980s, these were the textbooks I used, and they are the textbooks from which many of Junigau's love letter writers learned in their early years of formal schooling. There are standardized textbooks for each subject from the first grade all the way through college. The themes that come through most clearly from the textbooks' stories and pictures are (1) nationalism and development, which are presented as going hand in hand; (2) age and gender hierarchies; and, (3) hegemonic Hinduism.[1]

1. *Nationalism and development.*   Ever since the separate kingdoms that now make up Nepal were united in the eighteenth century, the central government has attempted to forge a unifying national identity that transcends differences in caste and ethnic background.[2] School textbooks used in Nepal during the 1980s and 1990s furthered this project, perfectly illustrating Robert Arnove and Harvey J. Graff's astute statement: "Literacy is almost never itself an isolated or absolute goal . . . [but] rather part of a larger process and vehicle for that process," namely, "nation building" (1987:7; cf. Anderson [1983] 1991). The first lesson of the first grade's social studies textbook presents the lyrics of Nepal's national anthem, which is incomprehensible to most students, and indeed to many Junigau villagers, because of its formal language. The lesson is accompanied by a picture of little girls and boys standing at attention in front of the Nepali flag while the Himalayas rise behind them. The king and queen are featured in many lessons, especially in primary and middle school English and Nepali social studies. The following poems, from the second grade social studies textbook, are examples of how the king and queen are presented to students as unifying national symbols. The poem titles are the full titles of King Birendra and Queen Aishwarya, respectively.

Shri Panch Mahārājādhirāj Birendra Bir Bikram Shāhadev
All of us Nepalis have
One common king.
The King who loves Nepal
Is everyone's king.
Just as his mother and father did,
The King acts with fondness.
The King is liked
By all of us Nepalis.
Our King travels around
To Nepal's homes and doorsteps.
The King understands
Nepalis' happiness and suffering.
The King gives us work, rice,
And happiness.
The King gives love
To everyone equally.
Our dear King wears
A crown on his head.
The King looks out for
Nepal and Nepalis.
                    (Ghimire 1986: 173–74)[3]

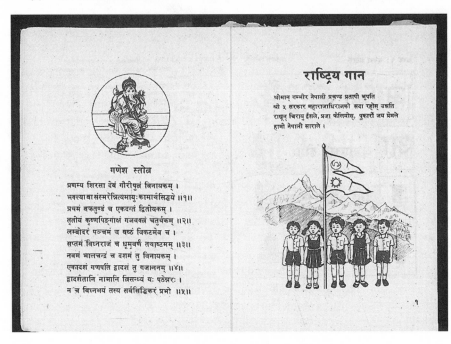

Plate 19   Pages from the *Mahendra Mālā* first grade textbook

Shri Panch Baḍāmahārāni Aishwarya Rājyalakshmi Devi Shāha
Our country's Queen
Loves us all.
Our Queen
Does service for our society.
The Queen of all of us
Writes beautiful, beautiful songs.
The Queen loves us all
As she loves herself.
Our Queen walks
Up and down steep hills.
The Queen understands
Nepalis' happiness and suffering.
The Queen celebrates
At Nepal's houses and homes.
Our Queen loves
All of us equally.

(Ghimire 1986: 177–78)

Other reading selections tell students of the scenic beauty of Nepal, its history, and its ancient buildings. Most salient for our purposes here, the textbooks also contain development discourse, starting from the very first page of *every* school textbook, where King Birendra, pictured atop the page, discusses his hopes for the National Education Plan:[4]

> This National Education Plan, which devotes itself to the policy of causing the national intelligence to flower and bear fruit and to making people's attitudes development-oriented, will, I hope, create within a few years an aware, industrious, and progressive society. (King Birendra, in Ghimire 1988)

Development discourse of this sort is found not only in the king's statement but throughout the textbooks. It is always linked, however, to the government's attempt to instill national pride in students. Development and nationalism go hand in hand in these textbooks. Unlike some of the magazines discussed later, government schoolbooks illustrate the government's desire to retain a strong Nepali identity rather than take on a Western one. When the topic of development is raised, it is done in a way that encourages students to feel proud *as Nepalis* for the progress the country has made in moving away from "backward" conditions toward "modern" ones. Several reading selections from English textbooks illustrate this point. The following is for seventh grade students:[5]

Changes in Our Village

Our village has changed a lot in the last ten years. The women used to walk to a stream for water every morning. Sometimes the water was not very clean. Now there is a tap in the middle of the village. The water from the tap is generally clean.

We had no school ten years ago. Pupils used to walk five miles every day to the school in Ganeshgaon. Now we have our own lower secondary school.

Ten years ago there was no market in our village. People used to go to the market in the nearest town every Saturday to buy and sell things. Now there is a market once a week in the village.

There did not used to be a road to our village. Now there is a road. A bus stops here twice a day.

We had no electricity. In the evening, we used to light oil lamps or candles. We had no doctor. Sick people used to buy village medicines or walk to Kathmandu to see a doctor. Now when we are sick, we can go to the village health centre. People are healthy now.

Our village has certainly changed a lot. (Vaidya 1982: 29–30)

Junigau underwent many of these changes during the 1980s and 1990s. Water taps were built, a high school was created, tea shops offered the opportunity to buy goods in the village, electricity arrived, and a health post was opened. Students observing these changes in their own village are encouraged to become cognizant of these changes as part of the country's attempt to become *bikāsī* and feel proud. In my observations of students in the 1980s and 1990s, it seemed that many of them were indeed absorbing the messages they were receiving from textbooks and other sources. Reading selections, such as the following from the seventh grade English textbook, echoed the ubiquitous development discourse on the radio, in village political speeches, and in the popular press that called for all Nepalis to improve themselves and their country by making their behavior more *bikāsī*:

How to be Healthy

Mr Subba is a health worker. The Pradhan Pancha[6] asked him to speak to the villagers about health. He asked all the villagers to come to a meeting at the school. Most of them came. [The drawing shows Mr. Subba with an audience of three men.]

At the meeting, Mr Subba said, "The most important rule of health is: you must keep clean. Wash your hands before a meal. Don't let flies touch your food. Drink clean water. You mustn't drink dirty water. The panchayat has made a tap for clean drinking water. Use that water."

"You mustn't empty your bowels in the fields on paths and near streams because flies will sit on this dirt. Then they will carry this dirt to food or other people. People will become sick. One sick person can make the whole village sick. Make a latrine near your house and use it. But remember, you mustn't make a latrine near a well."

Then he talked about food. One of the men said, "We have plenty of food in this village. There's enough rice and there are enough potatoes for all of us."

Mr Subba said, "Both rice and potatoes are good but you must also eat vegetables. You can easily make a vegetable garden in your field. Give your children green vegetables. They will be healthy and strong."

A woman said, "But mother's milk and a little rice are enough for small children."

Mr Subba said, "Mother's milk and rice aren't enough. Give your children porridge too. You can make it from roasted soybean flour, roasted wheat flour and roasted corn flour."

Finally, Mr Subba talked about smoking. He said, "Many people smoke in this country. Smoking is bad for your health. You mustn't let your children smoke and you must not smoke too." (Vaidya 1982: 65–67)[7]

Just as students are encouraged to credit the government with positive changes such as a new water tap, so are they implicitly urged to follow the examples of the characters in the stories, many of whom pursue formal education in order to improve their own skills. The following example is from the sixth grade English textbook:

> Ramesh had four children. Their names were Ram, Shiva, Laxmi and Jagadish. They lived in Bhojpur many years ago. Their father worked hard because he wanted to send his children to school. They all went to school and studied up to S.L.C.[8] Ram went to campus after his S.L.C. He studied there for four years. He works in a bank now.
>
> Shiva went to Birgunj five years ago. He became a teacher. He is teaching in Jhapa now. He is going to teach in Bhojpur next year. Laxmi went to Kathmandu three years ago. She studied medicine there and became a health worker. She is working in a health post now. Jagadish is in Bhojpur now. He is helping his father on his farm and he is learning a lot. He wants to be a J.T.A.[9] after a few years. Ramesh Prasad is very proud of his children. (Pradhan 1981: 100)

Note that the mother of the four children does not appear at all in the story. It is their father who works hard to send his children to school and then feels proud when they succeed in becoming more than just farmers. Furthermore, the children achieve "success" relative to their birth order, with the oldest child becoming a banker, the second oldest a teacher, the third oldest (the only daughter) a health worker, and the youngest a farmer and eventually an agricultural agent. This outcome mirrors the hierarchical relations expected among the siblings, which brings us to the next area of emphasis in Nepali textbooks.

2. Age and gender hierarchies.   As students learn how to read and write, they are also taught proper attitudes and behavior through the textbooks' pictures and reading selections. In addition to working for the development of their country by improving their own skills, students are explicitly told and shown where they fit in the country's age and gender hierarchies. Each social studies textbook contains a preface in which teachers are reminded that teaching morals is as important as teaching children how to read and write. Even if such a preface did not exist, however, the reading selections provide students with unmistakable lessons in cultural hierarchies. The following poem, accompanied by a picture of a boy bowing down to his parents, who are dressed in traditional Nepali garb, is from the first grade social studies textbook. It tells children to respect their elders, the gods, and education (in the form of books):

Good Habits
To Father, to Mother
We make respectful greetings
To the teacher's wife, to the teacher
We say/do *namaskār*[10]

To the gods and the earth
We worship and bow down
Bowing down to our books again
We repeat our own lessons

We love those who are small [i.e., junior to us]
We respect those who are large [i.e., senior to us]
Agreement with everyone
We do good work

Our own bag and things
We look after
Our own work, whatever there is,
We do it completely by ourselves

We learn good habits
We will be clean and pure
From childhood on
We do good things.

(Ghimire 1988: 142)

These admonitions are elaborated on in a similar second grade social studies reading selection:

Good Habits and Behaviors
Hari is in the second grade. His older sister Radha is in the fifth grade. They get along very well. The habits and behaviors of both of them are good. Both their customs are good. Hari and Radha's mother and father have taught them good habits and behaviors. At school, the schoolmasters and schoolmistresses [i.e., male and female teachers] have taught them good things and give them much knowledge.

Hari and Radha obey their father and mother. Hari obeys his older sister. Hari and Radha have one cousin [father's younger brother's son]. His is the older brother[-cousin] of Hari and Radha. Hari and Radha obey this older brother[-cousin]. They obey those who are bigger [i.e., more senior] than they are. (Ghimire 1986: 106–7)

This reading selection goes on to describe how punctual Hari and Radha are, how soft their voices are, how well they behave in lines and in crowds, and how well they get along with their friends, who may come from near or far, "but upon arriving at the school, they all become like older or younger brothers and older or younger sisters" (Ghimire 1986: 110). Although differences in caste and ethnicity are not mentioned explicitly, the implication is that for educated Nepalis their national identity should take precedence over their ethnic or caste identity and allow them to consider their schoolmates to be brothers and sisters. Age differences are not erased, however; children are told to treat their classmates like "older or younger brothers and older or younger sisters."

In addition to age hierarchies, existing gender hierarchies are for the most part reinforced by the government textbooks. Virtually all of the public figures featured in all of the primary and middle school textbooks—artists, politicians, writers, and so on—are men, with the exception of the queen (but even she derives her status from her relationship with her husband) and a few goddesses. While female students are mentioned and pictured occasionally, they often take a secondary role, as Radha does in the reading selection quoted earlier. As the accompanying drawing of boys playing soccer illustrates, the reading selection's main protagonist is Hari. Frequently, boys and men are depicted in public roles, while girls and women are depicted in domestic roles, such as in the following two reading selections from the fifth grade English textbook:

1. Mr Singh is in his classroom. He is telling the pupils a story. It's about Nepal. He is showing them a picture of Great King Prithvi Narayan Shah. [Illustration shows Mr. Singh in the classroom with two female and two male students.]
2. Now Mr Singh is walking home. He is wearing his black cap and he is carrying his bag. [Illustration shows Mr. Singh wearing traditional Nepali garb along with a suit jacket, and he is carrying a satchel.]
3. Mr Singh is sitting on a mat. Mrs Singh is giving him eggs, fish and meat. [Illustration shows Mrs. Singh leaning over to serve her husband food.]
    (Ministry of Education and Culture 1983: 73–74)

1. It is 6 o'clock. Ram's mother is bringing a pot of water from the tap. [Illustration depicts Ram's mother at the tap.]
2. It is half past eight. She is cooking a pot of rice on the fire. [Illustration shows Ram's mother cooking over a wood fire.]

3. It is 9 o'clock. Ram and his father are eating. Ram has got a small plate of rice. His father has got a big plate of rice. Ram is drinking a glass of milk. His father is drinking a glass of water. [Illustration shows Ram and his father sitting on a mat and eating. Ram's mother is not shown, but she is clearly the one who would be serving them, as Nepali etiquette and Hindu laws of purity require men to eat first and to be served by the cook.]

4. It is a quarter past 10. Ram is in school. He has got a bottle of ink. He is writing on a sheet of paper. [Illustration shows Ram sitting on a bench at school writing with a fountain pen.] (117–118)

Thus, in Nepali, English, and social studies textbooks from the 1980s, existing age and gender hierarchies are reinforced even as other cultural practices (such as attitudes regarding health and education) are challenged. One final area in which this is evident—an area particularly relevant to this book's major theme—is in the lessons devoted to teaching students how to write letters. In both the fourth and the sixth grade social studies textbooks, students learn how to address in writing those who are junior to or senior to themselves (Ministry of Education and Culture 1989: 28, 62–63; Acharya et al. 1988:19, 75). Each of these four lessons (two in the fourth grade book, two in the sixth grade book) starts with a reading selection written in the form of a letter. Examples include a boy writing to his father, who works in a different district of Nepal; a boy writing to a male classmate who was unable to go with the class on a field trip to Kathmandu; a boy writing to the headmaster to request a reduction in school fees; and a boy writing home to his father from a boarding school. All the letters in the textbooks are to and from males; no examples are provided of women or girls writing letters.

Unlike in the love letter guidebooks (discussed later), there are no explicit instructions as to how to write a letter. After the reading selection is presented, however, students are asked comprehension questions and then must write their own letters. Following the letter a boy writes to his headmaster requesting a reduction in school fees, for example, students are told to "Write a letter to the teacher of your younger brother, explaining why your sick younger brother was absent" and "Write a letter to the Headmaster asking that your younger brother be enrolled in fourth grade" (Acharya et al. 1988:20). Following the letter from a boy to his classmate, students are told, "Write a letter to your father, mother, or older brother about your experiences on a trip away from school" (Ministry of Education and Culture 1989:64). And after the letter a boy writes to his father from boarding school students are instructed, "Write a letter to your younger sister explaining the conditions and goals of the student hostel" (Acharya et al. 1988:76). All of these exercises implicitly yet firmly demonstrate to the students how to write to people junior or senior to them, using honorific pronouns and formal expressions where appropriate. From these lessons students learn the mechanics of letter writing, and in the process they are inculcated with cultural norms regarding age and gender hierarchies.

3. *Hinduism.*   Along with, and closely related to, nationalism and hierarchies of age and gender, students are exposed throughout their school years to Hinduism, the hegemonic religion of Nepal.[11] According to His Majesty's Government of Nepal, 85.5 percent are Hindus.[12] Ethnic and religious minorities dispute this figure, however, and, indeed, the number is almost certainly outdated if not simply incorrect. *The Statistical Pocket Book, Nepal, 1992,* which reports the results of the 1991 census, contains no statistics on religion or mother tongue, providing only outdated (1981) figures (National Planning Commission Secretariat 1992). Religion and native language are two very sensitive areas given the government's attempt to unify all Nepalis under one flag, one religion, and one language.

In any case, school textbooks contain many explicit references to Hinduism. On the first page of the first grade social studies textbook, for example, in addition to the quotation from the king quoted earlier, there is a prayer to the Hindu god Ganesh written in Sanskrit, which is utterly incomprehensible to most first grade Nepali students, especially those who are not high-caste Hindus (such as the Magars of Junigau). In the upper grades, reading selections feature summaries of Hindu epics such as the *Rāmāyana.* Even on the rare occasions when other religions are mentioned, their worshipers are represented as living in other countries. For example, in the sixth grade social studies textbook there is a reading selection about the Buddha entitled, "Messenger of Peace," the last paragraph of which I present here:

> The religion created by a Nepali person, the Buddha, a messenger of peace, is today practiced around the world. From Russia's Volga to Japan, from Siberia to Sri Lanka, the religion that Mahatma Buddha created is extremely popular. The stupa[13] built by Ashok twenty-three hundred years ago is still protected in Lumbini. From different countries around the world Buddhists make pilgrimage to Lumbini, and they make offerings of garlands as evidence of their faith. Contented, they return home, having said, "Buddham sharanam gachhami," "dhammam sharanam gachhami," and "sangam sharanam gachhami" [Buddhist declarations of faith in Pali]. In this way, a center for Buddhism is being created in our country. From the Buddha's birthplace of Lumbini, the name of one of our country's zones, Lumbini Zone, is taken. (Acharya et al. 1988: 53–54)

The main focus of this selection is on how the Buddha was born in Lumbini, which is located in the south of Nepal. That the Buddha "was a Nepali person" (an anachronistic assertion, since Nepal did not exist at the time of the Buddha) is yet another reason for national pride, according to the lesson. No mention is made of Nepal's thousands (perhaps even millions) of Buddhists.

All of the messages conveyed in Nepal's national textbooks are important influences on Junigau's constantly shifting structures of feeling. They both reflect and shape villagers' changing notions of personhood, agency, and social hierarchy. Similar themes underlie *Nāyā Goreṭo (New Path)*, the textbook used to teach female literacy in Junigau and elsewhere throughout Nepal. I turn now, therefore, to an analysis of its contents.

A "New Path": Instructional Materials for Female Literacy Classes

The text and images in the female literacy materials through which many Junigau women have learned to read and write differ somewhat from those of the textbooks used for formal education in Nepali schools, yet there are interesting parallels. Like the textbooks discussed above, *Nāyā Goreṭo (New Path)* stresses the need to become "developed," but while the formal school textbooks emphasize hegemonic Nepali nationalism and Hinduism and reinforce existing gender and age hierarchies *New Path* seeks to challenge some of those hierarchies. Interestingly, both the textbooks used in Nepali schools and *New Path* are government-sponsored textbooks, which proves that no government is univocal in its publications.

The text I will be discussing here is the fifteenth edition of *New Path*, published in 1994 (Ministry of Education and Culture 1994). The first edition was published in the early 1980s, just as female literacy classes in Junigau were beginning. Indeed, the timing was not a coincidence, as the headmaster of Junigau's school found out about the availability of the textbook and began the evening literacy classes as a result. From page one, *New Path* is steeped in development discourse. From the vocabulary words accompanied by full-page illustrations designed to raise students' consciousness to the serialized comic strip stories about villagers and their problems, the textbook clearly presents in unmistakably moral tones a correct—or "developed" (*bikāsī*)—way to live. In the chapters that follow, I explore to what degree literacy students or other villagers who read these materials (for the workbook is in wide circulation in Junigau) might accept, resist, or otherwise grapple with this image of the *bikāsī* Nepali. Here, however, I simply consider the contents of the textbook.

Although there are several "steps" (or volumes) in the *New Path* workbook series, only the first and most basic step has been widely taught and read in Junigau. The most recently revised 1994 version of this step has fifteen chapters, each of which introduces one or two keywords that are illustrated by a full-page picture (see table 4).

TABLE 4.   Vocabulary Words in the *New Path—First Step* Literacy Workbook

Nepali	English
kām	work
pāni	water
kheti	farming
chhimeki	neighbor(s)
mānchhe	person, people
lugā	clothing
garib	poor
paisā	money
goṭhālo	herder(s)
bikri garnu	to sell
pahiro	landslide
du:kha	suffering
sautā	cowife
jhagaḍā	argument
reḍiyo	radio
bhakāri	bamboo mat
thicho micho	oppression
ghus	bribery

Unlike formal Nepali schooling, which teaches children the Devanagari alphabet from first letter to last through rote chanting, the *New Path* workbook starts phonetically with simple consonant sounds and adds a vowel every lesson or two. There are phonics drills along with practice sentences, short reading selections, and comic strips that are designed to help students understand how Nepali writing works as a logical phonetic system. All of these components also seem designed to inculcate in the literacy student a desire to be like the "good" characters portrayed in the reading selections and to avoid explicitly stigmatized behavior. From the very first reading selection, entitled "Farming," an image is created of hardworking Nepali farmers who, though they may live in traditional, kinship-based, extended households, strive to become more *bikāsī* by learning new skills such as fish farming, weaving, and vegetable gardening.

Farming

Mother's Brother has neighbors. Youngest Brother and his wife are also nearby. The neighbor is at work in the fields. Mother's Brother is also in the rice paddy. Youngest Brother digs in the rice paddy. In the rice paddy there is water. Youngest Brother is surprised because there is a fish in the water. Youngest Brother eats a meal in the rice paddy. In his meal he eats fish. Youngest Brother's Wife also eats after working. Youngest Brother and

Youngest Brother's Wife are hard working. (Ministry of Education and Culture 1994:28)

In "Putali Is Self-Sufficient," there is an implicit message about gender relations as well as hard work. When Putali takes the initiative to learn how to weave, her husband supports her by buying the loom she needs to start a weaving business on her own, and furthermore he is proud of her. Note, however, that it is Putali's husband who evidently has control of the family's finances. Such income-generating activities are precisely the ones advocated by development-oriented Junigau residents like Pabi Sara and Dimi, whose elopements were described in chapter 5. Indeed, Pabi Sara and Dimi attended a training that taught them how to weave, thereby becoming as self-sufficient as Putali in the story "Putali Is Self-Sufficient."

Putali Is Self-Sufficient
Lalu is at the market. Putali is also at the market. Their neighbors are also at the market. Lalu buys the things for a loom because Putali is taking a training on loom work. After the training Putali will weave nice clothes. The neighbors are surprised at Putali's work. Lalu is proud. Putali is self-sufficient. (Ministry of Education and Culture 1994: 39)

In addition to presenting ordinary Nepali farmers who create better lives for themselves through their own hard labor and ingenuity, *New Path* sometimes lapses into outright proselytizing, using imperatives in an attempt to compel its readers to behave properly. In "Learn Skills," for example, readers are urged not to do "bad work" such as drinking alcohol or gambling. Instead, they should work hard and learn skills that will enable them to earn money by raising chickens, planting a vegetable garden, learning to weave, and getting along with people. The reading selection below ends with the proclamation "All people are equal," a statement perhaps meant to encourage the readers to think that, whatever their current circumstances, they have an equal chance to become *bikāsī* if they work hard and learn skills.

Learn Skills
Don't do bad work. Don't waste money on alcohol. Drinking alcohol is considered a bad habit. Don't ruin your habits by playing card games involving gambling. Prepare oneself for the sake of work. Learn skills and work. If one works, one earns money. Learn how to raise chickens. Also learn about the skill of a vegetable garden. Plant bananas. Plant cotton. Raise livestock for fertilizer. Get along with all people. All people are equal. (Ministry of Education and Culture 1994:52)

The characters in the workbook's reading selections not only earn money from working hard and learning skills; they also become happy. In "Bimala and Gopal," the reader meets the ideal Nepali family, one with which most Junigau readers would be familiar from ubiquitous family-planning campaigns and slogans: a nuclear grouping consisting of a mother, father, son, and daughter. It is not clear whether or not Bimala and Gopal's children attend school, but they do help with the family's development projects, thereby helping the atypically nuclear family to bring in money and remain happy. In all of these reading selections, capitalist activity is associated with attributes of personhood that readers are supposed to want to acquire, such as being "productive," "successful," and "independent."

Bimala and Gopal
Bimala and Gopal live in Gorkha. They have a son and a daughter. Gopal has a goat shed. In the shed are sixty or seventy goats. At the far side of the shed is a pine forest. Gopal's son takes the goats to the forest because there is no goatherd. Bimala raises fish. In the pond are very, very good fish. At the edge of the pond is a vegetable garden. Gopal spreads dung fertilizer on the garden. Bimala grows vegetables in the garden. Their daughter raises chickens. Bimala sells not only vegetables but also fish and meat at the market. Bimala and Gopal are happy. (Ministry of Education and Culture 1994: 75–76)

This happy nuclear, four-member family is contrasted with the family described in "Regret(s)." Narman insists on continuing to have children until he has a son, and when his first wife, Minu, only produces daughters, he marries again. The result is nothing but discord, hunger, and sickness for everyone. In the end, Narman regrets his second marriage.

Regret(s)
Minu's husband is Narman. Narman doesn't do any work. By Minu's hard work alone there is not enough food. Because of a shortage of food their daughters are skinny. But Narman marries Seti to have a son. Thinking of the suffering that could come after the wedding, Minu cries. Narman gets along with Seti really well. From time to time Minu and Narman have an argument. Minu is sad. Seti has argumentative habits. Seti and Minu don't get along at all. They both argue. After some years, Seti also has sons and daughters. Narman's wealth is not enough for food. The children keep fighting over food. Because of a shortage of food the children are skinny. Because she is pregnant every year, Seti is also sickly. Narman is also sad. Narman regrets that he had a second wedding. (Ministry of Education and Culture 1994:102–3)

सीप सिक

खराब काम नगर । रक्सीमा पैसा नमास ।
रक्सी खानु खराब बानी मानिन्छ । तास
खेलेर बानी नबिगार । कामका निम्ति कम्मर
कस । सीप सिकेर काम गर । काम गरे पैसा
मिल्छ । कुखुरा पाल्न सिक । तरकारी खेतीका
बारेमा पनि सीप सिक । केरा खेती गर ।
कपास खेती गर । मलका लागि बस्तु पाल ।
सबै मानिससित मेलमिलाप गर । मानिस
सबै समान छन् ।

Plate 20   Story, entitled "Learn Skills," from the *New Path* literacy textbook

In the following selection, "Landslide," the reader of *New Path* is told not only how to be a hardworking and happy nuclear family member but also how to be a good Nepali citizen—the "nation building" Arnove and Graff say is so important in literacy texts (1987:7). In "Landslide," readers learn that all Nepalis are farmers. While the vast majority certainly are, this selection, I believe, seeks to establish something more than a mere statement of fact. A certain subjectivity is proposed, one the text urges its incipiently literate villagers to accept: the subjectivity of a proud Nepali farmer who, by planting trees to stop soil erosion, acts responsibly for the sake of future generations. Once again, the text is attempting to influence villagers' conceptions of their own personhood.

Landslide

Farming alone is the main work of Nepalis. All Nepalis are farmers. But farmers suffer when they see the damage done by landslides. Every year small streams damage fields. Landslides destroy crops. Because fields are ruined, farmers suffer. Because the forest is used up, fields are also washed away. You have to plant trees on the banks of the streams. Trees will help to stop landslides and the washing away of fields. Landslides can be stopped by planting trees on the sides of streams and in grassy fields. If trees are planted, future generations won't have to suffer. (Ministry of Education and Culture 1994:91–92)

The world of *New Path* is almost entirely a self-contained, generic Nepali village. In only one reading selection is there any explicit mention of a city, and it comes in the story "Radio." Here the reader is introduced to the next step in the development process: what to do with the profits earned from all the hard work and capitalist activity. The answer is to become consumers, buying commodities, such as a radio, that will further one's ability to become *bikāsī*. In this story, Sitaram and his son, Gore, buy a radio with the money they earn from selling their woven goods, and when it needs repair they take it in to an unnamed city, where Gore decides to learn how to repair radios himself after watching the repairman (and it is indeed a repair*man* in the accompanying picture). The space of the city is distinctly masculine in this story; nowhere in *New Path* do we see women venturing as far afield as the city, never mind striving to become like city dwellers themselves, as Gore does in his plans to learn how to repair radios.

Radio

Sitaram is a hard-working farmer. After doing his farmwork, he weaves baskets, ropes, and mats. Sitaram is skilled at this work.

He takes the things he makes to the market and sells them. Sitaram's youngest son, Gore, also does weaving work with Sitaram.

One time Sitaram bought a radio with the money he got from selling baskets, ropes, and mats. Father and son both listen to various programs on the radio. After some time, the radio broke. Sitaram and Gore took the radio to the city to be repaired. Gore sees the radio repaired in the city. After that Gore too decides to learn how to repair radios. (Ministry of Education and Culture 1994:111–12)

Another reading selection takes place in a district center. In "Bribery," two brothers have a dispute over land inheritance. The older is cheating the younger and is bribing all the other villagers into silence. Nevertheless, the younger brother takes his older brother to court and wins the case. Thus, traditional kinship hierarchies are depicted as being superseded by the power of the state. The accompanying picture shows a space that, like the city scene in "Radio," is entirely masculine; in addition to the two brothers, there are three other males—a lawyer, a judge, and a police officer.

The only other reading selection in the first "step" of the *New Path* workbook series is one called "Sita's Suffering." In it, Sita becomes sickly after giving birth year after year, and her children and husband become ill as well. Her husband spends a lot of money trying to cure their sick children, but then he dies, leaving Sita ill equipped to support her family. Sita's troubles multiply when a wily neighbor convinces her that before her husband died he borrowed nine hundred rupees, which the wily neighbor is now demanding back. Sita doesn't have the money and so is forced to offer him one of her sons as an indentured servant instead. The story ends with the lines, "Because her son became a plow boy, Sita's heart/mind cried. What oppression this is. A false document made her son a plow boy. Not having thought in time, Sita and her family had to endure suffering" (Ministry of Education and Culture 1994: 125). Unlike the man whose brother is cheating him, Sita does not take her case to court. (Perhaps she was dissuaded from doing so when she peeked a few pages ahead in *New Path* and saw the picture of the all-male courtroom.)

By far the most popular and best remembered features of *New Path* among Junigau residents are the workbook's comic strip stories, in which gender relations, especially between spouses, are foregrounded. I have heard villagers refer to the comic strips' characters explicitly when faced with similar situations in their own lives. Presented in serial form throughout the workbook, the two main comics, "Suntali and Bire" and "Dil Bahadur's Suffering," depict severe antagonism between spouses, including violence at one point. The plots of the two stories, briefly, are as follows. In "Suntali and Bire," Bire is a stereotypically loutish husband who gets drunk, gambles, and then, when he loses, demands his wife's jewelry to pay off his debts. When Suntali objects, the bottle he throws at her narrowly misses her but hits their daughter in the head. Bire continues to

Plate 21   Pages from the "Suntali and Bire" comic strip in the *New Path* literacy textbook

threaten them with a stick, so Suntali takes her daughter and leaves. Bire, meanwhile, passes out drunk. When he regains consciousness, he goes to look for his wife at her natal home. He apologizes to Suntali, and the story ends with her being undecided as to whether to forgive him.

In "Dil Bahadur's Suffering," Dil Bahadur has two wives who do not get along. Food is scarce, and one of the wives, Nakkali (meaning "vain," "false," or "fashion conscious") gets angry when her cowife's son complains about the meal she cooked. After she throws food at him, his mother appears, and the two cowives engage in a fistfight. Dil Bahadur then shows up, and in the process of trying to break up the fight he is punched in the nose by Nakkali, presumably by mistake. In an interesting attribution of agency, the workbook ends the first segment of the comic strip by having Dil Bahadur think to himself while rubbing his head in dismay, "Ach! What sin have I committed?"

The story continues with Nakkali's departure (without permission) from the house to attend a fair, at which she hooks up with a man named Hem Lal and stays out all night. Dil Bahadur is seen remarking to his other wife, "Nakkali gives me nothing but trouble." The next morning Dil Bahadur confronts Nakkali about the rumors and tells her to leave, which she does, gladly moving in with Hem Lal. When Dil Bahadur refuses to allow her to take her jewelry, however, Nakkali, using the lowest form of *you* to address him, vows revenge. The final segment of the comic strip describes that revenge. One of Dil

Bahadur's bulls is driven away, reportedly by an associate of Hem Lal, but when Dil Bahadur visits a village elder to complain Hem Lal accuses him of letting the bull loose in his fields and destroying his crops. The elder believes Hem Lal, and as a result Dil Bahadur has to go into debt by signing a document in which he agrees to pay Hem Lal for the alleged damages. The segment ends with Dil Bahadur thinking, "It's all because of Nakkali that I have to suffer this oppression"—a total reversal of agentive attribution over the course of the story. The last segment even has a different title: "Poor Dil Bahadur."

I must emphasize that the ideology of *New Path* is not absorbed passively or unquestioningly by its Junigau readers. Nor is it by any means the sole source of development discourse in the village. Tracing individuals' actions and beliefs back to this particular text is therefore problematic, if not impossible. Nevertheless, I have heard Junigau residents use the comic strip stories as cautionary tales, especially regarding men with drinking problems and multiple wives, like Bire, or women who are dissatisfied with their fates and decide, as Nakkali did, to leave their husbands. Junigau women in particular disapprove of such behavior, at least in their public remarks.

Where *New Path* has contributed most to social change in Junigau, it seems to me, is in its advocacy of the ideological package involving self-sufficiency, hard work, development, success, and individual responsibility. Many of the same messages are being communicated in Sarvodaya School's textbooks and classrooms, albeit within a very different framework, which emphasizes patriotism, Hinduism, and filial piety. As Junigau residents acquire basic literacy skills, whether through formal schooling or evening literacy classes, they are encouraged to associate the acquisition of all kinds of skills with greater development, capitalist activity, independence, and agency. Jenny Cook-Gumperz recognizes this process when she states, "Literacy as a socially defined phenomenon is constructed through a process of schooling" (1986:6).

Looking more closely at the *New Path* workbook, we can use Umberto Eco's notion of a "closed" text. Of closed texts, Eco states:

> They apparently aim at pulling the reader along a predetermined path, carefully displaying their effects so as to arouse pity or fear, excitement or depression at the due place and at the right moment. Every step of the "story" elicits just the expectation that its further course will satisfy. They seem to be structured according to an inflexible project. Unfortunately, the only one not to have been "inflexibly" planned is the reader. (1979:8)

The structure of a closed text assumes a particular kind of "model reader," one with presupposed cultural and textual competence that may or may not be possessed by actual readers. Thus, Eco paradoxically concludes that closed texts "can give rise to the most unforeseeable interpretations, at least at the ideological level" (1979:8). Why should these texts be called closed, then? Eco answers that while they presuppose extratextual competence, they also work to build up such a competence by textual means. Even as female literacy students in Junigau were resisting some of the messages of *New Path* in ways that will be described in the following chapter, they most likely were absorbing others, becoming competent in the language of development. While the stories in *New Path* are open to a number of alternative interpretations, therefore, their almost rigidly univocal contents impelled readers to espouse at least some aspects of *New Path*'s worldview.

Magazines

Next to the textbooks used in the government school and in female literacy classes, the most popular reading materials in Junigau in the 1990s were magazines. Three main types were popular: (1) film magazines such as *Kāmanā*; (2) magazines such as *Deurālī* and *Yuvā Manch*, which focus on development, education, and entertainment; and (3) publications such as *Lāphā* and *Kairan*, which support the *janajātī* political movement. Each of these three genres of magazines will be analyzed in turn in the sections that follow.

Film Magazines

Of the various magazines to which Junigau young people had access during the 1990s, film magazines were perhaps the most widely read. Many types were sold in Tansen bookstores. Some magazines provided information about Hindi films and the Indian film industry more generally, while others focused on Nepali movies. All featured color photos of actors and actresses on their covers, and many also offered glossy centerfolds of scantily clad women or macho men ready for any kind of action. Tea shop walls were plastered with these magazine photos, and young people in Junigau often used them to decorate their rooms (if they were lucky enough to have their own rooms). The magazines also contained numerous full-page ads for soon to be released films.

In the following analysis of *Kāmanā*'s issue no. 104, published in the fall of 1996, I provide an overview of the contents of a typical film magazine. *Kāmanā*, meaning "wish, desire," introduces its readers to Nepali film stars—their glamour, their dreams, their disappointments. While readers learn about the real lives of their favorite actors and actresses, they also become steeped in the values of their world, a world in which appearances are all important and gender relations, while very much in flux, remain male dominated.

The cover of issue no. 104 features a photograph of a Nepali actress, Jala

Shaha, along with the headline "The Girls of Film Need Security." Inside, in the accompanying interview, *Kāmanā* asks Shaha why she always takes her mother with her when shooting a film. She replies that because she is only sixteen years old she needs to have someone more experienced around her. Nepali actresses need such security, she says. What kind of security, *Kāmanā* asks? All kinds, Shaha replies—economic, physical, personal.

The magazine is full of interviews with current stars and has-beens, all of them speaking in a question and answer dialogue format. Film stars are frequently chided if their latest movies have not been successful, and they always reply that in fact they *have* been successful, they *are* "moving forward." Here we can see the same concern for development, success, and progress that appears in many of Junigau's love letters. One interview is particularly interesting in this regard. Binod Chaudhari, one of Nepal's "most successful" businessmen, used to be involved in films as an actor, producer, and singer. When *Kāmanā* wants to know why he is no longer part of the film industry, he replies that if he had only himself to think of he would be, but he is responsible for "bringing forward" his own family business, the Chaudhari Group. He says he may become involved in the film industry again soon, once he has the time. *Kāmanā* clearly hopes so and states that Chaudhari's involvement would be the industry's best hope for greater success.

Aside from conveying ideas about progress, development, and success, *Kāmanā* also focuses on romantic love—in the films themselves, among the actors and actresses, and even among the magazine's readers. At the end of the magazine, an entire page is devoted to love poems sent in by readers, every single one of them bemoaning a lost love. Five young women and four young men have their photos and poems displayed on this page. They represent different castes and ethnic groups from all over Nepal, with one young Nepali man even writing from Dubai, where he is evidently employed. Two examples of these heart-wrenching poems follow (*Kāmanā* 1996: 48):

Stories and Misfortunes
There are unforgettable stories
On all of memory's pages;
There are unbearable misfortunes
All over the roof of the heart.
    —Kopila Lamichhane, Chitwan

Heart
Some say the heart is an open flower
Some say the heart is a broken-down bridge

Some say the heart is a flowing stream
But I say the heart is a bag for holding pains
—Tek Gurung, Kaski

These poems from around the country represent romantic love in a way that is reflected elsewhere in the film magazines, as well as in other media in Nepal, pointing to a widespread emergence of new structures of feeling. While romantic love has existed for generations in Nepal, these students are giving it new meanings by making their romantic feelings public and by emphasizing the great risk to an individual's happiness if a relationship does not work out. Their sentiments are echoed in the poems Junigau villagers include in their letters, such as the following, which is quoted from the second letter Bir Bahadur wrote to Sarita:[14]

The source of the water coming out of the hills can dry up,
But the tears coming out of my eyes cannot dry up.
You will be able to forget me, perhaps,
But I cannot possibly forget you.

While a thorough exploration of these trends throughout Nepal is beyond the scope of this book, the national distribution of Nepali film magazines (not to mention the films themselves) indicates that the changes occurring in Junigau are not unique to that village alone. Nor are these changes unique to Nepal. Two panels on romantic love at the 1999 American Anthropological Association meetings demonstrated the pervasive influence of Western ideas about romantic love in many cultures around the world—and yet in each case people were constructing culturally specific meanings for the new practices and attitudes regarding love, courtship, and marriage.[15]

*Magazines Focusing on Development, Education,
and Entertainment*

Also popular among young people in Junigau during the 1990s were magazines devoted to the education, development, and entertainment of their readers. *Deurālī* and *Yuvā Manch* are examples of this type of magazine. *Deurālī*, a magazine published in Tansen, has a unique organizational structure.[16] The magazine's editors set up reading and writing groups throughout Palpa District in the early 1990s, which were given free copies of each issue in return for occasional articles written by the groups' members. While there has never been an official *Deurālī* reading and writing group in Junigau, the magazine was nevertheless quite popular there because it contained a lot of local news and was written in easy to understand Nepali.

When we examine the contents of an issue from the fall of 1996 (25 Asoj 2053), all the articles in one way or another emphasize the importance of development, self-sufficiency, individualism, nationalism, and Hinduism. The cover depicts Muktinath Temple, an important pilgrimage site for Hindus. A letter from the editor urges readers to work hard during this harvest time so as not to allow earlier efforts to go to waste. Then the following articles appear:

- "In Dankuta, There Was a Journalism Training"—all about a new development center in eastern Nepal that was built by "hardworking youths"; the building is now used for all sorts of trainings and development activities involving drinking water facilities, income-generating skills, and other activities designed to "increase people's knowledge and understanding."
- "Serpent-God Statue Found"—about how a man found an idol depicting a serpent-god in a river in Syangjya District after having seen it in his dreams; people came from as far away as Kathmandu and Pokhara to worship it.
- "One Must Be Careful of Plastic Things"—an article warning readers that plastic, though very useful, takes many years to decompose, is flammable, and produces poisonous fumes when burned.
- "Man Who Made Vow Does Panchawali Worship Ceremony"—a Magar man from Palpa District makes a vow to conduct a special Panchawali worship ceremony if he gets into the army. The article reports that he does so when he comes home on his first leave, but the author is extremely critical of this practice and condemns the expense of the ritual. "We understand now that we must try to institute more trust in hard work than in pledges [to the gods]," the author writes.
- "2053's School Leaving Certificate Exam Starts on Chait 14th"—an article providing information about fees and exam schedules.
- "Sakil Wants To Teach Hair Cutting"—about a ninth grade Muslim boy who cuts hair in Tansen. Sakil's uncle believes in leaving everything up to fate, the article says, causing him to end up with a very large family and a small business. Sakil disagrees with his uncle's philosophy and abides instead by this saying: "A person doesn't survive by luck (*bhāgya*) but by his or her own work." The author of the article concludes by praising Sakil's industriousness and desire to get an education.
- "Let's Move Forward"—a poem by a Magar man from Palpa District. Contains the lines "Let's move forward for the sake of development / Along the road to prosperity / Let's go by the light of the education's torch / Through Nepali mud."

Plate 22   Cover of *Deurālī* magazine

- "Good Health Care Hasn't Reached the Villages"—a two-page article on the lack of qualified health care assistants and health posts in Palpa District.
- "Possibilities for Development In Eastern Palpa District"—the possibilities include (1) starting women's development programs, (2) opening a supply store where farmers can get fertilizer and seeds, and (3) opening a branch of Nepal's national bank.
- "The Fun of Festivals Isn't For Sale In Stores"—an article urging people not to spend too much money during the upcoming Dashain festival.
- "No One Should Hesitate To Stand on His or Her Own Feet"—an article about opportunities for women to gain skills through trainings so that they can contribute to their family's income. The authors, three women who have gone through such trainings, write about the benefits to women of

learning marketable skills: "There will be no arguments at home. Agreement and love will increase. No one will have to suffer from anyone else's nagging. No one should hesitate to stand on his or her own feet. . . . So, sisters, you, too, should learn these kinds of skills and increase your income. That's our advice."

- "Who Is To Blame?"—an article about the importance of taking responsibility for the exercise of authority under democracy. The author argues that a discussion on this topic is needed.
- "Conditions of Tenant Relationships"—a question and answer page about who has which rights regarding rented land.
- "Let's Do a New Search"—a poem about the need to change social institutions that keep people in poverty. It ends with, "Let's do a new, new search, let's search for new social institutions / If we remain like this, the road to prosperity will be closed."
- "Pride"—a comic strip for children about a hen and her chicks who are constantly being harassed by an egotistical rooster. Finally, the hen tricks the rooster into accompanying her up into the hills to fight another rooster that had allegedly bragged he could beat him, and there the rooster is eaten by a coyote. With the bothersome rooster gone, the hen and chicks live happily ever after.
- "A Funny Thing On Campus"—an article about wealthy students who fail the School Leaving Certificate exam and then buy themselves fake certificates from India and proceed to study at Nepali colleges.

Other issues contain a very similar array of articles emphasizing economic development, self-help, and progress. I want to point out just two more articles from other issues to illustrate *Deurālī's* concern with gender issues and public health concerns. The first, entitled, "We Are All the Same" (2 Kartik 2053), is a manifesto on behalf of women's rights, especially in the realm of equal pay for equal work. It begins, "Men and women are the same. There is no law that gives men a lot of rights and women few rights."[17] And it ends with demands such as: (1) "A factory must get the consent of a female employee if it wants her to work outside of the hours between 6:00 A.M. and 6:00 P.M."; (2) women must receive the same pay as men for the same work; and (3) a female employee must be given maternity leave of at least fifteen days. The final *Deurālī* article I will mention is one of many the magazine has published on health issues. This full-page article shows a cute picture of a smiling condom and contains explicit instructions on how to use condoms to avoid unwanted pregnancies and sexually transmitted diseases such as AIDS (21 Bhadau 2053).[18]

Yuvā Manch is another magazine popular among young people in Junigau. Like *Deurālī, Yuvā Manch* seeks to provides its readers with moral, philosophical, and economic uplift. Unlike *Deurālī*, however, *Yuvā Manch* is not published in Tansen and has no reading and writing groups associated with it. *Yuvā Manch* is a longer, more sophisticated magazine; while it has no color photos, it does have black-and-white line drawings illustrating many of its articles. One issue of *Yuvā Manch* from the fall of 1996 (Kartik 2053) provides a representative overview of the kinds of articles published in the magazine. It opens with an article about an ancient Hindu statue of the goddess Kali, once again implicitly enforcing Hinduism as the hegemonic religion. Sprinkled throughout the magazine are vocabulary and trivia quizzes, and at the bottom of each page is a famous quotation from sources such as Goethe, Mao, Carlisle, Thomas Fuller, Milton, Fielding, Virgil, Jefferson, Herbert Spenser, Pepys, the Buddha, Disraeli, Wilde, Gorky, Plato, Newton, Napoleon, and the Bible. Only two quotations are authored by Nepali men: one by the famous politician B. P. Koirala and the other by the famous poet Lakshmi Prasad Devkota. Not one of the quotations is by a woman, Nepali or otherwise. Merely by looking at the sources of these quotations, one can see one of *Yuvā Manch*'s main messages: truly valuable wisdom comes from men who live outside of Nepal.

Most of *Yuvā Manch*'s articles are explicitly educational in nature. They teach the readers about subjects such as the following:

- Darwin's theory of evolution
- What pregnant women should eat
- The ecological importance of trees
- Nepal's previous era of democracy
- Famous Indian writers
- How to treat hepatitis
- The solar system
- The history of elevators and escalators
- The effect on kidneys of urinary tract infections
- The Internet
- The Gulf War and the dangers of chemical weapons
- How airplanes fly
- The benefits of walking
- Egyptian hieroglyphics
- Brain diseases such as Parkinson's
- The historical and religious importance of Nuwakot Bazaar
- How to use one's abilities to achieve success
- Ayurvedic treatments for illnesses
- Pete Sampras, the number one player in men's tennis
- Napoleon's great achievements

- How to reduce infertility in livestock
- Health and legal advice

Of particular interest for our purposes is the tone of the articles, which assumes that all people need to do in order to become healthy, wealthy, and wise is to acquire the necessary knowledge. An article about the benefits of walking as a form of exercise concludes with the question "Once we have learned this, why don't we all take up the habit of walking every morning?" Similarly, an article about how to use one's abilities to achieve success ends with "Trying to achieve success without abilities is like trying to multiply zero. If this is so, why don't all people work on the development (*bikās*) of their own abilities in a step-by-step manner in order to climb the ladder of success?" Through statements such as this, individual readers are encouraged to become active agents in order to improve their lives.

Yuvā Manch may attempt to appeal to its readers without discriminating among them on the basis of gender, but it implicitly conveys to readers the male-dominated nature of the (especially Western) world by focusing solely on male scientists, authors, and military officers. Napoleon is valorized in this issue, as are Darwin and Devkota. Of the dozens of drawings in the Kartik issue of *Yuvā Manch,* only three depict women, all of them anonymous figures: one is riding an elevator (illustrating the article on the history of elevators and escalators), one is pregnant (illustrating the article on what foods pregnant women should eat), and one is crying (illustrating the article on how Ayurvedic treatments can cure illnesses). On a spread presenting readers' photographs and ideas about how the festival of Dashain should be celebrated, only four of the twelve respondents are young women; the rest are young men. And on the back page of this issue of *Yuvā Manch,* among the forty readers listed who would like a pen pal not one is a woman.

Deurālī and *Yuvā Manch* urge readers to adopt a development-oriented, success-driven, male-dominated worldview. To what extent readers actually absorb these ideological messages cannot be known, but because they are ubiquitous, not only in these publications but also in radio programs, Hindi and Nepali movies, and school classrooms, it is not surprising that these themes appear in Junigau love letters.

Political Magazines

Political magazines constituted the final type of periodical read by some residents of Junigau in the 1990s. During this time period, the *janajātī* movement, an attempt to unite all Nepalis of Tibeto-Burman origin under one political banner, gained many adherents in Junigau because Junigau Magars agreed with

Plate 23   Article on Napoleon in *Yuvā Manch* magazine

politicians such as Gore Bahadur Khapangi that upper-caste Nepalis had been discriminating against them for generations (Ahearn 2001b; Thapa 1993). Although political magazines were not very popular in Junigau during the 1990s, the *janajātī* adherents circulated their movement's literature fairly widely, and so I will describe it briefly here.[19]

The two magazines read by villagers in Junigau were *Lāphā Traimāsik* and *Kairan Māsik*. The former is addressed primarily to Magars, while the latter addresses an audience comprised of all Tibeto-Burman groups—Magars, Gurungs, Rais, Limbus, Sherpas, and others. The articles in these magazines passionately argue for a more equitable political arrangement, possibly along a federalist model that accords minority groups a certain amount of autonomy (*Kairan Māsik* 1992; *Lāphā Traimāsik* 1992–93). The magazines also urge their readers to take pride in their own indigenous languages and religions and to discard the hegemonic Nepali language and Hindu religion. Readers, these magazines argue, should develop a strong ethnic identity and take collective action in order to prevent further oppression at the hands of high-caste Hindus. Furthermore, readers are urged to avoid the social ills of Western culture—a sentiment rarely expressed in Junigau, although it is echoed in films such as *Kanyādān,* in which a woman who is "too Western" fails to win the love of the hero.

Even though these political magazines do not accept all aspects of Western culture, they still advocate a particular kind of individual and collective agency among their readers. The actions readers are encouraged to undertake are not the same, however, as the ones suggested by other types of magazines. The ideal worlds portrayed by the different magazines vary. In all cases, however, the magazines Junigau villagers were reading in the 1990s endorsed a view of agency that assumed the efficacy of an individual's actions rather than the inevitability of fate.

Love Letters—the Novel

Another type of reading material available to Junigau residents in the 1990s consisted of short stories or novels, but many fewer villagers actually read these materials because of their expense. They also lacked the appeal of magazines, which had more attractive graphics and prose that was easier for villagers to understand. The only work of fiction I saw in the village besides a few collections of folktales was a 1990 novel by Prakash Kovid entitled *Love Letters.*[20] Although none of the letter writers featured in this ethnography had read the book before they wrote their love letters, other young people in the village had, and the details of the plot were circulated fairly widely, as was the book itself. For this reason, I include a summary and short analysis of the plot here, as the novel both reflects and contributes to emergent structures of feeling surrounding romantic love in Junigau. Questions of modernity, success, gender relations, agency, and romantic love permeate *Love Letters,* echoing the tragic *Romeo and Juliet*–like quality of many of the Nepali and Hindi films that are shown in Tansen and viewed by virtually all young villagers. One word of caution: while the plot of *Love Letters* might seem implausible at best to Western readers, Junigau readers are more willing to suspend their disbelief and concentrate instead on enjoying the depiction of the characters' "developed" lives.

The book opens with a confusing scene that takes place at a young woman's funeral pyre in Darjeeling.[21] As a man is attending to the burial, he thinks he hears the corpse say, "Why are you burning me? He will certainly come . . ." The man recalls having seen the woman in the hospital when she was deathly ill, and

Plate 24   Cover of the novel *Prem Patra* (*Love Letters*)

at that point she had given him a packet and asked him to give it to her husband. Another man arrives at the funeral pyre and announces that he is the woman's husband, her "life friend," who could never be her actual companion. The first man gives him the packet, and the scene ends with his question, "What's inside this packet?" The rest of the novel is presented as the answer to that question.

The next part of the book goes back in time to when the husband, Narendra, is just a high school student. His mother, a widow, works hard to support her only son, who aspires to be an artist. One day, a wealthy family moves in next door. Their little daughter, Renu, and a teenaged niece, Menuka, live with the family. Narendra hears Menuka's voice as she is singing one morning, and he begins to fall in love. The family hires Narendra to tutor little Renu, so he spends an increasing amount of time at their house. When Renu's parents go away, they leave the girls on their own (an extremely unlikely occurrence in village Nepal), and both Renu and Menuka come down with typhoid. Of course, Narendra then becomes their nurse. At one critical point, Menuka becomes unconscious and starts to sweat profusely, so Narendra takes off all her clothes and sees "her nipples and her secret virgin parts." He is uneasy about this but does not dare to kiss her, only to wipe the sweat off her naked body and daydream about painting nude female bodies. Toward dawn, Narendra falls chastely asleep next to Menuka. She awakes to find herself naked and, while shyly looking for her clothes, realizes that Narendra had been the first man to see her "secret/covered body parts." She looks at him and "feels love." It is interesting to note that no mention is made of Menuka's feeling ashamed or of her wondering whether Narendra had taken liberties with her while she was delirious—sentiments most Nepali women would probably experience under similar circumstances. When Narendra awakes, he sees Menuka standing by the window, recovered from her illness and singing in her beautiful voice a song about his unselfish virtue. They embrace, kiss for a long time, and pour out their hearts to each other.[22]

Shortly thereafter, Menuka gives Renu, her little cousin, a love letter to deliver to Narendra. Note that here it is the woman who initiates the correspondence, while in Junigau everyone told me it is always the man who does so. Narendra sends back a response with Renu. When Renu's parents (Menuka's aunt and uncle) return home, they are extremely grateful to Narendra for saving the girls' lives; they remain ignorant of Menuka's episode of nakedness and are unaware of the growing love between Menuka and Narendra.

Two years go by in which Menuka and Narendra continue their studies. Narendra becomes a gifted artist, and together they join a group of other students who are starting a magazine devoted to Nepali literature and art. At a gathering of these students, one of their friends, a young man named Rasik, urges everyone not to consider women lowly because they are "the most important source of auspiciousness in a writer or author's life." He mentions Leo Tolstoy and Vincent Van Gogh as men who have been inspired by women. (Notice here the assumption that women themselves cannot be artists or writers.) Soon after this gathering, Narendra returns home one day to find that his room has been cleaned up and decorated—Menuka has been there in his absence. She has also locked his tin box, and when he finds the key to open it he discovers that she has bundled up all her love letters for him, leaving him a new one on top, which he reads. In it, Menuka says that she wants to be the "Mrs. Tolstoy, the Mrs. Van Gogh" for Narendra. She's waited two years already, she says; she'll come whenever he calls. She considers him God, worships him, and has already decided to be his companion, one who will work for his success. She asks him to meet her that evening at ten o'clock.

Narendra comes to Menuka's house that evening and waits for her to slip out in secret to meet him. They have a long walk, during which he tells her they can't marry until he gets a job. Menuka begs him to change his mind—he didn't steal her honor when he saw her naked, she says, so she considers him her "life friend." Before they can resolve this disagreement, Menuka's aunt discovers them, sends Menuka inside, and tells Narendra never to come by the house again—a reaction Junigau readers found understandable, if unfortunate.

Within a few days, Narendra discovers that the whole family has moved to Deradun and is distressed to learn that Menuka had said a tearful goodbye to his mother when he wasn't home but didn't leave a letter for him. He pours out all his grief into a painting and feels better. He resolves to tear up all of Menuka's letters but can't bring himself to do so because he remembers that Menuka had called them "a priceless autograph."

Months go by, and then it is time for Menuka to return to Darjeeling to take her final high school exams. She shows up at Narendra's door one day looking very sickly and says that she wants to buy some of Narendra's paintings to remember him by because her uncle is forcing her into an arranged marriage. After Menuka and Narendra take the final exams, Narendra's mother becomes very sick, and Menuka nurses her every day. Finally, Narendra's mother is well enough to limp over to Menuka's aunt and uncle's house to ask their permission for Menuka to marry Narendra because they love each other. Menuka's uncle rudely refuses, noting how poor Narendra's mother is, and as a result Narendra's mother's blood pressure rises and she barely makes it home in time to die in Narendra's arms.

While Narendra sits in formal mourning for his mother, Menuka looks after him tenderly. Her uncle doesn't dare interfere because he feels such guilt at having caused the woman's death. When the rest of the family returns to Deradun, Menuka refuses to do so and instead stays in Darjeeling to be with Narendra. It's not clear at this point whether they are living together, but they definitely have not married. When the test results are released, Menuka and Narendra both learn that they have passed in the first rank, and so they may attend whichever colleges they choose. Narendra chooses to study fine arts for six years in Calcutta, while Menuka decides to return to Deradun, where her aunt and uncle live, and wait for Narendra's return. They joke and kiss while Narendra packs for the trip, and she promises to provide moral and financial support for him.

Once Narendra is in Calcutta, he becomes lonely and writes Menuka over fifty letters in his first two months there. She replies that he should be patient and devote his energies to his art because he'll be a world famous artist someday. After this, Narendra stops writing love letters in class and begins to pay attention. He even begins to make friends among the other art students. They are all in awe of him for scoring first on the placement exam and for being a "born artist." The years go by, and soon Narendra is in his fifth year of art school, not having returned home to Darjeeling or visited Deradun once. (Presumably it's too expensive for him to do so.) He writes Menuka at this point, telling her that his paintings are selling well, so she doesn't have to send him any more money.

Narendra and his friends decide that in order to be true artists they need to practice painting nude portraits, and so they arrange with a pimp to be able to paint a prostitute, who turns out to be a Nepali woman named Maya. Narendra wonders how a "good Nepali girl" came to sell her body, and he asks her for her address. The next scene in the book describes the visit of Dhanuwar, a mutual friend of Menuka and Narendra, to Menuka. Dhanuwar tells her that he has been to visit Narendra in Calcutta—and he's married! But Dhanuwar says that Narendra's wife, Maya (the prostitute), hasn't received from Narendra "the kind of love a wife has the right to expect from a husband." Upon hearing this news, Menuka loses the will to live and stops eating. Her uncle curses Narendra, saying that "the poor will always be poor," but Menuka defends him, claiming that the fault lies in her karma, which she curses. Her cousin, Renu, tells her that the man her uncle had wanted her to marry is still willing to marry her, so Menuka decides to go to Calcutta to get Narendra's blessing for the marriage.

When Menuka shows up at Narendra's doorstep in Calcutta, he happens to be away in New Delhi for a month. Maya, Narendra's wife, invites her in, tells Menuka that she looks sickly, and explains to her (still not knowing who Menuka is) that Narendra and she only appear married; they are not in actuality husband and wife. He did her a huge favor by removing her from prostitution, but he doesn't love her. Maya tells Menuka the whole story of how he saved her from being arrested by telling the police she was his wife. Menuka promises Maya that one day she (Maya) will be Narendra's true wife.

That night Menuka bleeds from her mouth, and Maya promises to take her to the hospital the next day—the day that Narendra is supposed to arrive home. After Maya falls asleep, Menuka opens Narendra's tin box, finds all her old letters to him, and writes him a final one in which she tells him to marry Maya and wishes him a happy married life.

The final scene of the book shows Narendra and Maya, now truly husband and wife, scattering Menuka's ashes into the sacred Ganges River while performing a *pujā* and crying.

In *Love Letters* we see many of the themes present in the other reading materials available to Junigau residents in the 1990s, themes that also emerge in the love letters of Junigau young people. Romantic love is portrayed in *Love Letters* as an uncontrollable emotion that simply happens to people upon hearing a lovely voice or seeing someone's face. Narendra and Menuka fall in love suddenly and irrevocably. Romantic love is also depicted as being incompatible with arranged marriage; when Narendra's mother tries to arrange for her son to marry the woman he loves, Menuka's guardian refuses. In the same way, in Junigau love letter correspondences have almost never resulted in an arranged marriage, although many villagers speak longingly of the possibility of marrying the person they love while also retaining their parents' approval and involvement. Furthermore, like young people in Junigau, the protagonists in *Love Letters* associate romantic love with becoming "modern," "educated," and "developed." Menuka and Narendra take their schooling seriously, and Menuka asserts that her love will help Narendra attain success as an artist.

This emphasis on becoming successful is not applied equally to Menuka and Narendra, however. Despite the "modern" lives the main characters lead, gender relations in *Love Letters* shows some important continuities with previous eras. If Menuka has educational or professional goals of her own, they are not mentioned, nor does she ever question Narendra's decision to pursue his education in Calcutta and delay marrying her for six years. Menuka does use her literacy skills to initiate a love letter correspondence with Narendra, and she does support him financially, but she sublimates her desires to Narendra's. At the end of the book, however, Menuka is portrayed as exercising a powerful yet selfless agency by demanding in a letter to Narendra that he marry Maya once she (Menuka) dies.

Love Letter Guidebooks

Although most Junigau love letter writers have told me that they write only what is in their hearts/minds (*man*) and have never consulted a guidebook, the examples, rules, and sentiments contained in the love letter guidebooks that are sporadically available in bookstores in Tansen so closely echo Junigau love letters that I have decided to include an analysis of these texts here.

When I first heard that how-to books were available to Nepalis who wanted to learn how to write love letters, I asked one of the clerks at the Shrestha News Agency in Tansen for copies of whatever he had. Sorry, the clerk replied, they were sold out. I returned a couple of weeks later, but although they had received a new shipment of the guidebooks in the interim they were again sold out. By my third trip to the bookseller, the clerk recognized me and gave me an apologetic smile that acknowledged what he must have perceived to be my desperate need to learn how to write love letters. There were still no guidebooks. Finally, a few months later, I did manage to obtain a copy of Ara John Movsesian's *How to Write Love Letters and Love Poems* (1993) from the Shrestha News Agency, although in all my subsequent trips back to the store it never had any of the popular Hindi guidebooks in stock.[23] I found two more English guidebooks in Kathmandu bookstores, J. S. Bright's *Lively Love Letters* (n.d.) and Manohar's[24] *Love Letters* (n.d.). Whereas Movsesian's book was originally published by the Electric Press in Fresno, California, before being reprinted in India, both Bright's and Manohar's books were only published by presses in New Delhi. As a result, Bright's and Manohar's guidebooks contain more Indian names, situations, and examples, while Movsesian's consists solely of Western cultural references.[25] Nevertheless, there is a great deal of overlap in all three books. Because Movsesian's guidebook contains the most thorough treatment of love letter writing and because I found it in Tansen rather than Kathmandu, I will go into some detail in describing its contents. Tropes and themes similar to those of the Junigau letters presented throughout this ethnography will become apparent.

Movsesian opens his book with an original poem in which he states the main purpose of his guide: to provide the lovelorn with words to express their love in case they themselves are unable to articulate their feelings:

> *Pearls of Love*
> Words that fit your heart's intent;
>   Words that seem so Heaven sent;
> Words that flow with feelings true,
>   Are found within to be used by you.
>
> These letters, poems, quotes and such,
>   Are here for you to add your touch.
> Transform them well to suit your needs;
>   These words of love will do good deeds.
>
> So when the words are hard to find,
>   And you have really wracked your mind;
> Use these "Pearls of Love" to say,
>   "I love you" in a special way.
>   —Movsesian (1993: v)

In other words, Movsesian fully intends the letters, poems, and quotations in his guidebook to be copied verbatim by people searching for ways to express their love.[26]

In his guidebook, Movsesian puts forth the same philosophy of love that informs the Junigau love letters. According to this philosophy, love is an eternal centrality of life. At the same time, an evolution is posited that moves away from illiterate "backwardness" toward "civilized, refined" expressions of "Romantic Communication." The following passages from Movsesian's preface demonstrate the parallels with the love letters written in Junigau and the ideological assumptions regarding the effects of literacy:

> Verbal language has enabled individuals to personally express their love in a more refined manner than was earlier possible. Written language has provided lover's [sic] a very potent tool which, in turn, has given rise to two forms of Romantic Communication: The Love Letter and Love Poem.
>
> Both of these forms have been used by literate people everywhere for centuries to communicate their innermost passions, desires and emotions. Even Henry VIII and Napoleon wrote love letters to their sweethearts. The most famous legendary writer of love letters was Cyrano De Berjerac [sic] who wrote countless letters, not for himself, but on behalf of his close friends. (1993: vii)

Compare this passage to the first letter Bir Bahadur wrote to Sarita, which contains the lines, "Love is the sort of thing that anyone can feel—even a great man of the world like Hitler loved Eva, they say. And Napoleon, who with bravery conquered the 'world,' united it, and took it forward, was astounded when he saw one particular widow." Moreover, the very first letter in Movsesian's book, in the section entitled, "Love Letters from the Past," is from Napoleon Bonaparte to Josephine De Beauharnais, written in December 1795. It reads in part:

> I wake filled with thoughts of you. Your portrait and the intoxicating evening which we spent yesterday have left my senses in turmoil. Sweet, incomparable Josephine, what a strange effect you have on my heart! Are you angry? Do I see you looking sad? Are you worried? (1993:7)

Compare these lines to the many allusions to anger and sadness in the correspondence of Vajra Bahadur and Shila Devi. In the spring of 1990, for instance, Vajra Bahadur wrote, "Again, you'll probably get angry reading this letter. Whenever I see you, you're always angry. Why, oh why, when I see you walking, looking angry, does my heart get cut into slices?"

The letters of Junigau residents also resonate with the second letter in Movsesian's guidebook, another letter from Napoleon to Josephine, written in 1796. It contains the following words: "I ask of you neither eternal love, nor fidelity, but simply . . . truth, unlimited honesty" (1993: 8). In many of Junigau's love letters the same sentiments are echoed. For example, in July 1992 Bir Bahadur wrote, "If you also love truly, then there will be truth between us as well . . ." And in a December 1990 letter Vajra Bahadur wrote, "You [must] also tell me everything without hiding anything. If you hide [things], I'll get extremely angry at you."

I am not suggesting that Vajra Bahadur (or any other Junigau residents) copied ideas from Movsesian's and Manohar's books or even that he was inspired by such guidebooks, for he explicitly told me he had never seen one. Nevertheless, other Junigau love letter writers often spoke to me of learning from their same-sex friends how to write romantic letters. I believe it is very likely that examples of famous love letter correspondents like Napoleon and the expression of various emotions from the guidebooks get communicated orally from person to person. Even when a letter writer has not seen a copy of one of these guidebooks, therefore, he or she may still be indirectly influenced by their contents. Moreover, the guidebooks' ideologies of romantic love were found in many other Nepali texts and contexts in the 1990s. The sentiments expressed in all of these venues both shape and reflect changing structures of feeling for Junigau residents.

I will present three more excerpts from the many guidebook letters (including those written by historical figures and as well those made up by the authors) that feature themes also central in the love letters written by Junigau residents. All three excerpts address the issue of overcoming obstacles—love might make a letter writer feel powerless in the realm of romance, but it is portrayed as providing people with additional agency in other areas of their lives. Bright's guide contains a letter composed by the author, entitled "To the Cupid of Calcutta," which ends with this convoluted sentence: "There are hurdles to be crossed and I seek your help in crossing those hurdles; and you can depend on me to help you cross your hurdles; across the Howrah Bridge of our past and future lives" (n.d.: 20). Another letter in the same guidebook, entitled "Obstacles Are Blessings in Disguise," contains the following passage: "We must tackle all coming obstacles fairly and squarely like a deer at bay. With courage even a lamb can challenge a lion and with tact can ride over him" (62). Similarly, Movsesian's guidebook contains this excerpt from a letter that the author himself composed:

> Life seems to be full of trials of this type which test our inner strength, and more importantly, our devotion and love for one another. After all, it is said that "True Love" is boundless and immeasurable and overcomes all forms of adversity. In truth, if it is genuine, it will grow stronger with each assault upon its existence. (1993: 59)

Compare the foregoing statements to these two from Bir Bahadur's fourth and fifth letters, respectively: "But the connection between us binds so strongly that even life's most terrible cruelty couldn't cause a separation" and, "May our love reach a place where we can in our lives overthrow any difficulties that arrive and obtain success. Such are the feelings of mind between lovers." In all these examples, love is portrayed as enabling a person to overcome any and all obstacles. According to this formulation, fate is not the final arbiter that determines the outcome of a person's life; the lovers themselves are.

Of the three guidebooks, two instruct the reader explicitly as to how to write an effective love letter. As Movsesian notes, "If you were to analyze all the great love lettes of the past, you would almost always find the presence of 1) *strong emotions* and 2) *good writing ability*" (1993: 21; emphasis in the original). Movsesian therefore starts with the basics of grammar and provides guidelines such as the following: "Use words which are familiar to you," "Do not use too many *trite* words or phrases," and, "Use alternate words to create variety within a love letter" (23–24; emphasis in the original). This guidebook then goes on to teach the reader how to construct "Love Sentences" and "Love Paragraphs." Movsesian defines the former in this way:

> The Love Sentence is the basic unit of all thought expression and its importance cannot be overstated. Indeed, the success of any love letter depends greatly upon how well you can write the love sentence. . . . Every complete love sentence has two distinct parts: The Subject and The Predicate. (25)

On the other hand, Bright's "Golden Guidelines to Write Successful Love Letters" suggests following the nine rules (n.d.: 15–18):

1. Be humble.
2. Ego is a great killer.
3. Write as you feel. [Here Bright disagrees with Movsesian: "Don't worry about grammar on (*sic*) wrong spellings. Love writes freely. Love speaks freely" (16)].
4. Never feel dejected, whatever, [*sic*] the result.
5. Trust in God and be not daunted.
6. Proper use of pronouns. ["Avoid the use of 'I' as far as possible because it often creates a sense of bragging and boastfulness" (17)].
7. Follow your inspiration.
8. Learn from experience.
9. Age and temperament. ["In successful love correspondence don't forget the age and temperament of your correspondent. What you can write to a teenager, you cannot write to a thirty year old (*sic*) correspondent. Many poor young men have successfully won over rich widows and married them too. In USA it is customry (*sic*) for young girls to marry rich husbands; and when these girls become widows, rich and old, they look for young lovers" (18).]

In all of these books, good writing skills are associated with a certain kind of personhood, and this concept of personhood is in turn linked with romantic love. Assumptions about love, personhood, and agency permeate the guidebooks, and even though these books may not be directly consulted by Junigau correspondents they, like the textbooks, magazines, and other reading materials available to villagers, offer a window onto the shifting landscape of sentiment and the changing structures of feeling that were emerging in Junigau during the 1990s.

In the following chapter, I turn to the practices surrounding reading and writing in Junigau and explore various types of literacies in the village.

CHAPTER EIGHT

The Practices of Reading and Writing

Reading and writing are social activities, even when a person is alone while engaging in them. Here, I analyze the ideologies embedded in several of Junigau's new literacy practices, concentrating on the contexts in which villagers read the texts discussed in the previous chapter. New structures of feeling can be detected in the texts themselves and in the reading practices of the villagers that emphasize the right of the individual to act according to her or his own wishes, and there is a strong desire to become "developed." And yet at the same time some long-standing cultural values and hierarchical relationships are being reinforced. Even as new ideas link romantic love with development, economic success, nationalism, and individual rights, old ideas about unequal gender and age relations are being reinforced.

In this chapter, I describe some of the literacy practices in which Junigau villagers have engaged over the years besides writing love letters, for love letter writing does not occur in a vacuum. Rather, it takes place alongside other acts of reading and writing that are just as socially embedded. It is important, therefore, to note the various contexts in which these practices take place—in settings as diverse as schools, tea shops, bookstores, youth clubs, and movie theaters—and to indicate changes in practices and contexts over time. To begin with, I provide an overview of literacy trends in Junigau over time.

Patterns of Literacy in Junigau

There is a wide range of literacy skills among Junigau women and men, making any kind of measurement of literacy rates extremely challenging. Nevertheless, a sense of the overall distribution of literacy skills and formal education among Junigau residents can be seen in table 5, which is based on a survey I conducted in 1993 of all 161 ever-married people in Junigau's central ward.[1]

TABLE 5.   Rates of Literacy and Schooling among All Ever-Married Individuals in Junigau's Central Ward, 1993 ($N = 161$)

Sex	Illiterate	Some Informally Acquired Literacy Skills	Some Formal Education	High School Graduate	Some College
Female	65.4%	13.6%	18.5%	2.5%	0%
Male	6.9%	43.1%	20.8%	25.0%	4.2%

For the purposes of this survey I defined *literacy* as being able to sign one's name (a common point of reference in Junigau discussions of literacy).[2] The survey demonstrated that, according to this definition, 65.4 percent of Junigau married women were illiterate, whereas only 6.9 percent of Junigau married men were. Because of evening female literacy classes, 13.6 percent of married women had some literacy skills (ranging from being able to sign their names to being able to read and write letters). In contrast, the 43.1 percent of married men with informally acquired literacy skills gained them in the military. Overall rates of high school graduation in Junigau also differed greatly by sex, with married men being ten times as likely to have graduated from high school as married women (25.0 vs. 2.5 percent).[3] There were no married women in Junigau who had gone on to college as of 1993, but in 1997 one woman with a couple of years of college education married into the village.

Literacy and formal education rates in Junigau vary significantly by age as well. Tables 6 and 7 show the distribution by age of these rates among married women and men, respectively. While over 95 percent of Junigau married women born before 1951 were illiterate in 1993, in the most recent birth cohort, those born after 1963, almost two-thirds had some formal schooling or had even graduated from high school, and only 8.7 percent were illiterate.

The same trend of increased literacy and formal education can be seen in

TABLE 6.   Rates of Literacy and Schooling among All Ever-Married Women in Junigau's Central Ward, 1993 ($N = 81$)

Year of Birth	Illiterate	Some Informally Acquired Literacy Skills	Some Formal Education	High School Graduate	Some College
Before 1937	95.5%	4.5%	0%	0%	0%
1937–51	95.2%	0%	4.8%	0%	0%
1952–62	66.7%	26.7%	6.7%	0%	0%
1963–93	8.7%	26.1%	56.5%	8.7%	0%

TABLE 7.   Rates of Literacy and Schooling among All Ever-Married Men in
Junigau's Central Ward, 1993 ($N = 72$)

Year of Birth	Illiterate	Some Informally Acquired Literacy Skills	Some Formal Education	High School Graduate	Some College
Before 1937	26.7%	73.3%	0%	0%	0%
1937–51	5.9%	58.8%	29.4%	5.9%	0%
1952–62	0%	41.7%	29.2%	25.0%	4.2%
1963–93	0%	0%	18.8%	68.8%	12.5%

the birth cohorts of married men in Junigau. Whereas over a quarter of such
men born before 1937 were illiterate in 1993 and none had any formal education, all of those born from 1963 to the present had at least some formal education and more than three-quarters of them were high school graduates or
had some college education.

As these figures demonstrate, there has been a dramatic increase in the
number of women and men who have at least some literacy skills and/or formal schooling. Taken by themselves, however, these numbers cannot illuminate
the types of literacy practices in which Junigau residents engage or the meanings and values they attribute to them. This is the task of the remainder of this
chapter.

Literacy Practices before 1960

Prior to 1950, when Nepal was ruled by an elitist, isolationist series of Rana
prime ministers, there were very few schools in the country. Almost all of them
were located in Kathmandu and were for the purpose of educating elite, high-
caste boys (Bista 1991: 118–21). In Junigau, there was no school until 1959, when
a small school for boys was opened. This created the uneven distribution we
have just seen of literacy skills across the Junigau population according to
gender and age.

Before a school was opened in Junigau, most of the social practices requiring literacy skills involved official documents. The process of creating, receiving, and storing official documents pertaining to birth, death, taxes, citizenship, and army service was gendered. Junigau men were not only much more
likely to be literate at that time and therefore able to participate in the social
processes surrounding documents; they were also the only villagers involved in
the military and in local leadership roles. The government administrator in the
village, or *sachip*, who was in charge of recording births and deaths, was always

a man, as was the head of the village council, the *pradhān panch*. Women sometimes attended village meetings but only when there were no men present who could represent the family. According to villagers who remember these meetings, the women rarely participated in the discussions and never took part in the writing of resolutions that occasionally resulted from the meetings. (Indeed, this was still the case as recently as 1998.)

Aside from records of birth and death, tax receipts, resolutions, military discharge papers, citizenship papers, and other sorts of official documents, Junigau residents also participated in the creation and reading of papers associated with moneylending. In the past, most moneylenders were upper-caste men from other villages, and the borrowers of money were Magar men from Junigau acting on behalf of their joint families. (This continues to be the case.) It was always the moneylender who drew up the document, while the man from Junigau who was borrowing the money would add only his signature (or thumbprint if he could not write). Sometimes villagers would call upon the assistance of more highly educated neighbors or relatives in order to make sure the moneylender did not charge too much interest, but again all these activities were—and continue to be—considered the province of men.

According to Junigau residents, men have also always been in charge of drawing up lists of invitees for feasts associated with life cycle rituals. Senior male relatives are still the ones who write down the names of the heads of households (all men, except in the case of widows living alone) to be invited to the feast, and boys or young men have the responsibility for personally delivering each invitation. Unlike in Kathmandu or Tansen, the invitations to weddings and other events have never been written, although the list of invitees is almost always put in writing. It is carefully noted on the list whether the entire family is invited (*chulo nimtā*—everyone who eats at the same hearth) or just one representative of the family (*nimtā*). During the feast, senior male kin write down who actually attends in order to have a better sense of future social obligations. Women sometimes keep careful track of this in their heads, but they have never been the ones doing the reading or writing.

A few of the older men in Junigau have specialized literacy skills that have enabled them over the years to read astrological calendars for the purpose of choosing an auspicious date to commemorate a relative's death or hold a marriage. Complex astrological calculations, however, have always been conducted by *hāmro bāun* (our Brahman), the Brahman priest from a neighboring village who officiates at all the Hindu life cycle rituals in Junigau. While a couple of Magar families in Junigau have Hindu calendars and copies of Hindu scriptures in Nepali or Sanskrit, these materials are rarely intelligible to ordinary villagers, even to those who can read and write Nepali.

Another sphere of life associated with literacy in the past in Junigau was the military, where most men acquired and used their literacy skills in earlier times. Retired Gurkha soldiers from Indian or British regiments described to me how they learned to read and write Nepali, Hindi, and sometimes English in order to be able to read training manuals. One Junigau man, a former member of a British Gurkha regiment, participated in deciphering secret codes during World War II. By far, the most common literacy practice of soldiers before 1960, however, was writing letters home. Because very few married women were literate at that time, men or boys received and answered most of the letters to and from soldiers. Women sometimes participated actively by suggesting things to include in letters to their husbands, or even dictating entire letters. (Older women still do this at times.) Women were also occasionally the recipients of letters, even though they usually had to call upon a male relative to read them, but most often a soldier would address letters to his father or other senior male relatives. From the few older letters I have seen, and from what Junigau residents report, letters to and from soldiers in the past almost always contained only prayers for the well-being of everyone and occasional reports on crops, weddings, childbirths, or deaths. According to everyone I consulted in the village, there were no love letters, or even any written expressions of love, in Junigau before the late 1980s. While explicit expressions of emotion were not part of letters in the past, however (cf. Besnier 1995), the reading aloud of soldiers' letters reportedly served to communicate implicit feelings of affection and strengthen family bonds.

Other than soldiers' letters, official documents, and Hindu scriptures, there were very few reading materials in the village twenty or more years ago—no novels, few if any magazines or newspapers, no songbooks, no literacy texts, and only a few school textbooks, most of them based on models of religious learning conducted by Brahman *pandits*. Villagers did use their literacy skills to handle money, especially as the economy became increasingly monetized from the 1960s onward, and some report being grateful they could read the occasional signboard on stores or buses in Tansen or elsewhere. Again, however, these activities were gendered, as it was mostly men who traveled and conducted trade, although women often went along as porters on the weeklong treks to Butwal or Pokhara for supplies.

Before 1960, therefore, literacy practices in Junigau were mainly activities engaged in by men. Furthermore, these practices mainly involved the government, commerce, religion, or the military. Completely absent from these literacy practices were expressions of romantic love (or any other emotion), exhortations to become developed or modern, or rhetorical tropes emphasizing individual rights and identity.

Emergent Literacy Practices in Junigau, 1960–90

As Nepal emerged from a century of oppressive rule by the Rana family in the 1950s, the government began to accept massive amounts of development aid from the United States and Europe, much of it for the purpose of setting up an educational system.[4] By the 1960s, some of this money was making its way out to villages like Junigau, where new literacy practices began to appear once the Nepal Rastriya Primary School was opened up in the village in 1959. This first school had only one teacher, a Brahman *pandit* from a neighboring village, and its goal was to teach the Magar boys of Junigau basic literacy and numeracy skills using traditional Hindu texts. Three years later, in 1962, the school was moved and renamed the Sarvodaya Primary School. It offered only three grades of schooling until 1969, when grades four and five were added. In 1980, Sarvodaya became a middle school offering grades one through eight, and in 1982 it became a full high school by adding on grades nine and ten. In the early 1980s, there were not enough Junigau residents with sufficient formal education to staff the high school, so, although there were a few local Magar teachers (former soldiers) in the lower grades, most of the teachers in the upper grades were high-caste Brahmans or Chhetris from distant villages. Exceptions to this were an Indian science teacher, the headmaster of the school (a Junigau Magar), and myself.

At a time when the vast majority of Junigau residents were illiterate, the headmaster had obtained a master's degree in education from an Indian university. Instead of remaining in India or moving to Kathmandu, where he could probably have secured a well-paying job despite egregious discrimination against Magars, he returned to Junigau and took on the task of improving the quality of education at Sarvodaya High School. One of his first decisions, in consultation with the School Management Committee, was to request a Peace Corps volunteer. The headmaster and village leaders assumed (correctly, as it turned out) that the presence of a volunteer (who turned out to be me) would help them achieve the status of a fully accredited and therefore fully funded government school. My presence also helped the school obtain a Peace Corps Partnership grant, which, after long delays, funded the building of an addition to the school.

The new school building remains one of the most visible long-term effects of my Peace Corps service in Junigau. People still occasionally refer to it in my presence as "my" building. No amount of explaining or reminding will disabuse them of the idea that I single-handedly caused the addition to be built. Sure, they helped by carrying sand up from the river for cement, carrying rocks for the walls, mixing mud with their feet—but the building is still "mine." This sentiment, along with learning more about the local politics of the village that helped to delay the project's completion, led me to question whether any "de-

Plate 25   Sarvodaya High School students line up for class in the early 1980s

velopment project" can result in an avowal rather than an eschewal of agency on the part of the people affected by the project (cf. Pigg 1992). We were told in the Peace Corps that the best kind of help is that which leads people afterward to say, "We did it ourselves." I found it virtually impossible, however, to get the villagers to acknowledge their own contributions.

Once the school became accredited in 1983, primary education became free to all villagers, and Junigau families began to send their daughters as well as their sons to school in greater numbers, as the school, now funded by the government, no longer had to charge prohibitively expensive monthly fees. Still, throughout the 1980s relatively few of the students were girls. In 1983, only thirteen of class 4's forty-five students and only three of its twenty-seven class 10 students were girls (and all three of the class 10 girls were Brahmans from neighboring villages). The number of girls increased significantly as the years passed and as the number of students as a whole doubled, but well into the 1990s, the majority of the school's students in the upper grades remained boys and many were high-caste Brahmans and Chhetris from neighboring villages. Nevertheless, by the mid-1990s Sarvodaya High School was regularly graduating a handful of Magar girls from Junigau each year.

In the late 1990s, overall enrollments at Junigau's high school began to fall. Neighboring villages had built their own high schools, thereby siphoning off

Plate 26   Junigau girl on her way to school in the early 1980s

many high-caste students who would have attended Junigau's school. Furthermore, as an increasing number of Junigau families had disposable income from
family members with jobs in the military or overseas, and as villagers became
aware of the benefits of strong English skills more and more of them were
sending their children to private English-medium schools in Tansen. The children either walked three hours each way to and from Tansen every day or, more
commonly, stayed with relatives in Tansen during the week, returning to the
village for weekends and holidays. In 1997, a private English-medium primary
school opened up in Junigau itself, offering only the first couple of grades. As
of my most recent visit in 1998, the school was extremely successful, enrolling
between twenty and thirty students per class. Staffed by local Magars, many of
whom were once my students, the new English-medium school is likely to at-

Plate 27   Students attend an outdoor class in Junigau's new English-medium school in 1998

tract all but the poorest villagers in the coming years, and if it continues to add grades it may very well trigger a crisis for Sarvodaya High School. Indeed, during the summer of 1999 my Nepali family and friends told me by phone of a remarkable event: at a village meeting about the problems Sarvodaya was facing with enrollments, discipline, and national test scores, village leaders expelled most of the high-caste Brahman and Chhetri teachers from outside of Junigau and replaced them with Junigau Magars.

The advent of formal schooling in Junigau was accompanied by the headmaster's institution of female literacy classes in the school beginning in the early 1980s. In the early years, one of the local primary school teachers, a Brahman (though not the same man who taught in Junigau's first school in 1959) taught the class, then Junigau high school graduates took over as instructors in the late 1980s and early 1990s. I know of only one female beside myself who ever taught the class: a young woman who had recently graduated from Sarvodaya High School in Junigau taught the class briefly in 1995. My own involvement as an assistant teacher in the female literacy classes lasted for about six months during my Peace Corps years in 1983–84. During this time, the class was held in the winter evenings from 6:30 to 8:30, when because of the season local girls and women were less likely to be busy with farm work. There were about a dozen students in the class, ranging in age from twelve to twenty-five.

**Plate 28   Tulsi Kumari Rana weaves a bag, having learned the skill at a special train-
ing course for women**

Most were unmarried daughters of families who lived close to the school; a few
were daughters-in-law of those same families. The main teacher in those years
was a local Brahman man, and while he focused on teaching the girls and
women how to read and write in Nepali using *New Path,* the textbook that was
analyzed in the previous chapter, I had the responsibility for teaching them
basic numeracy skills (how to read and write numbers and how to add and
subtract). Toward the end of my stint, upon the request of the students, I
switched from teaching numeracy to teaching English. The girls and women in
the class recognized the status associated with being able to speak, read, and
write English, and they often told me that they enjoyed showing the members
of their families, especially the men, their notebooks containing English words.

For many reasons, the female literacy classes were at best a mixed success.
First of all, they were held in the evening, which meant that the students were
tired after a full day of work that had often begun before dawn. As a result, attendance was sporadic, and many of the students who did attend regularly were
too exhausted to learn. Second, there was an extremely wide range of abilities in
the class. Some of the students had attended a year or two of formal school,
while others had never tried to grasp a writing utensil in their lives. At one

point, we wanted to split the class in half to address the ability groups separately, but we had insufficient kerosene to do so. As it was, the kerosene lamp we used often malfunctioned and was never bright enough for all the students to write at the same time. The final obstacle to the female literacy class was cultural: many senior men and women would not allow their daughters or daughters-in-law to leave the house at night even if they did acknowledge the benefits of literacy for women (which, in 1983, many did not). Some of the village elders who did initially permit their daughters or daughters-in-law to attend the class rescinded their permission when they heard rumors (some of them true) that young men were hanging around the school hoping to see or talk to some of the young women in the class.

Nāyā Goreṭo (New Path), the literacy textbook described in the previous chapter, was inspired by the emancipatory philosophy of Paolo Freire (cf. Freire 1972; Freire and Macedo 1987). During Peace Corps training, our trainers introduced *New Path* to us and urged us to take on female literacy as a secondary project. We were told about Freire's philosophy of education and encouraged to put it into practice in our own female literacy projects. One of the most important Freirean aspects of *New Path* was the picture at the beginning of each chapter. Depicting various social ills, these pictures were designed to stimulate discussion of inequitable conditions and encourage collective action to fight oppression. Neither the female literacy students in the class nor the Brahman man who taught them were at all interested in using the text this way, however. Even when I tutored individual women using *New Path,* which I did from time to time, the women became impatient with any attempts I made to use the pictures as consciousness-raising tools. The women in the class wanted a "real" education, which to them meant learning the way their little brothers learned: by rote, without any explicit messages of social reform, and from the beginning of the alphabet to the end rather than starting with the easiest letter to form, as *New Path* does. Ironically, therefore, or perhaps not so ironically, Junigau women actively resisted the very elements of the *New Path* textbook that attempted to involve them as agents in the process of their own "development"— even as they absorbed many of *New Path*'s messages about development.

Junigau's Literacy Practices in the 1990s

Junigau's literacy practices from the 1990s on have become far more complex and numerous than they were thirty or more years ago. Many more villagers are reading and writing, and they are reading and writing different kinds of materials than in the past. Social practices surrounding literacy have also changed, although many of the older practices have continued and are for the most part still considered to be the responsibility of men. The social dynamics involved in producing and consuming literacy materials, as well as the contents of the materials themselves, have had a profound impact on the younger generation in Junigau. New structures of feeling are emerging that communicate novel sensibilities about how one should live, what gender relations should look like, and what it means to be a person in Junigau in the 1990s.

One very important new social context for literacy practices was created in 1990 when a group of young (in their late teens and early twenties) and unmarried villagers decided to create a "youth club" (*yuvā kalab*). In the spring of 1990, there was a democratic revolution in Nepal led largely by an active student movement. While no Junigau villagers participated in any of the demonstrations that eventually ushered in a constitutional monarchy, those students who were studying at the Tansen campus of Tribhuvan University at that time were undoubtedly influenced by rhetoric highlighting the importance of individual rights, economic development, and education. Because student strikes closed the campus in Tansen for months, several young men from Junigau, including Vajra Bahadur, whose courtship was featured in chapter 6, found themselves home in Junigau with little besides farming tasks to keep them busy. They decided to use their free time to start a youth club, which would raise money for various development activities in Junigau. During festivals, the youth club raised money by organizing *bhailo* singing during Tihar and games for the fair held on Dashain Purniya each year. Eventually, the club members succeeded in constructing a small meeting place for club activities, buying hundreds of stainless steel plates for villagers to borrow when they had feasts[5] and acquiring reading materials from charities for a youth club library. They also received permission to move many of the books from the school's "library" (actually a locked cupboard in the headmaster's office, inaccessible to students) into the youth club's library. These books included several dozen dated textbooks in English that I had procured from a charity in Darien, Connecticut, while I was in the Peace Corps and another dozen or so Time-Life science books that the Peace Corps had distributed to its education volunteers in the 1980s. I remember watching youth club members marvel over the Time-Life book's photos of the astronauts landing on the moon. Very few of the youth club members were able to (or even wanted to) read the books' difficult English prose, but almost all of them enjoyed looking at the pictures of "developed" Westerners engaged in science and everyday life.

While the club leaders were all young, highly educated men, they attempted to involve other young people in Junigau, including young women and other young men who had dropped out of school or joined the army. Many villagers still speak with admiration of the hard work the young men and women did in constructing the club building and meeting regularly to plan activities. After the initial construction of the building and the celebratory inaugural picnic (where Shila Devi and Vajra Bahadur first "exchanged glances"), however, the club-house essentially became a young men's space. Young women were still involved but only peripherally. For one thing, it was the young men who had much more time on their hands, as they were not expected to do as much work around the house or in the fields as were the young women. So, it was the young men who were able to congregate in the clubhouse, playing carom board games, making plans, and perusing the books and magazines the club had managed to purchase or have donated. Even after the campus reopened in 1991–92 and the club lead-ers only returned home on vacations, the clubhouse continued to be a meeting place for young, educated men in the village who engaged in "development talk" (*bikāsko kurā*), gossiped about who was courting (*mileko*) with whom, and flipped through the types of magazines I described in the previous chapter. Reading magazines became a central activity in the clubhouse. The magazines that club members were able to acquire were circulated so that the entire club— and even some nonmembers, including women—were able to read (or at least look at) the magazines.

After just a couple of years, however, the club began to suffer from a lack of conscientious leadership. Club funds were misplaced, the number of activities dwindled, and the clubhouse remained locked more often than not. During 1992, I attended several youth club meetings at which there was considerable discord, mostly surrounding the (mis)management of funds and the purpose of the organization. At one of those meetings, members decided that because some young men had been responsible the year before for losing or stealing (it was never resolved which) the proceeds from the games they organized at the Dashain Purniya this year they would put the female members (including my-self, as an honorary member) in charge of handling the money at the fair. All day long several other young women and I supervised the bottle toss, bingo, and other games at the fair, handing over several thousand rupees' (roughly three hundred dollars') worth of proceeds by the end of the day. Youth club members agreed to give half of the money they had raised to the village development fund. The other half they kept in order to throw a feast for their members. The young women who had spent all day overseeing the fair games felt this was a poor use of the money, preferring instead to spend the money on development projects and supplies rather than on a feast, and subsequently they became even less involved in the youth club. By the mid-1990s, the youth club had disinte-grated, its former members having joined the military or taken on other re-sponsibilities. Nevertheless, for a period of time in the early 1990s, the clubhouse provided an important space for some Junigau residents, especially young men, to engage in literacy and other social practices that both reflected and reinforced novel ways of thinking and behaving.

Plate 29   Tea shop patrons (Pashupati Rana, Hum Bahadur Rana, and Bijaya Thapa) with posters on the wall behind them

Many of the social reading practices that went on in the clubhouse moved to the half-dozen tea shops that sprang up in Junigau in the mid-1990s. The few that were opened by former members of the club became especially popular sites for the congregation of young people in Junigau. Young men were still the primary consumers of magazines, but young women told me that they, too, would sometimes sit in the tea shops looking at the magazines, occasionally borrowing copies to take home to look at and share with family members. Not only did Junigau's tea shops become places in which villagers read; they also became reading material themselves. Several of the shop walls featured posters and excerpts from magazines, and two even displayed signs written out by hand by the proprietors. These slogans emphasized the efficacy of hard work, even as they urged readers to trust in God. As such, they mixed older values with newer structures of feeling, indicating the emergence of a stronger sense of individual agency.

One magazine advertisement posted in a Junigau tea shop (and seen in a Kathmandu billboard) embodies a number of the newer ideologies that are appearing more and more frequently in the texts and images the villagers con-

Plate 30   Billboard in Kathmandu

sume. In this ad for Shikhar ("Summit") cigarettes, a man and a woman dressed in Western garb are embracing in a way that suggests more physical intimacy than is usually considered appropriate to display publicly in Nepal. They are both light-skinned, and he is holding a briefcase. The slogan, written in English, reads "The taste of success." This striking image, along with the accompanying slogan, which is echoed in Junigau love letters, point to new structures of feeling that link romantic love with economic success and Westernization.

In addition to the spaces in Junigau in which literacy practices took place, such as the clubhouse and the tea shops, I will describe several venues in Tansen (pop. 16,169),[6] the district center of Palpa District that is three hours' walk from Junigau. Like the sites in Junigau itself, the locations in Tansen that I will mention have facilitated the emergence of new practices surrounding reading and writing. By the early 1990s, a dozen or more Junigau young people—including Vajra Bahadur, Bir Bahadur, and Sarita—were attending college classes in Tansen. Some, such as Bir Bahadur and Sarita, lived in small, rented rooms in Tansen while attending classes at Tribhuvan University's campus there, while others, such as Vajra Bahadur, walked there and back daily (a four- to six-hour round trip, depending on how fast one walks). Even those residents of Junigau not attending classes at the Tansen campus went into Tansen frequently to buy goods at the bazaar and to attend Hindi and Nepali films at the cinema hall. Because Tansen was an increasingly important location for literacy practices in the 1990s, I will describe four specific spaces in which Junigau residents engaged in new forms of literacy: the college campus, the bazaar's bookstores and tea shops, students' rented rooms, and Tansen's cinema hall.

The Tansen campus of Tribhuvan University (TU), the only government-sponsored university in Nepal, offers students courses of study leading to intermediate (similar to our associate's degree) or bachelor's degrees in commerce (business) or nursing. Other courses of study available at Tribhuvan University's campuses elsewhere in Nepal (such as medicine, political science, or anthropology) are not available in Tansen. All of the Junigau students who studied at TU's Tansen campus in the 1990s chose commerce as their field. In their curriculum, they were required to take courses such as rural economics, math, accounting, and English. From my observations and from what Junigau residents attending TU told me, classes at the Tansen campus in the 1990s were huge (hundreds of students squeezed into cramped benches), only sporadically in session, and often taught by Indians whom Junigau students could not understand. Students relied on rote memorization of the textbooks, and professors rarely attempted to do anything more than read aloud the textbooks in class. When yearly exams approached, many professors offered expensive *tyusan* (tuition) classes on the side, and for many Junigau students these sessions were the only chances they had to listen to someone explain the material; most considered regular classes to be a waste of time.

The campus buildings in Tansen are bleak, uninviting, concrete structures that are cold in the winter and hot in the summer. Tansen's campus has no building comparable to a student union. As a result, most college students in the 1990s spent as little time there as possible, lingering instead in bookstores, tea shops, or their own rented rooms. It was in these spaces that new literacy practices emerged.

As of my most recent visit to Nepal in 1998, Tansen had a half-dozen bookstores. Most were small and stocked only the required textbooks for local schools. One, however, the Shrestha News Agency, has been around for decades, and in the 1990s it expanded to carry thousands of titles in Nepali, Hindi, and English, many of them concerning development. Magazines and newspapers were also available there, as were love letter guidebooks. Even after it expanded, the Shrestha News Agency was still a cramped space unsuitable for browsing; indeed, customers had to stand at the front desk and ask the clerk to get whichever reading materials they were considering buying. As a result, very little reading took place in the store itself, but the displays, the vast number of books and magazines available, and the mere fact of the store's existence (and expansion)

Plate 31 Tansen

in the middle of the bazaar conveyed messages about the increasing centrality of reading as an activity important for the country's—and each person's—development. Reading materials sold in the Shrestha News Agency and elsewhere were not cheap, however; most Junigau college students could barely afford to buy required textbooks. Whenever a student did buy something extra, such as a magazine, therefore, it was passed around from friend to friend.

Most of the casual reading and serious studying that Junigau college students did in Tansen took place either in their own rented rooms or in tea shops in the bazaar. In the tea shops, the scene was very similar to that described earlier for tea shops in Junigau itself. Tea shops were mainly, though not exclusively, a masculine space. On countless occasions, I witnessed male college students poring over magazines in Tansen tea shops. Poor lighting and constant disruptions must have dissuaded the students from studying in tea shops; I never saw any student open a textbook in one. Tea shops were therefore primarily spaces for informal perusing of magazines.[7]

Most Junigau students attending Tansen's TU campus in the 1990s studied either alone or in small groups in their rented rooms. As mentioned, formal education in Nepal requires a lot of rote memorization, so students' study techniques, which I witnessed frequently as I attempted to tutor Junigau college students, consisted mainly of reading and rereading (often aloud) the textbook for a particular class. Usually study partners would be same-sex, same-caste friends, but occasionally young people romantically involved with each other would find enough privacy in their Tansen rooms to "study together." Even though young people (especially young women) studying at the Tansen cam-pus most often lived with relatives, many of them were not supervised as closely as they would have been in the village, and thus in their own rooms they were able to meet with, or write letters to, their sweethearts. Controversy over exactly what took place during Sarita and Bir Bahadur's "study sessions" com-prises part of the next chapter.

The final Tansen space I want to discuss here is the cinema hall (cf. Liechty 1998). While very little, if any, reading or writing took place in the cinema hall, a different type of literacy, which we could call cultural or visual literacy, en-abled viewers of Hindi and Nepali movies to absorb, contest, or merely be ex-posed to emerging structures of feeling surrounding romantic love, develop-ment, success, and Westernization. Moreover, the cinema hall was not only a place where young people were able to observe new patterns of behavior on the screen; it was also a site for young people to act out some of what they saw in the films.[8] While young Junigau residents are not allowed to date openly, many Junigau college students and noncollege students, including many couples whose courtships are described in this ethnography, managed to meet their sweethearts secretly at the cinema hall.

Although Tansen's one cinema hall has existed since the 1970s, Junigau res-idents only began attending movies there regularly in the 1980s once Nepali-language films began to be shown, and even then most did so surreptitiously, since filmgoing was considered a disreputable activity, especially for women, well into the 1990s. Attitudes have changed dramatically in recent years, how-ever, as a result of the wide-ranging social changes occurring in the village. Whereas some of Junigau's older residents have never attended a film in Tansen, most younger residents now attend movies frequently and openly. Col-lege students from Junigau who live in Tansen are even better situated to take advantage of Tansen's cinema hall. They generally attend as many films as they can afford—and since some seats are extremely cheap, and the films change only once every few weeks, most Tansen students and many village residents are able to attend virtually every movie that comes to Tansen.

I remember vividly my first experience attending a film in Tansen's cinema hall. It was October 1984, and the women in my Nepali family and I had been trying for months to persuade my Nepali father to allow us to go to a movie to-gether. Finally, just before I was to leave the village for other parts of Nepal, he relented. The women (my Nepali mother, twelve-year-old sister, and seventeen-year-old sister-in-law) did their early morning chores as quickly as possible, and by 8:00 A.M. we were headed to Tansen on foot. We arrived just before the daily

11:00 A.M. showing and fought our way through the crowd to buy balcony tickets to a new Hindi movie. All the while, Didi, my Nepali mother, who had never before attended a film, was regaling me with stories of "ignorant villagers" she had heard about who, when seeing a film for the first time, assumed that when it was raining in the movie it was also raining outside. She would not be so foolish, she assured me. After the three-hour film full of song and dance numbers, fights, and chaste romantic interludes, I asked my companions what they thought. None of us had fully understood the plot, since the sound quality was horrible and the dialogue was in Hindi. Still, the three of them enjoyed the film. I was less enamoured of it. The hot, claustrophobic firetrap of a cinema hall made me nervous, and the extremely unlikely plot twists prevented me from being able to identify with the characters. My companions felt differently, however. Didi was amazed at how frequently the actors changed clothes, my little sister was taken by the Indian-style "disco" dancing, and Bhauju was still choked up by what were for her extremely emotional scenes. We talked as we walked the three hours back to the village, arriving home just before dark. I took many such trips with Junigau friends and family to see films over the ensuing years.

One Nepali film I saw with Bhauju at the cinema hall in Tansen in September 1993 contained many of the messages common to Nepali and Hindi (but especially Nepali) films. I will describe it briefly here, therefore, to give readers a sense of how themes surrounding development and romantic love often come together in the movies Junigau residents so frequently viewed in the 1990s. Like the novel, *Love Letters,* described in the previous chapter, *Kanyādān* requires a suspension of disbelief. Junigau viewers are not troubled by such unrealistic plots, however; many have told me that they enjoy movies for the song and dance routines, the depiction of "developed" lifestyles, or the lessons in fashion they invariably provide.

Kanyādān (Gift of a Virgin) opens with scenes depicting two eight- or nine-year-old high-caste children being married off by their parents. The little bride, Agati, is taken to her new home, but she soon becomes homesick for her natal home. Her mother-in-law, extremely supportive at this point, allows her to return for a visit to her mother and father's house. There all her friends admire her new clothes and jewelry. While Agati is at her natal home, her husband falls from a tree, and because the cut is not washed or shown to a doctor but just blown on by a shaman—the film is explicitly judgmental on this point—the boy dies. Thus, Agati very quickly becomes a child widow, forbidden to remarry and considered by all to be a sign of bad luck. At first Agati resists her status and is allowed to return to her natal home even though the mourning period is not yet over, but she becomes too much for her parents to handle, so she is soon sent back to her marital home. Agati's mother-in-law, embittered by the loss of her son, takes out her anger on her daughter-in-law. From then on, Agati submits to her fate and becomes an unhappy, uncomplaining young woman dressed plainly in a white sari to convey her permanent state of widowhood.

The film then jumps forward ten or so years. Agati is beautiful but without the spirit or spunk of her youth. Vikram, an old playmate of Agati's husband's, comes back from India and begins to harass Agati. She righteously refuses his advances but says nothing about them to her in-laws. At the same time, a doctor, whose name, unsubtly enough, is Bikas (development), arrives in the village. Bikas sets up shop and starts curing people immediately, dispensing medicine and giving injections left and right. Agati comes by to deliver milk to him and sees him cure a little boy whose leg had the same kind of injury that killed her husband. She cries. Bikas sees her crying and asks about her circumstances. From then on, he does his best to make her happy whenever he sees her.

But Vikram has not given up his scheming. When Agati accompanies a group of women on a pilgrimage to Kathmandu, she just happens to lose her way and just happens to be nearly run over by Bikas, who also just happens to be in Kathmandu. Vikram finds out and returns to the village to spread evil rumors about the two of them. Meanwhile, a cast is placed on Agati's leg and she is put up at Bikas's house in Kathmandu, where he lives with his widowed mother. Enter the competition—a woman named Bina who has an M.A. and dresses in scandalously short, Western-style clothing. Bina tries to eliminate Agati from contention by reminding her of a widow's place. This almost works, but the doctor insists that Agati accompany him to his birthday party (an event foreign to Junigau residents, who do not celebrate birthdays). Agati is the one who lights the candles on the cake instead of a fuming Bina. All of Bikas's Kathmandu friends speak English with one another, but they still need to be convinced by a speech from Bikas that a widow is a worthy wife and person.

Once Agati's leg is on the mend, she and Bikas return to the village, where, because of Vikram's rumors, Agati is almost not allowed back into her in-laws' house. Bikas insists, however, and this later emboldens Agati to fight with her mother-in-law over work and win. Meanwhile, Bikas's reputation has also been damaged, and he is asked to leave the village. He asks Agati to meet him secretly in the forest to tell her he is leaving and to ask her to go with him. Before she can answer him, though, Vikram and his cronies ambush Bikas and a violent fistfight ensues. After the fight, Bikas is left injured on the ground, while Vikram takes Agati back to her in-laws' house, where her mother-in-law ties her to a beam in the cowshed and starts to beat her. Vikram stops her but returns later to threaten Agati. When she spits in his face, he starts a fire in the cowshed, where she is still tied to the beam. Just in time, Bikas recovers from his beating and learns of Agati's plight. He rushes to save her from the flames, but when he finds her body he assumes (without taking her pulse or performing CPR) that she is dead. He delivers a speech to the crowd of villagers who have assembled, telling them that widows are people, too, and that early marriages and a ban on widow remarriage are wrong. Society must change, he passionately proclaims. Just then, Agati awakens. On the spot, Bikas's mother, who just happens to be present, suggests a makeshift marriage ceremony. Agati's contrite mother-in-law agrees, announcing to all that she is going to stage a *kanyādān* right there. She places Agati's hand in Bikas's, and the film ends.

As Bhauju pointed out to me on the walk back to the village after viewing *Kanyādān*, two of the film's messages were quite clear to her: (1) that child marriage is bad and (2) that it is not good to hate widows. But the movie conveyed other messages as well. Bina, the one educated woman in the film, is an unpleasant schemer. Agati as an adult passively submits to her fate, having to be rescued by Bikas, the male hero. The in-laws still get to "give away" their widowed daughter-in-law, and nowhere does Agati seem to make a choice on her own, except to exercise negative agency when she spits in Vikram's face.[9] Thus, when development (*bikās*) arrives in the village in the form of Dr. Bikas, residents can expect better health care, an end to child marriage, new possibilities for widows—but no fundamental restructuring of gender or age hierarchies. As to how Junigau residents reacted to the film, none of the people I asked about it liked it very much. It was too *dukha lāgdo*, they said; it caused them to be too sad. Still, many women admired Agati. Bhauju said, "She was so good, poor thing."

Films have an undeniable impact on structures of feeling in Junigau. They are arguably more influential in setting fashion trends and providing models for gender relations than any real life or written material. In one naturally occurring conversation I recorded between two young village women in 1992, one of them urges the other to go to more films in order to learn how to wear more fashionable attire. She exclaims: "*philim herera sikinchha ni!*" (One learns from watching films, you know!). And when the film *Gopi/Krishna* was popular during the summer of 1993, many boys in Junigau took to wearing their hair like the hero of the movie and playing a flute as he did. These are only some of the more obvious ways in which films had an impact on the behavior and attitudes of Junigau residents.

Some of the same influences and changing structures of feeling can be seen in the courtship of Sarita and Bir Bahadur, the subjects of the following chapter.

CHAPTER NINE

Wearing the Flower One Likes

Sarita and Bir Bahadur's Courtship

In the spring of 1992, Sarita and Bir Bahadur began a love letter correspondence. Sarita was a serious young woman of about twenty-one at the time, and Bir Bahadur was a year older. Sarita had been a student of mine when she was in the fourth and fifth grades, and once she was older she became a close friend. An only daughter, Sarita was (and is) dearly loved by her parents and older brothers. She was therefore able to convince them to allow her to stay in school much longer than is common for Junigau girls. While I have known Sarita and her family for more than eighteen years, I am only slightly acquainted with Bir Bahadur and do not know his family at all, for they live in a village quite far from Junigau. And yet it is Bir Bahadur's eighteen letters that I will mainly be discussing here, along with Sarita's verbal remarks about them, since Sarita's letters were not available to me.[1]

The Courtship Begins

When the correspondence between Sarita and Bir Bahadur began in the spring of 1992, both were in their first year of studies at the campus in the district center of Tansen. Sarita was living in a tiny rented room with her little nephew and a female cousin, while Bir Bahadur was living in another rented room on the other side of the bazaar with two schoolmates. By the time I arrived in Junigau for fourteen months of fieldwork in August 1992, they had exchanged half a dozen letters and had even met each other a couple of times in the company of two close friends who were apprised of their secret courtship. In a series of informal interviews during the fall festival season that year, I asked Sarita to describe how the courtship had begun. Eschewing responsibility for the courtship's initiation, she replied, "From the start? From the start . . . well, it was as if I had no knowledge about it whatsoever." Although they were taking the same classes at the campus, Sarita said, she had

had no idea who Bir Bahadur was until one day in February or March of 1992 when a relative of Sarita's asked Bir Bahadur to deliver a message to her regarding a textbook that he (the relative) had for her. Sarita and her best friend, Jhili, were walking back to their rented rooms after class that day when Bir Bahadur and his best friend, Vishnu, called out to them, asking whether one of them was named Sarita. Telling the story months later, Sarita said, "I answered, 'Why?' as if I were angry." Bir Bahadur replied that Sarita's relative had some textbooks for her that she should pick up, and then he quickly departed. When they had their first real conversation in person months later, one of the questions Bir Bahadur reportedly asked Sarita was why she had been so unfriendly during their initial interaction, and Sarita replied that she had thought he had no legitimate business with her and was merely seeking an "introduction" (English), which she felt she had to discourage in order to protect her reputation.

When Sarita's relative brought the textbooks to her himself instead of waiting for her to pick them up, however, Sarita was interested enough in Bir Bahadur to ask her relative about him. She learned his name, his natal village, the fact that he was a Magar, and the fact that there was no direct kinship relationship between his family and Sarita's. Two months went by. Then one day Radha, a Brahman girlfriend of Sarita's, asked her if it would be okay for Bir Bahadur to write her a letter—would Sarita accept it? Sarita recalls that she asked the friend whether Bir Bahadur was *sojho* (straight, honest), and when the friend answered in the affirmative Sarita agreed to accept Bir Bahadur's first letter. Here is the full text of that letter, written in the middle of June 1992:

> Dear Sarita,
>   Warm love.
>   Life is an infinite circle. I find that it has not been possible at any time to have enlightenment ever since that day when you[2] and I had our "introduction." In the whole "world" there must be few individuals who do not bow down to love. Sarita, I'm helpless, and I have to make friends of a notebook and pen in order to place this helplessness before you. Love is the sort of thing that anyone can feel—even a great man of the world like Hitler loved Eva, they say. And Napoleon, who with bravery conquered the "world," united it, and took it forward, was astounded when he saw one particular widow. Certainly, history's pages are colored with accounts of such individuals who love each other. In which case, Sarita, I'll let you know by a "short cut" what I want to say: Love is the union of two souls. The "main" meaning of loving is "life success." I'm offering you an invitation to love. If you are capable of accepting

it, then accept; otherwise, in this, my time of suffering and life's last moment, please return this revealing letter.

I have tried on many occasions to offer you an invitation to love, but there was no good time. Sarita, from the day I first saw you I gave you a place in my heart. Finally, waiting for a long time and even until life's last, ultimate limit in hope of a letter etched by your physical body, I take leave with uncertainty.

Bir Bahadur

There are many ways to interpret the meanings embedded in this fascinating letter. The references to Hitler and Napoleon, for example, can be read as curious anomalies, endorsements of totalitarianism, or attempts to accrue status by mentioning (in)famous Westerners. What did Bir Bahadur intend to convey, and how did Sarita actually interpret the letter? Here we must apply a practice theory of meaning constraint in order to eliminate unlikely interpretations, focusing instead on the meanings Sarita most probably took away from the letter. Regarding Bir Bahadur's intentions, I know very little directly, but judging from conversations I have had with him on other topics I believe it is likely that he referred to Hitler and Napoleon after seeing or hearing about them from magazines, textbooks, or from the many the guidebooks that instruct people in love letter writing, most of which present examples of great love letters written by "famous men" such as Napoleon and Hitler. Even if Bir Bahadur did not use a guidebook to compose his first letter to Sarita, he was no doubt aware of the discourse associating love letters and romantic love with prestigious Western ways of thinking and living. Indeed, the letter above contains numerous words in English: *introduction, world, shortcut, main,* and *life success.* Not only does the use of English potentially signify a highly educated letter writer, but it also serves to connect the sentiments expressed in Bir Bahadur's letter with development discourse pertaining to progress, success, and Westernization. Indeed, Bir Bahadur wrote, "The 'main' meaning of loving is 'life success.'"

Now, how did Sarita interpret Bir Bahadur's first letter? In a conversation in the fall of 1992 about the letters Sarita had thus far received from Bir Bahadur, she went over the letter line by line with me, stumbling over the pronunciation of the English words and names. When I asked her what she thought Bir Bahadur meant by these lines and other (often ungrammatical and/or cryptic) English or Hindi references in subsequent letters, she answered, "*ke ke ho, ke ke ho?*"—"What is it, what is it?" In other words, she had no idea. In Bir Bahadur's fifth letter, written in July 1992, he writes in English at the very end, "so that no success by other letter," and when I asked Sarita about the meaning of this phrase she was as puzzled as I was: "Whatever does it say? Who knows?" Sarita was similarly at a loss when attempting to understand a line written in English at the end of Bir Bahadur's ninth letter, written in August 1992: "O.K. by Sarita you get me any time." She finally explained laughingly that it probably meant, "'*Thik chha, . . . malāī bheṭa,' bhane chha*" ("All right, meet me," he says). And when it came to other phrases in Bir Bahadur's letters that were in English, Hindi, or literary Nepali Sarita breezily explained, "*eee—malāī māyā garchha bhanera*" (Oh, it just means he loves me). Thus, we see that the interpretive indeterminacy inherent in all communicative events allowed Sarita to fashion her own meanings from Bir Bahadur's letters.

How did Sarita answer Bir Bahadur's "invitation to love"? Although I have not seen the actual letter, in November 1992 Sarita summarized for me her reply to Bir Bahadur's first letter, written in June of that year:

> What kind of answer did I give him? Let's see, what did I say in that letter? Umm, umm, love, that is to say, if one is to cause someone else to love— right?—then one should not deceive that person. If one is to cause someone else to love, then one should love truly. I said that in the letter, see? Then that one [i.e., Bir Bahadur] really . . . liked it!

The only problem, according to Sarita, was that Bir Bahadur reportedly thought the letter was too good to be true. He suspected that Vishnu, his best friend, had composed the reply as a practical joke—a common enough occurrence, as the reader will recall from the experiences of Jiri. When Vishnu vehemently denied having written the letter, Bir Bahadur decided to write Sarita another letter but hand it to her in person in the presence of Vishnu in order to see whether Sarita would accept the letter and thereby confer legitimacy on the correspondence. On the day Bir Bahadur and Vishnu were to give Sarita the second letter, Sarita and her best friend, Jhili, were the last students to leave the campus, having gone to the library right after class ended. Bir Bahadur and Vishnu were waiting just down the road from the campus, and as the two young women passed Bir Bahadur called out politely, "Please stop!" When Sarita and Jhili did so, Bir Bahadur offered Sarita his second letter. To Bir Bahadur, Sarita's acceptance of the letter would primarily mean that she had actually written the reply that he suspected Vishnu of writing. To Sarita, however, her acceptance of the letter would mean committing herself to an ongoing correspondence with Bir Bahadur. Several months after the event, Sarita recalled, "I stood there thinking, should I take it or not? Should I take it or not?" Sarita took the letter without further conversation, ran back to her room, tore it open, and read it aloud to Jhili. Here is the full text of that letter:

Date: 2049/3/5
Time: Around 11:00 at night
Place: In a deserted room

Dear Sarita,

Extremely pleasant remembrances.

In particular: Actually, there is no news or novel presentations that must be written. Because you didn't return but instead accepted the first love letter I have ever written in my life, giving a "reply" in a contented manner, I am distinctly grateful. I received the "reply" you gave only today, so I couldn't finish a "second letter" before this. Yes, Sarita, love is not life's means for titillating [*romāncha*] trickery; one must love truly and actually. And so, let's do so, and let's keep doing so. Let's neither of us engage in deceitful actions. My true thoughts are none other than that. This is only the "second letter" of my life.

Sarita, also give me your photo, okay? All right, Sarita, what more should I write? After writing it's never finished, so for today I'll defer. The rest we'll discuss slowly when we meet. Awaiting your letter and trusting,

Bir Bahadur

The source of the water coming out of the hills can dry up,
But the tears coming out of my eyes cannot dry up.
You will be able to forget me, perhaps,
But I cannot possibly forget you.

Your friend who remembers,
Bir Bahadur

[Stationary has the following verses imprinted in English on its first page:]
'Tis better to have loved and lost
Then [*sic*] never to have loved at all.

Tennyson

The question of trust dominated the first half dozen or so exchanges of letters between Sarita and Bir Bahadur. As can be seen in the way that Bir Bahadur's letters echo what Sarita must have written in her letters, and as Sarita herself told me, she repeatedly warned him that she was only interested in "true" love. If he intended to carry on a courtship with her that was merely for the purposes of "titillating trickery" and eventual betrayal, she made it clear that she wanted no part of it. Why not? A double standard is in effect in most of Nepal that taints a woman's reputation if it becomes known that she ever engaged in a love letter correspondence, even if she never got together with the man in person for secret meetings. Furthermore, in Sarita's case I believe she was behaving cautiously because of previous negative experiences with love letters. Although she at first told me that Bir Bahadur was her first correspondent, later on I found out that she had been involved in at least two other correspondences, one of them quite prolonged and serious. In that relationship, Sarita wrote letters for years to a young man who fell into the classificatory kinship category of mother's brother's son—in other words, the "wrong" kind of cousin for marriage. The young man himself told me that Sarita had ended the correspondence when she decided that she could not go through with such a controversial marriage. He was at first heartbroken, he said, and sent her numerous letters full of pain and accusations, but later he began another correspondence that ended eventually in an elopement. None of the letters from this earlier correspondence still exist; Sarita and the young man returned their love letters to each other and both destroyed all evidence of the courtship. As we will see shortly, Bir Bahadur was quite upset when he learned of these earlier correspondences of Sarita's.

Epistolary Agency and Successful Love

Because of these past experiences, therefore, and because of Sarita's desire to ascertain Bir Bahadur's true intentions, her first letters focused on trustworthiness and true love. Bir Bahadur's letters mirrored these concerns, in the process providing a detailed description of what he considered to be the definition of true love, as the following excerpt from his third letter demonstrates:

> 049/3/11 Trust me, you are the first person I have ever loved. Love shouldn't be really steady on one side only; it must be steady on both sides. So, love truly, you also. I, too, will put aside my heart for you as long as my life lasts. Life is such an understanding of trust that if anyone moves forward to interfere with you and me, once we show that individual the actuality, it will no longer happen. Love is not the sort of thing that is an impudent person's means for titillating trickery.

True love, according to Bir Bahadur, is reciprocal. Moreover, it also acts as an agentive force that empowers lovers and enables them to prevent anyone from interfering with them. Finally, love is serious business; it is not merely for the sake of flirtation or "titillating trickery," or so claims Bir Bahadur. Some young men, especially those in their early or middle teens, told me otherwise. In fact, one young man in Junigau who was known for carrying on multiple romantic correspondences said that he considered the purpose of love letters to be exactly what Sarita feared. According to this young man, the main reason he writes love letters is to *ṭāim pās garnako lāgī* (to pass the time). The presence of this alternative set of meanings associated with love letters made it necessary for Sarita and Bir Bahadur to clarify exactly what they meant by choosing to communicate through letters. Bir Bahadur elaborates even further on these meanings in this excerpt from his fourth letter to Sarita, written at the beginning of July 1992:

049/3/16 Sarita, trust me, I'm not loving you in order to make a game out of your life. In my life this is the first time I have ever loved, and it's with you. So, I don't know many things. Yes, in your feelings that kind of hesitation may exist, thinking that I might deceive you, no......?

Make an effort to forget that kind of doubt. Let's not control each other's "life," making a game out of it. Let's make an effort to make true promises. Life will be bright.

Sarita, life is made up of trusting, trusting; without trust nothing will succeed.

Love is such a thing that between two lovers "life success" occurs. Don't you think as if life were desolate. In other words, it's not enough for only one person to give true promises. It's not enough if only one person gives one-sided love. Both must depend on truth, and only then will it be possible to find the road to nothing other than success.

Sarita, it seems to me that if two people allow feelings of mistrust and doubt to come between them, then in such a condition in which fears and apprehensions torment, love will only be partially complete and will continue to be so. Therefore, trust me. Yes, I can't say that I won't also have such feelings toward you, but moving those feelings far from me, I am offering you only true promises and will continue to do so. I'm helpless, Sarita, as long as you won't look toward me with feelings of trust. Until then I'll keep worrying.

Yes, there may be boys these days who have written letters only in order to gain experience with girls. I can't say that's not so. But the connection between us binds so strongly that even life's most terrible cruelty couldn't cause a separation. If you also love truly, then there will be truth between us as well, and if neither of us tries to make a game out of the other's "life," then between us there will certainly be the strongly binding connection of "life frind" [*sic*].

The future is bright if we continue to love truly. Wait, and I'll also wait. May separation never occur once a union has been created.

I will love you truly. Even if difficult actions torment me, I won't hesitate to give up my life for you. If you also want to spend your life together with me, then certainly the relationship of life friend will bind us strongly for sure. [crossed out: If you don't wish to love truly, then, still, nothing's been broken; separation can be prevented.] But let's not turn the future into darkness. I also want nothing but that; I love you truly. No matter how far away you might be, certainly you will have success if you create a life friend. Saying this much, for today I'll say goodbye. At a future time there will be complete union. Saying so with hope, goodbye.

In the foregoing excerpt, Bir Bahadur evinces a concern not only with reciprocal trust but also with "success" (often written out in English). What does it mean for romantic love to be equated with "life success"? For many young Nepalis, including Sarita and Bir Bahadur, one clear sign of success in a relationship is eventual marriage. Many have told me this explicitly in interviews. The relationship between love and success is more complex, however, than the simple desire to have a romance culminate in marriage. Students like Sarita and Bir Bahadur had at the time of their courtship been steeped in development discourse at their village schools and then at the Tansen campus for years. They had also internalized from many other sources (films, radio, magazines, etc.) the goal of making something of one's life by making one's own choices— academically, professionally, and romantically—and by carrying out tasks in each realm to successful completion. The following excerpt from Bir Bahadur's fifth letter, written in mid-July, illustrates this goal nicely:

049/3/23 Sarita, trust me; I won't deceive you. Touching my beating heart, I say that until my life's last moment I will keep you in my heart. Now, make an effort not to put on me the distressing responsibility for the titillating trickery or deceit of others in matters of love relationships because in my heart I absolutely despise such titillating trickery and such mimicry of love. "so that no because by other letter" [*sic*]

Yes, there are many boys and even girls who destroy each other's lives.

But may such a condition not exist between you and me. From me it will not be at all, trust me, but what there will be from you depends on you alone. Let neither of us between us do the sort of thing that would be a blow to the other's "prestige."

Life is awaiting those who love truly. Therefore, Sarita, the connection between you and me is getting closer and closer. Let's wait. Certainly, separation won't occur after a union has been created. Therefore, let's keep making an effort to lengthen the true road. Certainly, we will create a sign of success. May our love reach a place where we can in our lives overthrow any difficulties that arrive and obtain success. Such are the feelings of mind between lovers.

In this passage Bir Bahadur urges Sarita not to blame him for the deceits of others—in other words, he wants her to attribute responsibility for blame-worthy acts to the actual individuals who perpetrated them. Such an individualistic concept of agency is evident throughout Bir Bahadur's letters to Sarita. Furthermore, he asks Sarita not to do anything that would be a blow to his "prestige" (using the English word here). The passage ends with the wish that they both be able to overthrow all difficulties, thereby obtaining success, for "such are the feelings of mind between lovers." Such an extraordinary emphasis on individual responsibility and on the efficacy of individuals' actions for obtaining desired results, especially when it comes to marriage, shows up clearly in the following excerpt from Bir Bahadur's seventh letter to Sarita:

049/4/5 There's no proposal [from my parents] for me to get married at present; when my older brother marries, then they'll make a proposal. I intend to marry boldly on my own. But if your father and mother propose to give you to a rich, handsome boy and you don't consult me you'll commit a great crime. Remember this well. These days a marriage certainly won't take place without conversation between the boy and girl. Conditions used to be such that when a daughter's father and mother gave her away in marriage, she was forced to go. But under today's conditions, the law doesn't allow this, and it's against the law. These things you know as well because you're not uneducated. If you have a strong wish, no one can interfere contrary to it.

In this excerpt, Bir Bahadur explicitly discusses changing marriage practices and the agentive meanings he associates with them. While the majority of marriages in Junigau at the time of Bir Bahadur and Sarita's correspondence were still arranged by parents without the consent (or even knowledge) of the woman involved, times were changing very quickly, and Bir Bahadur wanted to make sure that Sarita, even though she was "not uneducated," knew that she did not have to go along with any match her parents made for her. In fact, representatives of several men had approached Sarita's parents over the years, hoping to arrange a marriage with her, but her parents had always sent them away, declaring that they intended to allow her to study for as long as she wanted to, and that they would never marry her off against her will—"We won't cause her to cry by giving her away," both parents told me.

Clandestine Meetings

Gradually over the course of their courtship Sarita and Bir Bahadur started meeting more frequently in person. Their first face-to-face conversation (aside from their brief meeting when Bir Bahadur passed along a message to Sarita and made her acquaintance) consisted merely of small talk, according to Sarita, and occurred after four or five exchanges of letters. For fifteen minutes or so between classes one day, Sarita, Jhili, Bir Bahadur, and Vishnu met, allowing Sarita and Bir Bahadur to exchange some basic information about their families. They also decided at that time that since Bir Bahadur had the same sub-clan affiliation (*thar*) as Sarita's mother, they would use the kinship terms *māmā-bhānjī* (unmarriageable cross-cousins) in addressing each other in public in order to deflect suspicion that they might be romantically involved with each other. In reality, however, there was no close kinship relationship, so, unlike Vajra Bahadur and Shila Devi, they never considered marriage to be problematic for kinship reasons.

Bir Bahadur's early letters frequently expressed frustration that he and Sarita had not yet been able to talk privately about their love and their plans for the future. The following two excerpts from Bir Bahadur's fifth and sixth letters, both written in early July 1992 after a few brief meetings, express his belief that letters alone cannot adequately convey feelings of love:

> 049/3/23 Therefore by means of just one letter the road of trust cannot be followed because one must explain one's own personal matters not only in writing but also verbally. We have already exchanged many things through letters, but we have never sat at any place and made our own personal feelings of mind clear and distinct. Because I'm helpless, let's sit in some deserted place and talk.

> [letter #6, no date] I can't discern your heart/mind's feelings. The reason for this is that even though we've exchanged many letters about our "Love" we still haven't talked verbally. In every letter I write that we should sit in a deserted place some time and make clear our real feelings about life. But you haven't paid any attention to this suggestion in any letter.

Although they had only chatted and had not had a heart-to-heart talk by this point in their courtship (early July 1992), Sarita and Bir Bahadur had in fact attended a film together—a fairly risky and still uncommon occurrence in rural Nepal. On 18 Asar, 2049 (the beginning of July 1992), Sarita was walking home alone from the campus, her best friend and constant companion Jhili having been sick. Bir Bahadur and Vishnu were waiting for her alongside the path and asked her to accompany them to a Nepali film called, *Sampatī* (Wealth). Sarita replied that she would only join them if she could find a friend to go with her; under no circumstances would she go alone with them. When she could not persuade either of two other friends to accompany her that day, she convinced Bir Bahadur and Vishnu to wait until the following day when she was sure Jhili would be feeling better. Several months later, as Sarita was telling me about their outing, she said of Jhili, "She'll do anything I say." Jhili did indeed agree to act as an unofficial chaperone the next day, so she and Sarita slipped away from their respective rented rooms to attend a matinee showing of the film with Bir Bahadur and Vishnu. When the young women arrived in the courtyard outside the cinema hall, there was, as usual, a huge throng of people, but they managed to find Bir Bahadur and Vishnu. Bir Bahadur had already bought tickets for the four of them, so they all sat together in the more expensive balcony seats.

Once the film was over, around five o'clock, Bir Bahadur urged Sarita and Jhili to join him and Vishnu for some tea. Concerned that they might be spotted by someone who knew them, Sarita at first declined, but after Bir Bahadur scolded her for displaying too much shyness and shame/modesty (*sarma*), she reluctantly agreed to have a quick cup of tea with Bir Bahadur, Vishnu, and Jhili. It must have been a very quick cup indeed, for in his next letter Bir Bahadur complained about it. Directly following the passage quoted above that begins, "I can't discern your heart/mind's feelings," Bir Bahadur continued, "Also, the day before yesterday you went to see the film only out of obligation, and you wouldn't agree to anything else, either." Assuming that "anything else" refers to socializing beyond having a quick cup of tea, it is clear that Bir Bahadur wanted to spend time talking with Sarita and getting to know her. For Sarita, however, such interactions jeopardized her reputation. Explaining her feelings in a conversation with me later that year, Sarita said,

> We don't usually talk in public. People would say, "They seem to be courting—they talk in public!" So, we don't talk much in public, right? If a girl and a boy talk and walk [together in public], then people will say, "There is 'love' between that girl and boy!" They think badly of that. So, for that reason, he [Bir Bahadur] brings a friend and I bring a friend to talk. If there are three or four people—and we are always four—there won't be that much suspicion, see?

Sarita's fear that the relationship would be discovered were completely justified, for by the time she returned home to her rented room that day after the first film she and Bir Bahadur attended together it was nearly seven o'clock and her nephew and cousin, Babu and Rima, with whom she shared the room, were wondering where she was. They were so curious, in fact, that they searched through Sarita's trunk, where they found and read Bir Bahadur's first five letters to Sarita and looked at the photograph he had sent her! Such a risk is inherent in love letters, as Bir Bahadur reminded Sarita in his third letter: "Sarita, love letters, even without the give and take of conversation, remain in the form of a true trace until the end of life." Once Babu and Rima knew about the courtship, Sarita faced not only merciless teasing from them but also the possibility that they would tell others, thereby ruining her reputation and/or causing an end to the romance.

As it turned out, however, the two youngsters proved to be willing coconspirators who delivered letters and provided Sarita with alibis when needed in exchange for the treats Bir Bahadur brought them later on in the courtship after he began to visit Sarita more frequently in her rented room. In the first few months of their courtship, though, Sarita and Bir Bahadur confined themselves mostly to letter writing. One time they did go (with Jhili and Vishnu again) to an evening showing of another film, but Sarita claims never to have met Bir Bahadur alone before the fall festival season, not even (or especially not) when he invited her to stop by his rented room.

Initial Misunderstandings

In mid-July 1992, Sarita and Bir Bahadur faced a minor crisis that called into question the trust that they were attempting to build between themselves. In class one day, Radha, the Brahman friend of Sarita's who had delivered Bir Bahadur's first letter to her, caught sight of a page in Bir Bahadur's notebook that appeared to be a love letter to another woman, and she told Sarita about what she had seen. Sarita questioned Bir Bahadur pointedly about it in her next letter, and Bir Bahadur responded by denying any wrongdoing. The letter in which he does so, his sixth to Sarita, is so worn from having been read and reread that is illegible along the folds, and the date is no longer discernible, though it had to have been written in mid-July. Clearly, this letter marked a turning point in their relationship. The passage pertaining to this controversy follows:

> [letter #6, no date] Sarita, if you think such things about me, it will be a great sin. In my whole life my heart/mind probably hasn't suffered so much. The stuff in my "English note" notebook—the four or six lines about a love letter, or about marriage—that letter was written by a [Brahman] "Teacher" from my village. He requested permission to marry a girl there, it seems. The girl's father and mother didn't like him. Maybe the girl

didn't, either. . . . That Brahman girl [the one who told Sarita about the entry in his English notebook] can't understand Magars. That you should have made such a terrible thing out of such a small matter—forget it. There's nothing else to say. I don't even know that girl, never mind saying anything about "Love"! In the end, the teacher didn't marry that one; he married someone else. That's all there is to this matter. Trust me, Sarita, this is only the first time in my life that I have loved anyone, and it's you alone.

Bir Bahadur does not explain why the Brahman teacher's letter is in his notebook. I can only speculate that Bir Bahadur might have been using it as a template, much as the guidebooks do with love letters by famous people. The controversy over the Brahman's letter was not, I believe, the reason why Sarita (and probably Jhili, Babu, and Rima, if not others) read and reread this letter so many times. What made this letter so important was that directly after the explanation of what Sarita's friend had seen in his notebook Bir Bahadur goes on to propose marriage explicitly for the first time:

[letter #6, no date] I certainly want it to get better and better. In the end, if you don't make an effort to forget me or to deceive me, you alone will be my "Life friend." I will definitely marry you if you agree to do so. Yes, I also trust that you won't deceive me, but what's in your heart/mind depends on you alone.

Sarita, the reason I said I gave you my photo only under compulsion was because it's a little bad, not because I didn't want to give it to you.

Sarita, let's both make clear to each other in a trusting manner the matters of our heart/minds. And let no one have a "mood change." My "Habit" is to continue with an action once it's started and to worry about it. Why shouldn't I worry? My habit is to quit it only after it's complete. Why shouldn't someone make a difficult request of me? I'll make an effort and with competence will obtain success.

I have complete trust in this.

In this passage, Bir Bahadur combines his "can-do" attitude and confidence that he can obtain success with an explicit promise: "I will definitely marry you if you agree to do so"—that is, if Sarita agrees not to forget or deceive him. The fragments of the rest of the letter are difficult to patch together, but after studying them and talking about them with Sarita it seems that in the remainder of the letter Bir Bahadur turned to the question of how and when they should get married. Warning Sarita that their studies would be disturbed if they married too soon, he advocated waiting until after their second-year exams. (They were only halfway through their first year at that point.) Bir Bahadur also stated a preference for obtaining the approval of their parents. Both these statements proved to be of major significance months later during a critical phase of the courtship.

In conversations during the fall of 1992, Sarita described a talk she had with Jhili about her reactions to this letter and others proposing marriage. She told Jhili that she did not intend to marry right away and probably not even at the end of their second-year exams, as Bir Bahadur suggested. Jhili, who had already been married off to a man from a distant village who was in the Indian Army, was amazed that Sarita could get Bir Bahadur to agree to wait that long. Sarita described to me part of this conversation she had with Jhili on the topic:

> [I said] "He also agrees to postpone our marriage." Then Jhili asked, "He even agrees to that?" And I said, "Shouldn't he agree to what I say?" And Jhili said, "Wow! How agreeable he is!"

As this controversy indicates, Sarita seemed to be less committed to the relationship than Bir Bahadur was during the first six months or so of their courtship. She even admitted as much to me in the following conversation, which took place in November 1992. I had asked Sarita whether she would miss Bir Bahadur if he succeeded in joining the Indian or British Army as a Gurkha soldier. (Bir Bahadur, like most other young Magar men except Vajra Bahadur, viewed becoming a Gurkha soldier as one of the only routes to economic well-being and so was trying out for recruitment at the time.) In response to my question Sarita laughed hysterically and said she did not know whether she would miss Bir Bahadur; after all, she said, she did have his photo! The conversation continued:

> *LMA:* Do you love him already?
>
> *S:* No, not yet.
>
> *LMA:* How would you feel if he broke it off?
>
> *S:* Who knows? There are so many others like him! If he broke it off today, tomorrow there would be another one, and if that one broke it off, there would be still another one. Who knows? He probably won't break it off. If anyone does, it will probably be me. Who knows? He probably won't break it off.
>
> *LMA:* So, he loves you more than you love him?
>
> *S:* Uh huh. [agrees laughingly]
>
> *LMA:* So, in that case, he's just okay to you?
>
> *S:* Yes. It'll be okay with me whether he breaks it off or not. His village is far away, see? Very far. His house is so far away. Our village is this close to Tansen, but=

LMA: =So, if you lived there, you wouldn't be able to return here?

S: No, not whenever I wanted. . . .

. . . *LMA:* In your reply to Bir Bahadur's last letter, did you say, "I also love
you very much"?

S: In the letter I wrote the other day?

LMA: Yes.

S: Uh huh! [agrees laughingly]

LMA: But you said it would be okay whether he breaks it off or not!

S: Yes, I made my mouth say the right thing.

One of the reasons Sarita was so ambivalent about the future of her relationship with Bir Bahadur at this time was that they had been dealing for several months with ostensibly minor but actually quite significant misunderstandings that had arisen between them. One of these issues arose at the end of
July 1992, when the need for secrecy became a central theme in Bir Bahadur's
letters. Evidently, Sarita delivered a letter to Bir Bahadur herself one day instead
of using her nephew or girlfriend as a *hulākī* (letter carrier), and two other
classmates of theirs saw the transaction. After being teased by them, Bir Bahadur scolds Sarita for her actions in his eighth letter:

> 049/4/8 Sarita, I also know that they shouldn't find out in our section. In
> case you and I become weak, it's because of that backward/old-fashioned
> reason. There's no question that they shouldn't find out, but often they al-
> ready know, but they can't say. While giving a "letter," don't take it out of
> your book or notebook, no matter how carefully. Yesterday they saw it. Two
> boys were watching you take it out at that time. Later I forgot and went out-
> side, and they had the opportunity to look at it. Why should you have given
> it to me yourself, why?

Instead of risking discovery by delivering letters in person, Bir Bahadur
suggests that they meet more often in person, thus obviating the need to write
so many letters. Although meeting in person carried with it its own risks, Bir
Bahadur argued that it would be more fruitful and less dangerous than continuing to send letters frequently. Once again Bir Bahadur also urged Sarita to
discard her modesty and talk to him in person:

> 049/4/8 Between two people who love each other existence is not possible
> from just "letter[s]." Actual knowledge must also be verbal. Your shy "hebite"
> [i.e., habits] are a blow. Change a little bit. . . . What to do, Sarita? Now, I
> tried many times to suggest that we write letters a little less often and meet
> in person instead because if we meet every day we can write less often.

Bir Bahadur includes in this section a warning to Sarita about the possible consequences should their courtship be discovered:

> 049/4/8 Even more than the boys in our section, outsiders like my and your families—if they find out about this at home, then I won't be allowed to study here next year; they'll transfer me.

The letter then goes on to discuss other "unconscious mistakes" Sarita and Bir Bahadur have made, mistakes that have jeopardized their relationship. The first mistake, according to Bir Bahadur, is that Sarita has mentioned in her letters to him that she carried on correspondences with other young men in the past. He finds this extremely upsetting, as is evident in the following excerpt from his eighth letter. He is afraid that Sarita accepted his first letter thinking that it had been written by another suitor, and he is worried that she might be using her greater experience to toy with him. Bir Bahadur makes it clear that this is not acceptable behavior:

> 049/4/8 Sarita, in the future don't write things such as, "So many boys have written me letters, but I didn't go along with them!" Fine, you didn't go along with them—either you didn't wish to or else they or you broke up after only a short time. It depends only on you. In this matter, "no consold" [i.e., I'm not consoled? Sarita did not understand this phrase when we went over the letter together]. What I want is for the relationship between you and me to be clear. May the difficulties that occur in the future not last. Also, I'm surviving in the hope of a successful love. . . . Sarita, the boys who wrote the letters aren't in our section, are they......? In that case, if you accepted my letter under unconscious circumstances, then the love between us in our relationship isn't under mature circumstances, is it......? I can't understand your true feelings; you illuminate some things clearly, while others are unclear. Since this is the first time I have loved, I can't understand such roundabout words because I don't have the experience. Some girls are even the kind whose appearance is such that they deliver a shock to a "simple" boy's "life"—they make a momentary sexual relationship seem like a large feeling. That kind is extremely disgusting.

Bir Bahadur then turns to an "unconscious mistake" that he himself made. Evidently, he stood outside her windows and called out to her from the street when it turned out that she had relatives visiting. In the following passage from the same letter (his eighth), Bir Bahadur begs for forgiveness but also tries to excuse his actions as only human:

049/4/8 The reason I called out to you at 3:00 was that only the thirsty one drinks. Because I didn't know that your "uncle" and younger cousin-brothers were there and will come there from now on, forgive me. I didn't call out to you in words suggesting a love relationship or a relationship of dishonor. Never mind. Between people who love each other there will certainly be unconscious mistakes because we're human.

Bir Bahadur finishes this important letter by urging Sarita once more to make their love successful. He also alludes to the right that they both have to admonish each other. Indeed, he says in the following excerpt, he is taking her advice to heart and is giving up chewing tobacco. As Sarita and I read this letter together, she explained that just as Bir Bahadur had quit chewing tobacco when she asked him to she had moved into a different rented room because he had asked her to. (He claimed that the Tansen neighborhood in which she had been living was too "rough.") Bir Bahadur's eighth letter ends with a statement about the importance of forgiving each other:

049/4/8 Sarita, life is eternal. If you worry, it won't be possible to achieve success with anything. Remember these sound words—how to achieve "life success," how to make "love" succeed. Sarita, we can admonish each other for the mistakes we make in what we do, or if we take a worthless path, not just because we love each other but also because we are "class fried" [i.e., class friends]. That's okay—I'm quitting chewing tobacco not because I feel coerced but because I want to myself, starting with the time of the writing of this letter. All right, I want to say goodbye at this point in my short letter. If there are small mistakes between those who love each other, let's make an effort for one of us to remember that they were unconscious and forgive the other because if we illuminate the malevolent feelings when one of us is obsessed then remorse will be felt. Saying this, finally: let's not pervert feelings of true love. Not from happiness but from suffering is a person made. If I've illuminated mistaken feelings, consider it unconscious.

About two weeks later, at the beginning of August, Bir Bahadur wrote Sarita yet another letter (his ninth) urging her to trust him. He bemoans the fact that she still seems to be withholding her affections and trust from him. Generalizing from his own feelings of powerlessness and insecurity, he makes the following statement about gender differences:

049/4/21 What to do, Sarita? Girls don't have to endure as much difficulty as boys do. This is what I want: may our separation not occur.

Bir Bahadur then proceeds to explain how he felt when she (along with Jhili) did not meet him as they had arranged. For the first time in their correspondence, anger—or lack thereof—becomes a central issue:

> 049/4/21 You said that I was angry because you didn't come to Tundikhel Field. I didn't feel that way, Sarita. Yes, I didn't know that your "reletive" [i.e., relatives], related people, come there, so...... They were there only for "some time." The actual reason was nothing, but you had the wrong feeling. It's nothing. If you have that kind of feeling, you yourself will suffer.
>
> Again, at that time, when I gave an "arder" [i.e., order] to write letters less frequently, it was natural for you to anger quickly and have feelings of suffering. Yes, the reason I said we should write letters less often wasn't because I was angry, Sarita, because they can illuminate one's feelings every day. If we speak and laugh in class, everyone will say there's "love," and that's okay—you can say it, I can say it, or anyone else can.

Bir Bahadur once again suggests that instead of writing letters, Sarita should become less modest and agree to meet with him alone so that they can discuss matters of the heart. Despite the fact, however, that, according to Bir Bahadur, Sarita is "extremely shy" and has "no desire," she evidently felt bold enough to invite him to see a film with her (still chaperoned by Jhili and Vishnu). Bir Bahadur turned her down, however, perhaps because his main goal at this time was for them to sit down in private to discuss their feelings.

> 049/4/21 Forgive me for not being able to see a film when you suggested it. Again, we'll see it—there's plenty of time. Otherwise, there are other films left to see. Again, "exam[s]" are approaching. Let's study, okay, as much as possible. Sometimes entertainment is necessary. It's not good to be too absorbed. Sarita, during the time of exam break, we'll sit down one day and have a discussion about true love, okay? "O.K. by Sarita you get me any time."

Spending More Time Together

By August 1992, Sarita finally acceded to Bir Bahadur's wishes and began meeting with him in person more often to talk. As a result, their letters became fewer and fewer, and ceased altogether by January 1993. In his tenth letter, written toward the end of August, Bir Bahadur remarked to Sarita that, far from creating distance between them, their less frequent letters had deepened their relationship because the two of them met more often. Furthermore, according to Bir Bahadur, Sarita had begun to lose her shyness.

049/5/8 The main thing is that when I told you the reason we should write letters less frequently, those suggestions made you think things might change. But the misfortunes you thought might happen never occurred. You'll even forget you thought such things, right? Where is the sense of separation? I don't feel anything from my perspective. . . . When I told you not to write letters so often, I said so with an extremely unkind heart because I wanted to understand whether you didn't want to meet in person because you were shy or because you didn't want to. But these days your shyness has decreased, hasn't it?

Throughout the early autumn, Jhili and Vishnu were still always present during Sarita and Bir Bahadur's talks, but by late autumn Sarita and Bir Bahadur were meeting alone at times, usually in the semiprivacy of Sarita's new rented room. Because her nephew and cousin moved with her, however, and because they, like Sarita's other friends and relatives, were likely to burst in at the most inconvenient moments, Sarita and Bir Bahadur had to be extremely careful while they were together. One of them usually watched out the window to make sure no unexpected visitors were approaching. Occasionally, they escaped up into the forest known as Srinagar, a place with a reputation for harboring ghosts, thieves, and lovers. Besides talking, I have no idea what Bir Bahadur and Sarita did while they were alone on these outings together. While Sarita herself told me repeatedly that all she and Bir Bahadur ever did together was talk or study, others were by this time beginning to spread rumors that they were doing *narāmro kām*—"bad activities"—together. There is a cryptic reference in one of Bir Bahadur's letters that I read as possibly alluding to "improper" behavior, which could be anything from holding hands to kissing to having sex. Alternatively, Bir Bahadur could be referring to a suggestion to go to the movies or something else equally innocuous. Here is the passage in question:

> 049/5/8 Sarita, just the other day in relation to that...... It seems to me that you felt bad because I did it. Because this is the first time in my life that I've loved and that I've had a relationship, I, too, felt so...... But between those who love each other truly, this sort of thing seems to me to be "vary simple" [*sic*] because since we're human, to ask for and receive forgiveness is no big thing. Even though it was my suggestion, you went along with it reluctantly. Right? Whatever happened, if I made a mistake, please forgive me. "Sarita— I expect love is not happy to youg thong so that real love is can abou done do not" [*sic*].

When I asked Sarita about this letter, her response was to laugh continuously as she read it out loud to me. In particular, she laughed at Bir Bahadur's remark that she had lost her shyness—"*mardār!*" ("dead body!"—a semi-obscene expression) she exclaimed good-naturedly. As for the cryptic passage just quoted, her response was noncommittal; she hardly seemed to react to it at all and had no explanation to offer me as to how she interpreted the sentences ending in ellipses. She did react, however, to the following few lines from the letter:

> 049/5/8 Sarita, memories of you come to me, too, at all times. Love is like this, it seems. I'd rather have memories of my family—younger brothers, younger sisters, as well as my father and mother—because such memories wouldn't come so often. But memories of you make me feel guilty at all times and under all circumstances. When I have memories of you I look at your three former photos when I'm alone. Because of my daydreams I also keep seeing you in my nighttime dreams. What to do?

Although Bir Bahadur's first sentence above makes it sound like Sarita has admitted that memories of him keep coming to her as well, in her conversation with me she chose to distance herself from such expressions of emotion toward Bir Bahadur. "Well, *I* never see *him* in *my* dreams!" she told me. The only other comments Sarita made concerning this tenth letter were metalinguistic. She remarked that Bir Bahadur certainly had written a lot of long letters. Then she asked me to translate the last line of this tenth letter, which Bir Bahadur had written in English: "I hoped in your letter. Sarita you meet me any time thank you your lover by B.B." It remains unclear to me, therefore, to what exactly Bir Bahadur was referring in the passage.

Whatever Bir Bahadur meant to convey in the excerpt, in his next letter to Sarita, written two weeks later, he wrote at some length about his dreams becoming a reality, beginning with the following remarks:

> 049/5/23 [S]ince your love has become an actual representation, not just a daydream, I can give particular consolation to my own beating heart.
>
> Yes, human life demonstrates the life cycle, it seems. When unacquainted people are introduced, "young" men and women become loving couples. Also, even in that condition there is a sense or a possible sign of lifelong love, it seems, right......? The relationship between you and me is slowly...... developing that kind of feeling.

Their love is deepening, Bir Bahadur writes, because they are finally meeting in person more often. This shift bodes well for their relationship, he thinks. After all, Bir Bahadur tells Sarita in his eleventh letter, "If we keep on creating 'Real' [English] feelings, then certainly true and right feelings will shine clearly

and capably." Ending this letter by reassuring Sarita about the inevitability of
their marriage and urging her to study for the upcoming final exams, he writes:

> 049/5/23 What to do? Love and memories come not only to you but to me
> also. What's the point of being in a hurry to marry? Because we are young,
> there's plenty of time. Let's spend our days, months, and years laughing,
> talking, and exchanging letters like this. Then I'll certainly marry you.
> Moreover, if my family makes a proposal on my behalf to marry someone
> else, I won't agree . . .
>
> All right, we studying students—let us study, and after studying we will
> certainly be successful, not unsuccessful, right......? . . . I live with daydreams
> of living with you. First, let's get through "2nd year," and then we'll have a
> discussion and make a decision, okay?

Bir Bahadur wrote his next three letters, his twelfth, thirteenth, and four-
teenth, from his own village because the campus was closed for almost a month
during the September-October Hindu festival season. For the first time, Sarita
and Bir Bahadur sent their letters through the post office instead of delivering
them personally or sending them through messengers. Since letters sent by regular post in Nepal are often opened and read by other villagers, Sarita and Bir
Bahadur sent their letters by registered mail. As a further precaution, they did
not use their own names in the return address portion of their envelope. So as
not to arouse undue suspicion by receiving mail from a member of the opposite sex, Bir Bahadur sent his letters using Jhili's name, and Sarita sent hers
using Vishnu's. Finally, they kept the contents of these letters as unincriminat-
ing as possible in case they were opened by others. As a result, the three letters
written by Bir Bahadur during this period merely report on his activities at
home during the festival season and his continued attempts to be admitted
into the British or Indian Army. Although they all begin with phrases such as
"unbreakable remembrances and boundless love," "with a full heart of affection and ties of love," and "heartfelt remembrances and affections of the past,"
they quickly move on to mundane details. Bir Bahadur's final letter from this
period contains an invitation for Sarita to meet him at a soccer field in Tansen
the day before classes started up again. Despite the ambivalence Sarita had expressed to me about the relationship, she eagerly made plans to return to
Tansen from Junigau in time to meet Bir Bahadur, telling her parents that she
needed to file some forms for school.

Following the festival season vacation, Bir Bahadur wrote Sarita only four
more letters before the month-long winter vacation that stretched from the
end of December 1992 until the end of January 1993. Because they were meeting more often in person, they seemed to feel less of a need to correspond. The

first letter Bir Bahadur wrote Sarita after the fall break, his fifteenth to her, was written at the end of November—over a month after the last letter he sent from his own village. They were both back in Tansen by this time, studying at the campus. The impetus for this fifteenth letter of Bir Bahadur appears to have been a letter Sarita wrote him asking if the fact that he had neglected to speak to her after class one day indicated that he was angry at her for some reason. Bir Bahadur replies as follows:

> 049/8/10 Sarita, I was really trying to meet with you at the campus to talk, but because the boys wouldn't have allowed me to say much I couldn't meet you. For that, I beg forgiveness. It wasn't because I was angry at you at all. I don't feel that way toward you. It is both our decision and our belief that this fortunate union should not be terminated. I don't love in a way that will destroy any woman's life. This, our love, will be our companion until the end of our lives.

And Bir Bahadur ended the letter with the following words in English:

> 049/8/10 I Love you Sarita. No I am not angray [angry] in our realetion [relation] Love life—Thank you I weat [await] your letter O.K. by Bir Bahadur [*sic*].

Earlier in this same letter Bir Bahadur had acceded to Sarita's wish that he study in the afternoon session with her instead of the morning session, which he had planned on doing. He writes,

> 049/8/10 All right, I'll also attend classes in the afternoon; I'll abide by your decision. Until now I was attending "morning class," but as of now I'll quit.

It is clear in this passage and others that both Sarita and Bir Bahadur were gradually modifying their daily routines and habits to suit each other. They were arranging their daily schedules so as to be near each other as often as possible during the day, although they still had to take care not to raise too many suspicions. Small misunderstandings still arose, but Bir Bahadur's letters demonstrate an increased level of confidence and comfort in the relationship. In his letters, he seeks to reassure Sarita that his love for her is pure and not merely a momentary feeling based on lust. For example, in his sixteenth letter to Sarita, written in the beginning of December 1992, Bir Bahadur states the following:

> 049/8/16 It always feels to me like you trust me, and I, too, trust you. I don't love you in the way that some love is—like a momentary basket of flowers

that, after being filled up once, can't bloom again in the basket; after picking them, they rot. Similarly, if one were to love out of sexual passion only, how much...... Therefore, I love you with pure promises and pure feelings.

In this same letter, Bir Bahadur alludes to yet another incident that made Sarita think he was angry at her. He assures her that he was not angry and then goes on to say that he hopes Jhili was not under a similar impression. This, then, leads him to ask Sarita to express to Jhili his gratitude for having acted as their go-between. Indeed, it is quite possible that their relationship never would have gotten off the ground if Jhili had not been willing to accompany Sarita during her initial meetings with Bir Bahadur. From the following passage we can also infer that it has become customary for Bir Bahadur to drop by Sarita's room after classes or as they returned from an outing:

049/8/16 The other day while watching the film I wasn't angry, believe me. I just headed off to my room for no reason. Having said this, if you forgive me for worrying you with doubts about my anger, in the future I won't do it again at all. I was just walking in a clattering way. You seemed to feel bad that I didn't come into your room. Sarita, don't feel bad. And if Jhili also felt that way then I want to ask her for forgiveness. Please also remind Jhili for me that I consider her like my own sister. She has helped us so much. As long as I live I'll never forget that quality. Think for yourself: Jhili is our life benefactor. What help is there for wretched me to give her? Life is a struggle; if there ever comes a time when I can help her in any way, I will.

Bir Bahadur ends this, his sixteenth letter to Sarita, by reasserting his intention to marry her:

049/8/16 Sarita—all right, I love you, loved you, and will love you. It's our decision since long ago to have a "marrige" [sic], and it really will happen.

This intention to marry has evidently been solidified by the time Bir Bahadur writes his seventeenth letter to Sarita, written in mid-December 1992. They plan to be married after their second-year exams in October 1993, and until then Bir Bahadur encourages both of them to study hard in order to attain success:

049/8/26 We'll marry only after taking our exams. Let's both await that time with great anticipation. . . . Pay close attention to studying. A student's main work is to study and only then to do other things. . . . But being a student means that only studying is my "main" aspiration. A student's life is a poor but merciful life. To take trouble cautiously is a student's duty. I am yours. I love you purely. I won't deceive you. Right. Since you also support these feelings, make an effort to study in order to be successful at higher education. We'll both be successful. Let's become educated people, and then the future will be bright. . . . I'm immersed only in my studies, and I seek to obtain success. If some humans have already produced such complicated, complicated things in this world, then we are also humans, so why wouldn't we be able to succeed at our worthless, ordinary education? . . . An ordinary life must have lofty thoughts. You, too, should give me suggestions; I'm content to follow them.

The development discourse evident in the passage above is echoed in Bir Bahadur's eighteenth and final letter to Sarita, written just before their winter vacation at the end of December 1992. After noting that they will not see each other for 25 days, Bir Bahadur concludes his letter on an up beat:

049/9/9 Yes, Sarita, because of love the world looks bright. While we don't see each other it will be unpleasant. Memories of the past will torment us. Our love I find to be true love. It is indescribable. We are students. Because our main vocation is to study, in order to reflect more, it is necessary to study. Yes, we love each other truly. This union cannot possibly be broken up. Therefore, let's put more effort into studying. This is the path toward progress.

Once again, Bir Bahadur connects romantic love with education and progress and attributes to himself and Sarita the agency necessary to achieve success.

Love after Letter Writing

The six-month correspondence of Sarita and Bir Bahadur ended in December 1992, but their courtship continued for another ten months. They did not resume their letter writing after they returned from their winter break in January 1993 because they were meeting in person nearly every day, and neither felt the need to correspond any longer. Meeting in person held less of a risk than it had earlier in the courtship because nearly everyone knew of their relationship, and those who knew either approved or looked the other way. Sarita had even told her mother by this time, and once her mother had checked out Bir Bahadur's family background she was entirely in favor of the match. One of the only people who remained unaware of the relationship was Sarita's father, a gruff former soldier in the Nepali Army who drank a lot of *raksī* and evinced great pride in his only daughter's educational accomplishments. Sarita was afraid that if her father found out about Bir Bahadur he would demand that she drop out of college and marry someone he chose for her. As a result, she was careful to hide the relationship from him whenever he came to Tansen, and she urged those who knew about Bir Bahadur not to share their knowledge with her father. Sarita's mother readily acceded to her daughter's wishes because, having endured many unhappy years with Sarita's father, she wanted her daughter to end up in a better marriage than she herself had had. With the complicity of a number of people, therefore, Sarita and Bir Bahadur's courtship continued for months after they had stopped writing letters.

On two occasions, however, events threatened their relationship and nearly caused a breakup. Eventually, though, both incidents ended up deepening their feelings for each other. The first crisis occurred at the beginning of February 1993. I had just arrived back in Tansen after a week in Kathmandu and was surprised not to find Sarita in her room when I got there at about 6:00 P.M., intending to stay overnight with her. Babu and Rima, Sarita's nephew and cousin, who shared the room with her, had no idea where she was, nor did any of her other relatives who lived in neighboring rooms. After dinner, Sarita had still not arrived back home, and we were all beginning to worry. At around 8:30 P.M., long after it had gotten dark, I went outside to use the latrine and recognized Sarita and Bir Bahadur standing in the shadows not far from the entrance to the house in which Sarita rented a room. As soon as I greeted them, Bir Bahadur sped off toward his own room, and Sarita returned with me to where Babu and Rima were awaiting her. Refusing to tell them where she had been, Sarita curled up on her bed complaining of severe menstrual cramps. Later that evening when we were alone together, I asked Sarita where she had been all day, and she replied that she and Bir Bahadur had gone by tractor to another part of the district so that Bir Bahadur could try to get some money back from a friend who had borrowed it. She complained about the bumpiness and dustiness of the tractor ride but said nothing about why she accompanied Bir Bahadur, missing several classes and enduring significant discomfort.

The following day, Sarita remained in bed with severe cramps and was even passing sizable blood clots. Although menstrual blood is normally considered to be highly polluting and shameful by most Junigau residents, on this occasion Sarita washed her soiled rags and sheets outside in full view of the public. Even Daya, Sarita's sister-in-law, who happened to be in Tansen that day, said she had never seen Sarita treat her menstrual period so openly. Sarita had suffered from painful cramps for years and had even had a shaman conduct a ritual on her behalf the previous year that involved the sacrifice of a baby chick in order to alleviate some of her symptoms, but she had always been as secretive as possible about these woes. Knowing that Sarita had skipped a period the previous month and worrying that she should seek medical attention if the bleeding was the result of an abortion or miscarriage, I broached the subject gently with her in private. Her response was nonchalant enough to allay most of my fears, although I continued to worry about her until her period was over.

Several days later after I had returned to Junigau, I discovered that I was not the only one who had suspected that Sarita had had an abortion or miscarriage. Daya, Sarita's sister-in-law, shared with me her speculation that Sarita had gone with Bir Bahadur to a clinic in a different part of the district for an illegal abortion. (All abortions are illegal in Nepal.) She worried that Sarita was jeopardizing her education, her future job prospects, and her relationship with Bir Bahadur. Gesturing around her to indicate the cooking fire, the mud hut, and all the work associated with being an uneducated daughter-in-law, Daya said that education and a job were the only avenues available to Sarita to escape what Daya herself had to endure every day of her life. If it became known or even rumored that Sarita had gotten pregnant by Bir Bahadur, no other man would ever agree to marry her, Daya feared, and, moreover, it would be such a disgrace to the family that Sarita's father would in all likelihood disown her, forcing her to rely on Bir Bahadur or her own devices to support herself.

Part of what Daya and I feared did transpire: soon many of the women in Junigau were discussing whether or not Sarita had gotten pregnant, had had an abortion, or had had a miscarriage. The mothers of some of Sarita's cousins who lived near her in Tansen became worried about her exerting a bad influence on their children, and when they expressed this concern to Sarita's mother and sister-in-law a feud developed in the extended family. For several weeks in March-April 1993, some of these women stopped speaking to Sarita, her mother, and her sister-in-law. Eventually, however, the incident blew over, and there were no serious repercussions. Sarita's father did not learn of her relationship with Bir Bahadur, and after a while, since the story could not be confirmed or refuted with certainty, Junigau residents lost interest in the matter.

Several months later, I asked Sarita whether she and Bir Bahadur had ever discussed or experimented with sex, and her reaction was immediate: no, they never did anything sexual or even talked about such *narāmro kām*—"bad activities." He was just as shy as she was about the subject, she claimed. "*lāj, sarma lāgchha,*" she giggled—"We feel shyness, shame/modesty." How would she feel about sex if she eloped with Bir Bahadur? Sarita replied,

I'd feel scared, you know, of course! My body goes *jaring jaring* [shivering sound] right now just thinking about it. Just talking about getting married makes my body get all flushed, with my heart going *ḍhuk-ḍhuk, ḍhuk-ḍhuk!* How much more so will it be when it's time to get married!

During the spring and summer of 1993, Sarita and Bir Bahadur continued to meet as often as their class schedules would allow. They continued to attend Hindi and Nepali films together, often with Jhili and Vishnu as unofficial chaperones, and also spent a great deal of time together alone or with Babu and Rima in Sarita's room. Once they even went for a ride together on a ferris wheel that was part of a traveling carnival that came to town. A couple of times during this period, Sarita told me that she intended to break off the relationship, but she always changed her mind because, she said, it was difficult to break up when they were both still in the same place. If one of them ever moved elsewhere, then maybe they would break up, she explained to me.

The Crisis

Things continued to go more or less smoothly in the relationship until mid-August 1993, when an uncle of Sarita's who lived near her in Tansen and who had known about the relationship for months decided to tell Sarita's father (his brother) about it. The precipitating factor, according to the uncle, was that he had seen Bir Bahadur in Sarita's room after ten o'clock one night. Not only did the uncle tell Sarita's father about Bir Bahadur, but he also told him that Sarita's mother had known about and had even facilitated the relationship. Sarita's father was livid and immediately consumed enough *raksī* to become quite drunk. The first person on whom he took out his anger was his wife. Accusing her of "selling" their daughter, he likened her to a pimp. Sarita's mother retorted that she had done nothing of the sort and indeed had not even known about the relationship until recently. She also claimed (not quite truthfully) that Babu and Rima were always present when Sarita and Bir Bahadur studied together late at night. On the night in question, when Sarita's uncle had burst into Sarita's room unannounced, Sarita and Rima had been cooking a late meal for Bir Bahadur that included meat from a ritual sacrifice they had conducted earlier that day. Bir Bahadur had been lounging on the bed, waiting for them to finish cooking. As Sarita's mother attempted to explain to Sarita's father, Sarita's uncle apparently had assumed that Bir Bahadur was staying the night and decided it was time for his brother to learn of the alleged affair. In justifying to me her tacit endorsement of Sarita's relationship, Sarita's mother made the following statement, which resonates with new structures of feeling in its attribution of agency to an individual (her daughter) rather than to fate:

> Daughters can't spend their lives in their natal homes. Once they've become old, everyone will call them "Old Woman." No one likes them. Instead, let them go [elope]! If a boy and a girl both like each other, it's bet-

ter that they go [elope]! If the girl stays unmarried until she's old, who will like her, after all? How many women there are around here who have become old without marrying! If Sarita experiences suffering after marriage, it will be she herself who earns it, and if she experiences happiness it will also be she herself who earns it. We won't be the cause.

For days after Sarita's father learned of the relationship, there were shouting matches—audible throughout the village—between Sarita's parents and also between Sarita's mother and uncle. If there had been anyone in the village who had not known about the courtship at that point, they certainly found out, as Sarita's father staggered drunkenly all over the village, alternatively bemoaning the disgrace that had fallen on the family and angrily vowing to rip Bir Bahadur to shreds. He claimed he would take Sarita away from the campus (and from Bir Bahadur) and bring her back to the village, along with both Babu and Rima.

Sarita found out early on that her uncle had told her father about Bir Bahadur, but her first reaction seemed to be nonchalance. She knew that her father's drunken rages usually resulted in very little concrete action. Indeed, her father did not even go into Tansen to see her until several days after he learned about her relationship with Bir Bahadur, and he only went then because he had business to conduct in the bazaar. He said not a single word about the incident to Sarita.

At this time, Sarita was studying hard for her second-year final exams and did not even tell Bir Bahadur at first that her father had found out about them. When I visited Sarita in Tansen about a week after her father had learned of Bir Bahadur, she seemed much more concerned with working on her math problems than speculating about the impact her father's knowledge would have on her relationship with Bir Bahadur. She still had not told him that her father knew of their courtship. After all, she said, with final exams only a little over a month away, they had no time to do anything but study. Besides, what was she to say about such a subject to Bir Bahadur? No, she answered in response to my question, Bir Bahadur had never spent the night in her room. Her uncle was merely "making something big"—in other words, making a mountain out of a molehill. When I asked her if this latest development would precipitate an early elopement, and whether she would continue to study after her marriage, Sarita merely answered, "Who knows?" She then added, "Nothing is certain; even a breakup is possible."

During the next few weeks, fights continued between Sarita's parents in Junigau, while Sarita herself remained relatively unaffected in Tansen. She eventually told Bir Bahadur that her father had found out about their relationship, and he was quite concerned that dishonor (*beijjat*) had landed on

both families. In Bir Bahadur's village, it turned out, dishonor had also occurred because a woman whom Sarita's mother had asked for information
about Bir Bahadur's family had told his family about Sarita. When the woman
also described Sarita's father's displeasure upon learning of the courtship, Bir
Bahadur's family, Sarita reported to me, felt extremely dishonored as well.

Everything came to a head in mid-September 1993, just a couple of weeks
before Sarita and Bir Bahadur's second-year final exams—and the time of their
tentatively planned elopement. On Monday, 13 September, 1993, Sarita's mother
and I walked the three hours into Tansen to buy some supplies at the bazaar and
to see how Sarita was doing. Sarita's father also had business in Tansen but was
leaving the village a little later in the day. When Sarita's mother and I arrived in
Tansen, Sarita told us that representatives from Bir Bahadur's family had arrived
in Tansen and were planning on traveling out to Junigau later that day to discuss a match between Bir Bahadur and Sarita in order to restore the honor of
both families. Knowing how volatile her father's moods could be, Sarita was reluctant to send the representatives out to meet with her father until she had as-
certained how receptive he might be to their offer of an arranged match. When
the representatives (Bir Bahadur's maternal uncle and a nonrelative, high-caste
villager) had arrived in Tansen the day before, they had summoned Sarita to
their quarters to discuss with her how to proceed. They also wanted to hear
from her what her wishes were—did she want to continue studying, was she
able to help with work such as the harvesting of rice back in Bir Bahadur's village, and would her father be likely to agree to an arranged marriage even
though she and Bir Bahadur, not their parents, had initiated the match? Sarita
reported that she had not felt embarrassed at all to speak up during this discussion. Nevertheless, she told her mother and me that she was extremely reluctant
to broach the subject with her father, who was due to arrive in Tansen momen-
tarily. Once again, Sarita heatedly defended her actions to us:

> Who's done anything bad, after all? Right? All we've done is laughed and
> talked. He...if he [i.e., Bir Bahadur] doesn't have a book, he asks me for
> mine, and if I don't have a book, I ask him for his, see? That's what we do—
> we exchange books, study. And Jhili, too—the three of us are all really good
> friends, see, Jhili and the three of us. And we also do that .[i.e., borrow
> books] with Jhili also. And that one [i.e., her uncle] says, "The boy comes
> here and stays ALL night!" Now, if he did stay here "ALL night," Rima and
> Babu are here, aren't they? What would he do? WHAT bad, bad talk there
> is! It makes me SO angry!

As the discussion progressed, it became more and more urgent to decide
how or even whether to inform Sarita's father of the presence of representatives

from Bir Bahadur's family, for Sarita's father was supposed to stop in at Sarita's room at any moment. Sarita and her mother decided on a plan to which I only reluctantly agreed. Sarita's mother would leave, since her presence would likely anger her husband, and together Sarita and I would apprise her father of the situation and assess how receptive he might be to a formal proposal from the representatives for an arranged marriage. The theory was that he would be less likely to dismiss the idea out of hand if I were there supporting Sarita. As uneasy as I was about my role in the matter, I was unable to refuse Sarita's pleas. As a friend and fictive older sister, I felt obligated to do what I could to help her. We decided that I was to raise the subject with Sarita's father—but only if he appeared sober upon his arrival. If he seemed drunk, we all agreed that it would be wisest to say nothing.

Sarita's mother left, and soon her father arrived. While he did not seem too inebriated, he had evidently been drinking, and I was unsure whether I should open the discussion or not. After some nudges from Sarita, however, I brought up the subject as respectfully as I could. "Some people have arrived," I said to him, and I proceeded to explain that Bir Bahadur's representatives had come to ask him for his permission to arrange a match between Bir Bahadur and Sarita in order to erase the dishonor that had come to both families. Sarita's father's reaction was immediate: "Let that good-for-nothing, campus-studying boy come and fight me himself!" He saw no need to talk to any representatives about any kind of respectable marriage, especially given what he had heard about Bir Bahadur and Sarita's behavior. At this point, Sarita, who had been laughing nervously at first, interrupted her father angrily and defended their actions. After arguing heatedly for about ten minutes, Sarita and her father came to an impasse. Her father kept saying that if he were going to give his only daughter away in marriage he would require any petitioner to come see him seven, ten, even twelve times before he would grant permission. Furthermore, he himself would visit the petitioner's village in order to make sure that he was who he represented himself to be. He cared too much about his daughter, he implied, to agree to a match just because it saved face. If Sarita and Bir Bahadur wanted to elope, that was fine, he said, just as long as she did not come running home crying, "Daddy, Daddy!" to him if something went wrong. "I'll feel happy, I'll even feel light if you elope," he said. "What the broom should have had to sweep up, the wind has swept away!" he added, quoting a well-known saying. At one point in the discussion, Sarita's father got all choked up as he said again that it would be fine with him if she eloped. She should just remember, he warned Sarita, that he would not be willing to help her in the future should the marriage turn sour. If the flower she was seeking to wear wilted and fell off, Sarita's father stated, he would not be there to look after her.

After a tense, fifteen-minute conversation during which neither Sarita nor I was able to convince her father to consider talking to Bir Bahadur's representatives about an arranged marriage, the discussion came to an abrupt end when Babu burst into the room. Sarita's father then quickly excused himself and left.

Sarita was uncertain about what to do. Should she send the representatives home without their having met with her father? Or should she risk having them meet with him when it was likely that he would be extremely unreceptive or even rude to them? If this happened, an elopement would become a much less acceptable alternative, since Sarita would end up having to live with Bir Bahadur's family after her father had shamed them. On the other hand, if she and Bir Bahadur eloped without the representatives' having met with her father, then her father had indicated he would accept the marriage as long as Sarita did not expect to be able to come running back to her natal home if the marriage did not work out. Her father had even said he would grant a *dhobhet*, a blessing ceremony that would acknowledge the marriage and enable Sarita to come back home for visits whenever she wanted. Unsure of what to do, Sarita asked me for advice, but on this subject I was both unable and unwilling to help her. She would have to decide for herself, I said. As she debated the alternatives, Sarita framed her decision not as one that would reflect her own wishes but as one that would be forced on her by circumstances:

> *S:* Now it's gotten difficult. "If you wish to, then go [elope]!" my father says. But really, it's not because I wish to, it's because of the circumstances.
> *LMA:* What kind of circumstances?
> *S:* Circumstances—well, very, a lot of dishonor has occurred, a lot of, um, see? It's not that I seek to go [elope] because I'm pregnant, you know. People say, "She's pregnant, they do bad things"—that's what others say, right? And that's NOT true, there's NOTHING bad that we've done. Dishonor has occurred because rumors have begun to spread all over the place. And after such talk, if the boy breaks it off . . . and if someone comes from somewhere else to ask permission to marry the girl, some-one—either the boy's brothers and other relatives, or others, will say, "No, that . . . that girl used to have a 'love.' So-and-so's daughter used to have a 'love,' it is said, and that boy left her." And then that boy's father will say, "WHAT?!? You won't marry that one! Kill the negotiations!" Yes, that's what I mean by saying dishonor has occurred. That's what I mean by saying that I seek to marry only because of circumstances, see?

In our conversation on that day and during subsequent weeks, Sarita repeatedly refused to attribute agency to herself at the very same time that she was debating what she should do. This paradoxical relationship to agentive attributions is quite characteristic of the decision-making processes of Junigau residents, especially young women. Although they increasingly take on actions and make decisions that in the past were done or made for them, they nevertheless hesitate to attribute responsibility for those actions or decisions to themselves. It is still considered unseemly in Junigau for anyone, especially a woman, to admit to a strongly felt desire, whether the desire is to have seconds at dinner, to dance at a songfest, or to elope with a lover. As Sarita grappled with the decisions she had to make, she increasingly connected her plight to that of other women in Nepal. During the 13 September 1993 discussion, she said:

> In Nepal, women experience MUCH suffering! Extreme suffering! . . . I'm finally finding out what others mean by saying that women experience extreme suffering!

Sarita elaborated further on these sentiments a few days later:

> What to do? Once one has taken on a daughter's life [i.e., once one is born as a female]—a daughter's life is unfortunate, isn't it? In other places, there's not so much sadness for daughters; it's only in Nepal that there's so much. And what is it that is said? After taking on a daughter's life, one MUST go to another's home [i.e., marry], right? . . . Those who stay at their natal homes and remain pure—right?—now, once they're twenty-two, twenty-three, or twenty-four years old, that's as old as a woman's age gets before she's too old to marry . . . And after she is an old woman, that woman's youth is GONE, see, GONE, you see? I think—maybe I won't marry, right? But what to do?

Eventually, Sarita decided to send Bir Bahadur's representatives back to their own village without having them talk to her father. She decided it was extremely unlikely that her father would receive them courteously, and even if he did who would return seven, ten, twelve times to request permission to marry her, as he had said he would require? It would be better, she decided, to elope with Bir Bahadur right after final exams as they had initially planned and then hope that her father would grant them a *dhobhet*. Sarita was a bit concerned about not being able to return to her natal home after eloping should the marriage turn sour, but she figured that her fate was indecipherable anyway:

> Who knows how to tell what one's fate will be? As for one's karma, one could end up rich or one could end up poor, right? Who knows, after all? Everyone has her/his own luck/fate [*bhāgya*]. Whatever is written on one's forehead is what one has to bear, right? That's what one will bear.

Just a few minutes later in the same conversation, however, Sarita's fatalism shifted to a position that favored individual agency:

It's up to one's *own* wishes, it is! You should wear the flower you like, you know. You should wear the flower that *you yourself* like. If a woman's father and mother choose for her and something bad happens, then it'll be difficult for the daughter. Now, if the daughter elopes with someone she likes and something bad happens, then it'll be difficult for her parents. The daughter thinks about this, and the parents think about this, right? They think about it this way and that. *But it's the daughter's life! It's not the father's life!* That's why there's this issue! Oh, how I think about it, how I think about it! Sometimes I think I'll go crazy!

In the end, Sarita and Bir Bahadur eloped as they had originally planned on the last day of their second-year final exams, 6 October 1993. Sarita's father granted them a *dhobheṭ* within a week. A little over a year later, Sarita gave birth to a daughter, and two years after that a son. The son was born at Sarita's marital home with no skilled midwife in attendance, and sadly, the son was deprived of oxygen, making him severely developmentally disabled. When I last saw them in 1998, Sarita and Bir Bahadur said they had suspected something was wrong because their son, who was by then a year old, could not even sit up on his own. We went into Kathmandu together to get the child tested, and the diagnosis was that he would never be able to take care of himself and might not ever be able to walk. In a country that has no special schools for developmentally disabled children, this meant that Sarita and Bir Bahadur would have to care for him at home. It also meant that their plans to have a small family (as the ubiquitous family planning posters urge) had to be changed. Without a son to take care of them when they are old, Sarita and Bir Bahadur decided to have at least one more child. In 1998, though, Sarita was still weak from the difficult birth and from taking care of her son. She had recently gotten a job teaching in the primary school in her village, but she had to carry her son there and back and try to take care of him while teaching. In July 2000, I talked to Sarita on one of my monthly phone conversations. She happened to be in Tansen because she had just given birth to her third child, another son, and wanted to have him checked out at the Mission Hospital there. He turned out to be healthy—so far, anyway—so Sarita and Bir Bahadur will probably stop having children.

Neither Sarita nor Bir Bahadur resumed their studies at the campus. While Sarita has continued with the teaching job, Bir Bahadur has had no luck enlisting in any of the armies. For a while, he wanted to become a politician, but he lost the election. All of these life changes and challenges seem to have taken their toll on Sarita and Bir Bahadur's marriage. When I asked Sarita by phone recently if she thought she had made the right decision in eloping with Bir Bahadur, she merely responded philosophically, "What to do? Life is like this."

CHAPTER TEN

Love, Literacy, and Agency in Transition

Studying Social Change

The stories of Sarita, Bir Bahadur, and other Junigau couples provide us with a picture of social change *as it is occurring*. This ethnography thus illustrates how, as Marx famously noted almost 150 years ago, people "make their own history, but they do not make it just as they please; they do not make it under circumstances chosen by themselves, but under circumstances directly found, given and transmitted from the past" ([1853] 1978:595). The preceding chapters focused on exactly how Junigau villagers' actions have been reconfiguring and reinforcing, challenging and accepting, attitudes and practices surrounding love, gender, literacy, social change, and agency. Some of the reasons for the emergent structures of feeling were also presented, including an increase in formal education, which exposes students to the ideologies embedded in the textbooks; greater exposure to reading materials such as magazines, love letter guidebooks, and novels; and the viewing of Hindi and Nepali films.

Using various kinds of data, I have tried to present a multifaceted account of social change that acknowledges complexities, contradictions, and indeterminacies. In order to provide a picture of social transformation as it is occurring, I engaged in repeated stints of fieldwork over an eighteen-year time period. I gained further temporal depth by learning about the history of the community before I arrived and by recognizing that change would not stop when I left. Perhaps even more important than long-term fieldwork was the kind of rapport that I developed once I became fluent in the language and because I lived with a family in the community, thereby demonstrating trustworthiness over time. Many models have been proposed in recent years for anthropological research, such as those involving multiple field sites and archival research, and most of these models can lead to interesting, informative ethnographies. (Indeed, I conducted fieldwork in two sites, Junigau and Tansen, and engaged in some archival research.) There is still a great deal of value, however, in looking at a single community over time. By placing the love letters of Junigau residents in the context of their beliefs and practices, and by presenting the villagers' own words and actions, I hope I have made it possible for readers to understand the broader significance of new courtship practices in Junigau for the study of social change wherever it occurs.

Gendered Agency through Literacy

None of the love letters discussed in this book would have been written if literacy skills among Junigau women had not increased dramatically in the 1980s and 1990s. When parents started sending their daughters to the village school, and when young women began to attend evening literacy classes, they acquired skills that were put to use in a way that teachers and parents never intended.[1] The unintended uses of literacy by Junigau young people demonstrate the need to consider the specificities of literacy practices in each incipiently literate society. It is not true, as Goody, Ong, and others have suggested, that literacy is a neutral technology that brings with it identical cognitive and social consequences. Rather, it is necessary to look at the full array of literacy practices within an incipiently literate society in order to understand the meanings and values people come to associate with being literate.

In the case of Junigau, the textbooks, magazines, novels, films, and other materials that young people were reading, viewing, and discussing in the 1980s and 1990s advocate particular ways of being, thinking, and acting (cf. Skinner et al. 1998). While the various genres differ somewhat, they are all examples of a development discourse that became ubiquitous in the village during this time period. As I have shown throughout this ethnography, development is not simply a set of economic and educational projects; it is also a set of ideas about how to think and be. In the process of acquiring and using their literacy skills, Junigau young people also therefore acquired and displayed a certain type of cultural literacy. Even though they did not absorb the messages in books, magazines, and films unquestioningly, exposure to this sort of development discourse familiarized them with new structures of feeling that:

- Associate romantic love with educational and economic success and development
- Advocate a type of nationalism that incorporates Hinduism as the state religion

- Reinforce certain gender ideologies even as others are challenged
- Portray individuals as being powerless in the face of love and yet paradoxically empowered by love to achieve success in other realms of life[2]
- Propose a new conception of individual agency that attributes responsibility for events to individuals rather than to fate
- Espouse a more individualistic notion of personhood

That these structures of feeling show up in the love letters of young Junigau residents such as Bir Bahadur, Shila Devi, and Vajra Bahadur should come as no surprise. Love letter writers have been steeped in such development discourse for most of their lives.

Conceptions of Personhood and Agency in Transition

Throughout this ethnography I have painted a picture of social change as it has been occurring in one small community and in one particular area of social life: marriage. Junigau residents, especially the younger ones, sought in the 1980s and 1990s to become different kinds of people.[3] "Modernity," Anthony Giddens writes, "opens up the project of the self, but under conditions strongly influenced by standardising effects of commodity capitalism" (1991:196). As I have argued throughout this book, far from representing a trivial, personal, or idiosyncratic practice, love letter writing in Junigau reflects significant changes in many areas of social, economic, and political life. Moreover, it also promises to reconfigure social relations and transform villagers' conceptions of their own personhood and agency. And as Aparna Rao notes, "Questions of agency, self and person are of increasingly ideological importance and political relevance in a world where conflicts are surfacing as perhaps never before" (1998:324).

A new theory of agency—a set of ideas about the efficacy of human action—has been emerging among villagers, and love letters both reflect and influence this new theory. Note that I am not arguing that there is now "more agency" or "less agency" among Junigau residents. Such attempts to quantify agency are misguided. It is far more illuminating to explore how villagers' ideas about their own and others' agency are changing—how they attribute responsibility for events,[4] what they identify as the constraints on and possibilities for action, and how they view themselves as individuals and members of various social groupings.

Even as a new theory of agency has emerged in Junigau, however, other, more fatalistic notions of causality persist, providing an example of what Raymond Williams calls "the residual." Williams writes,

The residual, by definition, has been effectively formed in the past, but it is still active in the cultural process, not only and often not at all as an element of the past, but as an effective element of the present. Thus certain experiences, meanings, and values which cannot be expressed or substantially verified in terms of the dominant culture, are nevertheless lived and practised on the basis of the residue—cultural as well as social—of some previous social and cultural institution or formation. (1977:122)

The change occurring in Junigau, then, is not a simplistic movement away from fatalism toward and individualistic theory of causality. Many villagers do express the new, more individualistic sense of agency, but the same individuals may also, depending on the context, express residual ideas regarding fate. These ideas are often generationally distributed; older Junigau residents tend to espouse more fatalistic ideas about agency, whereas members of the younger generation who have grown up immersed in development discourse tend to adhere to a more individualistic theory of human action. Pierre Bourdieu calls these generational differences "the hysteresis effect," commenting that are caused by "conditions of existence which, in imposing different definitions of the impossible, the possible, and the probable, cause one group to experience as natural or reasonable practices or aspirations which another group finds unthinkable or scandalous, and vice versa" (1977:78). Thus, many older villagers bemoan the arrival of the *chhucho jovāna,* a selfish, mean, or backbiting time period, while younger villagers celebrate the additional choices they view themselves as having. As Collier remarks about changing courtship practices in Andalusia, however, the discourse about freedom and individual choice in the realm of marriage in the 1980s and 1990s actually masks social expectations and obligations that can be even more onerous than those of previous generations (1997:104).

Not only can the new practices and structures of feeling bring with them onerous obligations; they can also reinforce certain preexisting attitudes, hierarchies, and behaviors. Indeed, as I have noted throughout the book, the alteration in structures of feeling in Junigau is being accompanied by a strengthening of existing gender hierarchies and ideologies that may cause the shift to be detrimental to village women. The picture is much more complicated than the simplistic notions emanating from some development organizations might lead one to believe. The case of Junigau demonstrates that increased female literacy rates do not necessarily lead to increased choices and better lives for women— or men. Furthermore, the shift away from arranged marriage and capture marriage toward elopement in the village shows that such a transformation does not lead inevitably to the elimination of coercion in marriage. In the remainder of this chapter, I speculate on some of the broader implications at the structural and individual levels of the changes and continuities in literacy, love, and marriage. In all these cases, consent and coercion go hand in hand.

Consent and Coercion: How Are They Related?

Throughout this book, I have dealt with the complexities of human agency, especially as young villagers initiate, consent to, or are coerced into, marriage.[5] In considering the question of the relationship between consent and coercion in the ongoing shift in structures of feeling in Junigau, it is necessary first to consider what villagers might mean when they emphasize the importance nowadays of obtaining the "consent" of both parties to a marriage. The words I have translated as "to consent" in the love letters and narratives of marriage excerpted in previous chapters actually have various other connotations that help us to understand more fully the significance of the recent emphasis on the term in Junigau. The Nepali verb *mānnu* can mean not only "to consent" but also "to obey," "to listen to," "to agree," "to accept," "to go along with," "to respect," "to heed," "to think," or "to feel." So, for example, when speaking of an obedient child or animal, villagers say, *mānchha*—"he or she obeys, listens, minds." Another frequent usage of the verb occurs in the phrase, *srimānlāī mānnu parchha*—"[a woman] must respect/listen to/obey [her] husband." The sense of "to think" or "to feel" is operative in the common question, *junigāū kasto mānuhunchha?*—"What do you think/feel about Junigau?" (or "How do you like Junigau?"). All these usages are current in Junigau, along with phrases denoting consent or agreement such as *heram, mānchha ki nahī*—"Let's see if he or she agrees." Another example, appearing frequently in the narrative excerpts, is *maile mānina*—"I didn't consent." Likewise, when Khim Prasad and others insist that "The girl's consent must also exist," the Nepali phrase is *keṭiko pani mañjur hunu parchha.* (Note that the noun/adjective *mañjur* has a much narrower range of possible meanings than the verb *mānnu*.)

What does it mean to have a semantic connection in Nepali between *consent* and *obey?* To start with, *consent* already contains within it, both in English and in Nepali, a connotation of passivity; someone must first make a suggestion or initiate an action in order for another person to consent to it. John Hoffman, a political philosopher, writes that *consent* "suggests an element of passivity, a *willingness,* an agreement to accept the initiatives of another" (1984:124; emphasis in the original). I would therefore argue that when the term can also denote obedience, as it does in Nepali, an even stronger association with passivity results.

Thus, the recent insistence that a woman must "consent" to her own marriage in Junigau constitutes less of a rupture than it may seem from the previous assumption that a woman would simply obey her parents in the matter of her marriage. The man is still the one who must try to persuade (*phakāunu*) the woman to elope, whether in person or through love letters. This construction of women as passive recipients of others' proposals dovetails neatly with the dominant gender ideology that dictates that women (especially but also men sometimes) should deny their desires, sexual and otherwise, by not acting upon, admitting to, or even experiencing them. While in practice there are many exceptions to this ideology in Junigau, it nevertheless exerts a strong influence on women and men alike. So, for instance, villagers at a songfest, especially women, rarely get up to dance without being persuaded, urged, or coerced into doing so by others, usually men (cf. Ahearn 1998). It is also considered inappropriate for guests, again especially women, to accept with alacrity offers for seconds when eating. Persuasion and coercion are thought to be necessary in this situation as well. So common is the phenomenon of a person turning down an offer when he or she actually wants to accept that there is a verb to describe such pretending: *ḍhāchā pārnu*—"to pretend not to want to do or take what one really wants." In sum, it is expected in Junigau that consent is usually obtained only as the result of coercion.

This is not to imply that there is no difference at all between, on the one hand, the practice of forcing a woman to go along with her parents' or future husband's wishes in the matter of her marriage and, on the other hand, asking for her consent. On the contrary, even if the request for a woman's consent is still almost always either coercive of pro forma, a space is nevertheless created for her potential refusal. A lived hegemony is never total or exclusive. Williams remarks that hegemony "does not just passively exist as a form of dominance. It has continually to be renewed, recreated, defended, and modified. It is also continually resisted, limited, altered, challenged by pressures not all its own" (1977:112). The fact that the consent of both parties to a marriage is increasingly considered necessary in Junigau indicates a restructuring, if not a weakening, of hegemonic forces in the village. Indeed, Gramsci noted long ago that the key to the continued domination of the ruling class is its ability "to win the active consent of those over whom it rules" (1971:244).

The question of the relationship between consent and coercion is one that has been debated in Western philosophy for centuries, if not millennia. Although this is not the forum for an exhaustive treatment of the issues surrounding free will versus determinism or the relevance of equality and freedom to the phenomenon of coerced consent, a few concluding remarks on the nature of consent and coercion may help to illuminate the emergence of new structures of feeling regarding human agency in Junigau. L. T. Hobhouse, a scholar of liberalism, states that "true consent is free consent, and the full freedom of consent implies equality on the part of both parties to the bargain"

(1964:50). The problem with this formulation is that it posits the existence of completely autonomous individuals who are unencumbered by all social constraints. Such "free consent" is an illusion, however, as every individual is a sociocultural product subject to social, political, economic, historical, and cultural constraints. Nevertheless, this is not to say the actions of individuals are completely determined. Neither pure spontaneity nor pure mechanicity exists (cf. Hoffman 1984:66). Ortner prefers to think of actors as "loosely structured" agents whose actions are influenced but not rigidly determined by the social structure and historical context (1989:198; cf. Parish 1994:292–93). An individual therefore never consents completely freely, nor does coercion ever rob one entirely of one's agency.

The relationship between consent and coercion is a dialectical one, according to Hoffman, because each implies the existence of the other, even as it shapes the other's qualities: "Consent can be defined as the conscious recognition of the coercion of relationships—a mechanism without which coercion could not be sustained and through which coercion is itself transformed" (1984:126). This analysis of consent as a dialectical negation of coercion holds for all forms of social coercion, Hoffman maintains (128). As provocative as Hoffman's explication is of consent and coercion, I find it least useful in its insistence on a consenting individual's "conscious recognition" of the coercive nature of social relations. One need not adhere to a notion of false consciousness in order to conclude that we are all often unaware of the extent to which our actions are steeped in the sociocultural structures from which they arise. What I find valuable in Hoffman, and what I would like to emphasize here in conclusion, is the transformative potential of consent (and, indeed, of any social action). Hoffman writes that

> consent, although the relatively passive moment of a relationship with another, is never simply a fatalistic acceptance of what "is." To consent is also to transform, for in "consenting," the individual enters into a relationship and by participating in such a relationship, social reality becomes something *other* than what it would have been, had the act of consent not occurred. (124–25; emphasis in the original)

Such a nuanced understanding of coercion and consent is necessary in order to appreciate the ways in which Junigau residents' conceptions of their own and others' agency have changed over the years. While many villagers increasingly accord individuals the power to affect their own lives, they realize that this power is not unlimited. Indeed, many of the letters and narratives cited in previous chapters explicitly acknowledge social constraints, such as village rumors, inappropriate kinship relations, and attitudes toward "unseemly" behavior by women. The force of these constraints should lead us to the realization that the new structures of feeling arising in Junigau do not indicate that there is total autonomy for young people now in the realm of marriage—or even that villagers think there is such autonomy. It is possible that the emergent emphasis on consent may eventually enable Junigau women and men to subvert current relations of domination within marriage, thereby transcending and transforming the structures that have hitherto constrained them. If someone were to ask me to speculate, however, on what marriage practices will look like in Junigau in 2020, I would have to reply that while most, if not all, marriages by then will probably be elopements involving the "consent" of both parties, possibly expressed through love letters, many of the deeply rooted structural inequalities between women and men in the village may very well remain fundamentally unchanged. Other hierarchies and alliances in the realm of kinship might be reconstituted, but hierarchical gender relations seem tenacious enough to persist in Junigau indefinitely. An overview of changes and continuities in the realm of marriage will help to illustrate the likelihood that gender relations will remain hierarchical even as new structures of feeling emerge.

Marital Transformations

In considering the shifts in Junigau social relations during the 1980s and 1990s, let us recall how they are manifesting themselves in the practices and discourses associated with the three main forms of marriage in the village: arranged, capture, and elopement. The transformations that are occurring in the ways in which these types of marriage are performed and perceived by villagers have potentially significant ramifications for the Junigau social structure in general and for the everyday lives of village residents. As the trend toward elopement and away from arranged marriage and capture marriage accelerated dramatically in the 1990s, the effects of new structures of feeling could be seen even in the few cases in which marriage practices seemed "traditional."

Arranged Marriage

In arranged marriage ceremonies and the narratives of marriage about them, what emerges most clearly is a mixture of consent and coercion, resistance and accommodation. Women who refuse to make the offerings themselves at their wedding ceremonies and/or who fight the application of the red powder to their hair do so in a manner that emphatically registers their disapproval of the marriage without jeopardizing the successful completion of the ceremony. Women's agency is constrained, therefore, but not eliminated by arranged marriage. How is it constrained? Junigau parents rarely if ever consult their daughters when ne-gotiating their marriages; by the time most young women find out that they are to be married off, the agreement has already been finalized. Thus, they have only two extreme choices: to comply or to defy—comply with the choice of their par-ents and go along with the marriage or defy their parents by eloping with an-other man or running away to stay with distant relatives. Since few women have men waiting to elope with them, and since utter refusal to marry would most likely result in a woman being disowned by her family, the vast majority of women who discover that their parents have arranged a marriage for them comply. In a community such as Junigau, in which women must depend on their fathers', brothers', or husbands' land or wages for subsistence, unambigu-ously rebellious defiance is an unattractive option (cf. Jeffery and Jeffery 1994:162). Nevertheless, in the course of complying with their parents' wishes many women inject elements of opposition into their arranged marriage cere-monies. Although young village women have few opportunities, if any, to influ-ence their parents in the timing of their marriage or the choice of a husband, they do have some leeway in how they perform their arranged marriage cere-monies and how they narrate the events afterward.

When a woman such as Pancha Maya fights the application of red powder to her hair, she is carving out a space for herself as an active agent who resists, however ineffectually, what she considers to be inevitable. Such actions are redolent of multiple meanings and motivations, serving on one level as indica-tors of the woman's displeasure with her fate and on another level as markers of her propriety, in that they allow her to demonstrate her disinclination to marry (and consequently become sexually active). On the one hand, therefore, oppositional acts may merely reinforce the gender ideologies that delineate what a "good" woman should be like. On the other hand, however, in the ever-changing contexts of village life, the space occupied by these actions has the potential to be utilized and reconfigured by women seeking to subvert the au-thority of their parents and avoid the marriages that have been arranged for them. Especially in the light of shifting structures of feeling that increasingly emphasize the need to obtain the consent of both parties before arranging a marriage, behavior such as that of Pema Kumari, for example, who wrote her father a letter threatening to have him jailed if he went through with plans to marry her off, becomes more likely to challenge the status quo successfully. Nevertheless, it seems to me that actions by Junigau women at the time of their arranged marriages are improbable catalysts for dramatic change in the near future. I agree with Patricia and Roger Jeffery, who state of Indian women:

> For the most part, women's struggles are more likely to be individualistic attempts to ameliorate their situation within the system, rather than

confrontational insubordination that challenges the very basis of the system. Generally, women's resistance is severely channeled by the structures in which women are located. (1994:162)

There is a tendency, Jeffery and Jeffery note, for scholars to treat South Asian women either as passive and oppressed victims or completely free agents (130). The latter type of "wishful thinking," as Jeffery and Jeffery term it, appears frequently in Raheja and Gold's 1994 book. Despite the lip service Raheja and Gold pay to the constraints placed on Indian women by dominant discourses and power relations, their book valorizes what they identify as resistance. In the following passage from Raheja's introduction to the book, she both acknowledges this imbalance and attempts to justify it:

> If in this book we direct our attention more to the resistance exhibited in expressive traditions than to the power relations that place women in subordinate positions, it is because we wish at first to counter colonial, and some anthropological and feminist, assumptions about the passivity of Indian women, just as the *Subaltern Studies* historians have generally had as their first priority the study of subaltern resistance, in order to question pervasive assumptions about peasant inertia, the internalization of structures of domination, and the "harmony" of Indian village society. (1994:17)

Surely, however, it must be possible to counter assumptions about South Asian women's passivity while at the same time acknowledging the powerful structures that are active in their lives. A more balanced approach would entail withstanding the "romance of resistance" (Abu-Lughod 1990) and recognizing that a woman "may both resist her oppression and also be an agent in her own coercion" (Jeffery and Jeffery 1994:130). Mohanty expresses the same sentiment:

> The relations of power I am referring to are not reducible to binary oppositions or oppressor/oppressed relations. I want to suggest that it is possible to retain the idea of multiple, fluid structures of domination which intersect to locate women differently at particular historical conjunctures, while at the same time insisting on the dynamic oppositional agency of individuals and collectives and their engagement in "everyday life." (1991a:13)

Thus, Khim Prasad can at one and the same time express his resistance to arranged marriage without the consent of the woman *and* provide as his reason the possibility that some other man might have a claim on the woman, potentially causing her to run off with him after marriage, thereby disgracing the family. So, while Khim Prasad can state categorically that, "The most important thing, the 'main' thing, I said, was that the girl must consent to the boy. It's not right for there to be only the boy's consent," he reinforces notions of family honor and men's rights over women when he explains why the consent of the woman is so crucial. Furthermore, if Khim Prasad's elders had followed his instructions and asked his future wife if she consented to marry him, how would she have responded? Given the configurations of power surrounding her in 1993, she most likely would have echoed Pancha Maya, who, when asked by her own male relatives *after* the marriage negotiations were finalized if she consented, replied with the rhetorical question, "What should I say to that??" Merely asking a woman if she consents to an arranged marriage, therefore, might have little significance if her options remain as limited as they have been.

Capture Marriage

In the area of capture marriage, the ongoing shift in structures of feeling in Junigau is having a strong impact on the ways in which villagers perceive and experience abductions. The incidence of capture marriage has decreased noticeably over the past thirty years as parents have become unwilling to facilitate their daughters' abductions and as villagers in general assert more frequently that a woman's consent is essential before marriage. So stigmatized has capture marriage become in Junigau that some villagers claim it no longer occurs there, while others such as Ram Bahadur deny that their own marriages were by abduction, preferring instead to maintain that they married "properly."

Junigau narratives of capture marriage share with those of arranged marriage the tendency of the narrators (male or female) to depict themselves as resisting what they deem to be their inevitable fate. Struggle as they might, however, the women eventually give in, and, as opposed to the idea of marriage as the men might start out to be, they either relent and bring home a bride by abduction to appease their parents or go along with their parents' abduction of a bride for them. Coercion and eventual consent have therefore both been present in the capture marriages of many women and men in Junigau. In recent years, though, the few abductions that have occurred have been more at the initiative of young men than of their parents. It seems likely that such capture marriages will continue to take place in the village, but at what rate and in what manner remains to be seen. A follow-up study of capture marriage in Junigau in the coming years, as well as research into similar practices in other societies, will begin to fill in the gap left by anthropologists since the days when marriage by abduction figured so prominently in the evolutionary theories of nineteenth-century ethnologists.

Elopement

What is most striking about love letters and narratives of elopement from Junigau is the degree to which almost all of the narrators and letter writers, particularly the women, eschew responsibility for their marriages, claiming to have been coerced into consenting to the elopement. Whereas some older women lay the blame for their marriages on spells that were cast on them, younger women assert that insistent matchmakers or the suitors themselves simply refused to take no for an answer. Others claim it was all a matter of fate that they eloped with one particular person as opposed to another. "It was probably written [i.e., fated], you know!" Rita Sara exclaims. Thus, in many respects Junigau women appear to experience, or at least describe, their marriages similarly, as involving at least some degree of coercion, no matter what type they were.

This is beginning to change, however, as Junigau residents are increasingly attributing their actions to their own agency rather than fate. Thus, Pabi Sara at first maintains that it was her karma to elope with Kul Bir after knowing him for only an hour but then proceeds to describe the decision-making process through which she went in order to determine whether or not she should marry him. Likewise, Shila Devi both attributes her elopement to the fact that it must have been "written" and scolds herself for her foolish act, stating, "Remembering my wedding, the day of my wedding, I get angry at myself!" Vajra Bahadur, Shila Devi's husband, sums up this middle phase in the shift from one structure of feeling to another, a time when the new pattern is still "in solution" (Williams 1977:132): "In a way, I say sometimes that this was probably written to be my fate. In actuality, we do it ourselves, but it's like that, see? Our fates are written."

Despite their emphasis on fate when describing the outcomes of their elopements, however, villagers depict themselves in their narratives and love letters as anything but fatalistic during the process. In this sense, their descriptions resemble those of Junigau residents whose marriages were arranged or by abduction. Both men and women, but particularly women, emphasize how vehemently they resisted the elopement. Pabi Sara, for example, describes her response to Kul Bir's proposal: "'I won't do it, I won't marry,' I said. 'I won't marry; I have no wish to do so. I don't like you,' I kept saying and saying." And Shila Devi repeatedly rejects or ignores Vajra Bahadur's appeals in his letters to elope by a certain date. By portraying themselves as strongly resisting their elopements, these women achieve the purpose (intentionally or not, whether they actually are or not) of appearing unwilling to marry, for in Junigau anyone, especially a woman, who seems eager to marry invites others to cast aspersions on her character. A common thread connects arranged marriage brides' acts of ineffectual opposition with elopement participants' disavowals of responsibility in their narratives and love letters.

Although many villagers experience, perceive, or at least describe their various forms of marriage similarly in some respects, in other respects the meanings and values Junigau residents attach to marriage practices are changing significantly. This is especially evident in Junigau love letters, which contain many instances of development discourse, which correspondents use to attribute responsibility to individuals for improving their own lives and making their loves "successful." There are several components of the recent shift toward elopement and love letter correspondences in Junigau that signal some potentially meaningful changes in the everyday lives of villagers. As these are only just beginning, it remains to be seen whether these new structures of feeling will be reabsorbed into the dominant matrices of power or instead substantially reconstitute those hegemonic relations. One important change that has been occurring in recent years is the lengthening of courtships in Junigau, the possible consequences of which are far-reaching. In the sentiments expressed in the love letters exchanged during lengthy courtships are the kernels of a dramatic realignment among individuals within village households, for in their emphasis on "true love," "life friends," and "life success," the letters create expectations of a companionate marriage rather than a union based merely on economics, procreation, convenience, obedience, or momentary urges. A closer tie between spouses has the potential to disturb both hierarchies and alliances within Junigau's joint families as men who have professed "true, undying love" for their wives find their loyalties to the patriline called into question.[6] Indeed, after some recent elopements the couples have established neolocal residences, either in Junigau itself or elsewhere in Nepal where both spouses can find employment. On an everyday basis, such a change in residence means that young married women are no longer subject to the direct supervision and authority of their mothers- and fathers-in-law. Some women prefer this relative freedom, while others consider the responsibilities of running a household single-handedly (assuming their husbands work outside the village) to be too burdensome. If this trend toward neolocal residences continues, kinship relations, possibilities for spousal intimacy and companionate marriage, and hierarchical relationships within the extended family could be significantly reconfigured.

Another possible challenge to kinship structures within the village is the novel practice of eloping with extremely "wrong" kinds of cross-cousins. While only a minority of villagers, even among the oldest residents, have married "actual" first cousins, many continue to marry people who are either distantly related to them in the "appropriate" way or who are not related to them at all, in which case a de facto cross-cousin relationship is established. Problems occur, however, when someone marries a "wrong" kind of cross-cousin—that is, when a man marries a woman who is his father's sister's daughter or when a woman marries her mother's brother's son.[7] Junigau residents complain that such marriages "mix up" or "ruin" the kinship terminology, since terms of address for particular kin presume a matrilateral cross-cousin match (or at least a match that does not preclude the creation of matrilateral cross-cousin ties retrospectively). As young villagers increasingly value their individual desires in selecting a marriage partner over the desires of their relatives and marry "inappropriately," the kinship-based social structure of Junigau is likely to be reconstituted—or dismantled entirely. Already villagers complain that they do not know how to address people whose near relatives have reversed the direction of marriage exchange for their two lineages, and in some cases they have even stopped interacting with such people. Although *dhobhet* ceremonies smooth over the minor discrepancies in kinship terms after slightly "inappropriate" marriages such as the one between Vajra Bahadur and Shila Devi, such ceremonies cannot reconcile blatantly contradictory relationships. It seems likely that the move away from kinship-based interactions will accelerate in the coming years. Thus, we might expect—and indeed are already seeing—a greater use of names instead of kinship terms for address and increasing reliance on wage laborers instead of kin to help build houses or work in the fields. Although other factors besides "wrong" marriages are certainly influencing these trends, the level of distress villagers display with regard to such matches is evidence of their perceived impact on social relations within Junigau.

On an individual rather than a structural level, the potential ramifications of the increase in elopements are more complex. While longer courtships and love letter correspondences may establish stronger ties between spouses, the relationship in almost all cases is still a hierarchical one. Many women who have eloped in recent years drink their husbands' foot water, for example, unlike many older women of all marriage types who have given up the practice. Similarly, all elopement couples address each other using asymmetrical forms of *you* (usually two levels apart, sometimes only one). The trend toward elopement in Junigau therefore poses little threat to certain aspects of the hierarchical relationship between wife and husband.

Another feature of elopement may serve to reduce a woman's options and authority should her marriage become troubled: the reduction in, or termination of, her natal family's support. Especially in cases of "wrong" elopements, a woman's parents and other kin may deny her the right to return to her natal home if she is subject to abuse or is otherwise made to suffer in her marital home. The reactions of particular parents vary, but the loss of her parents' unconditional support is a probable outcome of a woman's elopement. Whereas parents who have arranged a marriage for their daughter often feel an obligation to intervene on her behalf in case of difficulties, parents of women who have eloped usually communicate to their daughter the equivalent of "You've made your bed, now lie in it." As I reported in the previous chapter, Sarita's father maintained that he had no intention of providing moral or material support to her if she ignored his wishes and eloped. Dutiful daughters who add to the honor of their families by complying with their parents' plans to marry them off in *kanyādān* (gift of a virgin) ceremonies earn the right to expect assistance from their natal kin should their marriages turn sour. While not every family actually provides such assistance, women who elope forfeit this right altogether.

The Indeterminacy of Meaning and the Politics of Representation

In attempting to interpret love letters, development discourse, and the practices surrounding them, I have applied a practice theory of meaning constraint. Although meanings will always be to some degree indeterminate, if only because they are continually changing over time, I was able to constrain the range of possible interpretations people might take away from a text (such as a love letter) or an event (such as a songfest) by collecting as much ethnographic, historical, spatial, interpersonal, and linguistic information as possible. The trends I have noted—the rise in literacy rates among women, the increase in elopements, and a shift in the way villagers are conceiving of themselves and their actions—are not necessarily unidirectional or irreversible, but they have led to the emergence of new structures of feeling that are already causing significant changes in the ways in which Junigau residents think and act.

In writing this book, I have felt the enormity of the responsibility I have to the women and men whose stories and letters I present here. Some scholars, such as Gayatri Spivak, believe that the voices of those in other societies, especially the voices of poor women, cannot be detected in ethnographies such as this one. Spivak writes:

> On the other side of the international division of labor, the subject of exploitation cannot know and speak the text of female exploitation, even if the absurdity of the nonrepresenting intellectual making space for her to speak is achieved. The woman is doubly in shadow. . . . The subaltern as female cannot be heard or read. (1988:288, 307)

Spivak's assertion that subaltern people cannot be heard or read because they cannot speak is, I hope, at least partly belied by the voices in this ethnography.[8] Admittedly, the voices of Junigau women and men are filtered through a process of selection, transcription, translation, and interpretation, but I contend that they are still audible. To say that subaltern people cannot speak is to deny them agency, to render them mute by the very assertion of their muteness. Ortner writes, "The anthropologist and the historian are charged with representing the lives of living or once-living people, and as we attempt to push these people into the molds of our texts, *they push back*" (1995:189; emphasis in the original). The meanings that emerge from Junigau residents' words and actions may be multiple and on some level indeterminate, but that does not mean that patterns cannot be discerned (Eco 1990:6). In speaking about the lives and loves of Junigau residents and in using their voices in this account of their love letter correspondences, I have tried to do justice to the complexities and inconsistencies of their lives, particularly with reference to the social transformations that their love letters are in the process of both shaping and mirroring. I have also attempted to ascertain the structured regularities embedded within the words and actions of villagers, the patterns in emergent structures of feeling that have the potential, as indeterminate as they are in this incipient phase, to challenge, reinforce, or reconfigure conceptions of agency, gender, and personhood in ways that shed light on processes of social change around the world.

Notes

Chapter 1

1. Words in quotation marks were written in English.

2. Bahadur is a common middle name for Magar men; it means "brave." (Kumari and Devi, meaning "goddess," are common middle names for women in Junigau.) Although most Junigau residents stated that they would not mind having their real names used in this book because the courtships described have long since resulted in marriage, in order to protect the few who asked for anonymity I have used pseudonyms for all love letter correspondents as well as for others who shared their narratives of marriage with me. I do not use composites or fictional characters but do omit or change minor details on occasion that would definitively identify someone. In keeping with anthropological convention, Junigau itself is also a pseudonym.

3. Akhil Gupta notes that colonial discourse "bequeathed a set of dichotomies that were unusually 'productive' in a Foucauldian sense" because they enabled the construction of a sociology built on them (1998:9). That Junigau villagers themselves use such dichotomies as developed/backward or modern/traditional speaks to the complexities and ironies inherent in what Gupta calls "the postcolonial condition." As Stacy Pigg notes, "Whether or not this [traditional/modern] dichotomy serves us well in social analysis, the fact is that these terms are thriving in the world we aim to describe and interpret. We need, then, to track the terms of the discourse of modernity as people adopt, deploy, modify, and question it" (1996:163–64). See also Collier (1997:213) on how "modernity" and "tradition," are best seen as subtraditions of a wider post-Enlightenment European culture.

4. Desjarlais (1992:164) reports that the same adage is common among the Tibetan ethnic group with which he did his research. They end the saying with an additional phrase, however: *kasari dekheko?*—which Desjarlais translates as "How can it be seen?" A similar belief in the writing of one's fate on one's forehead at birth is also prevalent in other parts of South Asia. See Divakaruni (1999) for a novel about India based on this premise.

5. Williams (1977). I will define and discuss structures of feeling in greater detail in chapter 3.

6. See Ahearn (2000b) for a summary of the main themes of this ethnography.

7. There is a whole literature on development discourse written by scholars whose main objective is to destabilize the naturalness of development projects, categories, and assumptions. (See in particular Escobar 1991, 1995; Ferguson 1990; Hobart 1993; and Pigg 1992, 1996.) Recently, the use of the term *discourse* has been criticized for being too unitary and simplistic a concept, one that was not sufficiently sensitive to local interpretations and challenges (e.g., Gardner 1997; Grillo 1997; Kingsolver 1991; Rutherford and Nyamuda 2000; Sivaramakrishnan 2000; Woost 1997). As Sivaramakrishnan argues, "Development's stories are rife with a micropolitics often obscured by the consistency or more orderly progression implied by the terms *discourse* or *narrative*" (2000:432; emphasis in the original). For the purposes of this ethnography, I have retained the term *development discourse*, as I seek to point out consistent patterns of expression in the love letters and the other written materials analyzed in chapter 8. Nevertheless, I hope I have also demonstrated in my case study chapters and throughout the book that I consider development discourse to be a set of linguistic and cultural practices that are constantly being reconstituted or reinforced by the Junigau residents themselves (cf. Gardner 1997:154).

8. See Abu-Lughod (1986:9–24) for a discussion of the advantages and disadvantages of assuming the role of a daughter during fieldwork.

9. Later the son joined the Indian Army. The average household in Junigau has seven members (Ahearn 1994).

10. *bhāuju* means "older brother's wife" in Nepali. This is what everyone in my Nepali family called the son's wife.

11. Since democracy arrived in Nepal following the People's Movement of 1990, the local governing body previously termed the *panchāyat* has been renamed the *gāu bikās samitī* or Village Development Committee. Junigau residents still often use the older terminology, however.

12. The one non-Magar family was Brahman. They lived on the far edge of the village close to a neighboring mixed-caste area. In the 1980s, there was also one family of untouchable tailors; they have since moved.

13. For other work on the Magars, see Adhikary (1993); Chemjong (1967); Hitchcock (1961, 1963, 1965, 1966); Jiro (1974); Krauskopff and Lecomte-Tilouine (1996); Lecomte-Tilouine (1993); Molnar (1981); de Sales (1987); Shepherd (1982); and Thapa (1993).

14. Gore Bahadur Khapangi Magar, personal communication, 18 August 1993.

15. The anthropological literature on Nepal is too vast to cite here. The works that have most profoundly influenced the shape of this ethnography are Acharya and Bennett (1981); Adhikary (1993); Bennett (1983); Fricke (1984); Hitchcock (1966); Jones (1973); March (1979); Ortner (1989); and Watkins (1996).

16. See, for example, Burghart (1984); English (1985); Höfer (1979); Hutt (1994); and Regmi (1978).

17. Jane Collier reports the attitude toward the arrival of democracy in Andalusia, quoting what had become a cliché by the 1980s: "Now that we have democracy, people

do as they please" (1997:5). See also Anthony Giddens's discussion of intimacy as democracy (1992:184–204).

18. Hindi and Nepali movies will be discussed further in chapter 8 as evidence of the development of a new form of cultural literacy among Junigau villagers.

19. In the early 1800s, during the Anglo-Nepal War (1814–16), the British, impressed with the bravery of the Nepali soldiers, began recruiting them for their own military. In 1947, after India became independent, the ten regiments of the British Gurkha Brigade were divided, with four remaining with the British and the rest becoming part of the Indian Army. Today, Junigau men try to join the British Army first, as the status and pay are best there. Failing that, they try to join the Indian Army. The Nepali Army and Nepali police force are considered final resorts for young men seeking employment in security forces. Junigau men who are unable to enlist in any of these forces generally leave Nepal to work in factories in India or the Middle East. For more on Gurkha soldiers in the area surrounding Junigau, see Adhikary (1993:174–205). For information about Gurkhas elsewhere in Nepal, see Caplan (1995); Collett (1994); Des Chene (1991); Hitchcock (1961, 1966); and Höfer (1978). See also special issues of *Himal* on migratory labor in India (1997a) and Gurkha soldiers (1997b).

20. Caplan (1995:38) and Des Chene (personal communication). Adhikary claims that the minimum period of service is seventeen years (1993:185).

21. Collier argues that a similar shift has occurred in Andalusia; changes in courtship practices there "reflect the shift from following social conventions to thinking for oneself that occurred as people from Los Olivos replaced a discourse of inherited property with one of occupational achievement" (1997:68).

22. High schools in Nepal end at tenth grade, after which students must pass the national School Leaving Certificate (S.L.C.) exam if they want to study further at the college level. There is a move currently to add two grades to high schools, but thus far Sarvodaya High School ends at tenth grade. As soon as Sarvodaya became a high school, it became eligible to request a Peace Corps teacher, which the headmaster and the School Committee immediately did.

23. See Adhikary (1993:182–83) for a discussion of school attendance and performance of Brahman and Magar students at Sarvodaya High School from 1983 to 1988. Adhikary notes that Brahman students graduated at a disproportionately higher rate than Magar students during those years.

24. See Maggi (1998) for a fascinating analysis of changing practices involving menstrual impurity among Pakistan's Kalasha people.

25. *Bāḍne* means "to separate" or "to divide." It is the term most villagers use to refer to menstrual seclusion practices.

26. The strands of hair that are washed are those in the front of the head on either side of the part. As I discuss in chapter 5, the part of the hair symbolizes the vagina in the wedding ceremony in which the groom ritually deflowers the bride by tracing red powder down the part of her hair. It is therefore fitting that a woman should bathe the strands surrounding her part in order to cleanse herself symbolically at the onset of menstruation.

27. Other Junigau women use small balls of clay they call *mātengro*, which they wash as if they were their husbands' feet, or else they use water that they have poured over their glass bangles, which are symbolic of their married status.

Chapter 2

1. Given the multiple ways in which villagers are related, however, it is not uncommon for a person to be addressed in a seemingly inconsistent manner by members of the same family.

2. I am not by any means the only person to have made this transition. Schwimmer and Warren (1993) have compiled a volume of personal accounts written by anthropologists who were once Peace Corps volunteers.

3. I am using their real names (with their permission, of course). They deserve to be named for their enormous help to me over the years.

4. The one woman who requested that I use a pseudonym for her did so because she was fearful that she might suffer retaliation from the man she accused of having cast the spell on her that made her willing to elope.

5. I used three dictionaries in translating the love letters: two Nepali-English (Meerendonk 1960; Turner [1931] 1990) and one Hindi-English (Tiwari et al. 1990).

Chapter 3

1. See Collins (1995) for an excellent review of this debate.

2. See McCollum (1998) and Quinn (1982, 1996) for analyses of Americans' ideas about love and marriage.

3. There is an ongoing debate, for example, as to the causal relation between the Industrial Revolution and the emergence of romantic love as a cultural ideal in Europe. Some scholars see the former as a necessary precursor to the latter, while others see the latter as a necessary precursor to the former. See Giddens (1992); Goode (1959); Lindholm (1995); Macfarlane (1979, 1986); and Shorter (1977).

4. Junigau babies are named by a Brahman priest who has done astrological calculations to ascertain the most auspicious first letters for a name; parents usually have no say in their children's formal names. Most of the time this is irrelevant, however, for Junigau residents are most often addressed using kinship terms or nicknames. Only in school are children regularly called by their given names.

5. Rebhun reports a similar borrowing of the English word *love* in Brazil, pronounced there as *lovi* (1995:255–56; 1999b).

6. Recently, however, feminist theorists have maintained that sex itself is socioculturally constructed. Pointing to the existence of intersexed individuals with ambiguous genitalia, Bing and Bergvall write that, "like gender, sex is socially constructed and better described as a continuum rather than a dichotomy" (1996:3).

7. This section is a revised version of Ahearn (2000a) and is elaborated upon in Ahearn (2001a).

8. See Ortner (1996) for an interesting discussion of the intersections between feminist theory and practice theory. McElhinny's (1998) essay engages with Ortner and provides insights into the relationship between linguistic anthropology and practice theory, especially in the realm of gender relations.

9. See Ahearn (1998) for an expanded version of this discussion.

10. The Nepali legal code (Muluki Āin) requires the informed consent of both the bride and the groom. See Gilbert (1992:748). In practice, however, arranged marriage brides in Junigau are rarely informed of their impending marriages, never mind asked to consent. For more about consent and coercion in Junigau marriages, see Ahearn (1994) and the final chapter of this ethnography.

11. Magars practice preferential matrilateral cross-cousin marriage, which is described in greater detail in the next chapter.

12. Unlike the situation in more orthodox Hindu villages, widows in Junigau do sometimes remarry, especially if they are young and childless. Nevertheless, remarriage does not erase the stigma of widowhood. See Bennett (1983) on the status of widows in Hindu communities.

13. I have heard, however, that some of the same young men were involved in a similar incident in which they sent one of their friends a fake letter supposedly from his girlfriend, who purportedly expressed the desire to break off the relationship. The young man was extremely hurt by this news, and it was months before the relationship was back on track. To my knowledge, they are still corresponding—presumably with greater care.

14. This is a perfect example of what Junigau residents mean when they say, "Weddings pull weddings" (*bihāle bihālāi tānchha*). Villagers looking to elope often meet their future spouses at someone else's wedding.

15. Villagers use this phrase to refer to the *kaliyug,* the fourth or iron age, which Hindus believe began on 18 February 3102 B.C.E. and will end on 18 February 428,898 C.E., when the world will be destroyed (Turner [1931] 1990:79).

Chapter 4

1. Bennett (1983:144–45). There is a vast literature on the gift in South Asia and on *kanyādān* marriage in particular. See Raheja (1988) for a review of these materials. P. V. Kane (1974) summarizes the Hindu scriptures in Manu (3:27–34), providing a list of the eight forms of ancient marriage. Note how closely they resemble the three main types of marriage practiced in Junigau (arranged, capture, and elopement): (1) *brāhma,* which is the "gift of a daughter, after decking her (with valuable garments) and honouring her (with jewels &c.), to a man learned in the Vedas and of good conduct"; (2) *daiva,* which is when "the father gives away his daughter after decking her (with ornaments &c.) to a priest"; (3) *ārsa,* when "there is a gift of one's daughter, after taking one pair of cattle . . .

only as a matter of fulfilling the law (and not as a sale of the girl)"; (4) *prājāpatya*, which is the "gift of a daughter, after the father has addressed (the couple with the words 'may both of you perform your religious duties together') and after he has honoured the bride-groom"; (5) *āsura*, when "the girl is given away at the father's will after the bride-groom gives as much wealth as he can afford to pay to the relatives of the girl and to the girl herself"; (6) *gāndharva*, the "union of a girl and the bride-groom by their mutual consent . . . which springs from the passion of love and has intercourse as its purpose"; (7) *rāksasa*, the "forcible abduction of a maiden from her house, while she weeps and cries aloud, after her kinsmen have been slain (or beaten), wounded and (their houses or fortresses) are broken open"; and (8) *paisāca*, when "a man has intercourse with a girl stealthily while she is asleep or intoxicated or disordered in mind (or unconscious) . . . which is the basest and most sinful of all the forms" (1974:517). As Kane notes, in the first four forms there is the "gift of the girl (*kanyādāna*) by the father or other guardian" (ibid.), making these the approved forms of marriage. The latter four—bridewealth, elopement, capture, and rape—are generally condemned by ancient Hindu scholars (520; cf. Trautmann 1981:277–93).

2. In practice, however, there are often differences in how individual daughters-in-law are treated within a household. Although the hegemonic rhetoric of equal treatment is quite strong, there is one type of daughter-in-law who most villagers agree receives special treatment: the mother-in-law's actual brother's daughter. While this might seem to make such marriages more attractive in terms of the relative status of the daughter-in-law, most Junigau residents said they would hesitate before giving their daughter to her actual father's sister's son because of the resentment she would be likely to have to endure from the family's other daughters-in-law if she received special treatment from her aunt (who would also be her mother-in-law).

3. Ahearn (1998). On Tij in Nepal, see also Holland and Skinner (1989, 1995); Skinner and Holland (1990); and Skinner et al. (1994).

4. See Caplan (1995:101–7) for a discussion of how masculinity was attributed to Gurkha soldiers.

5. I never heard of any homosexual relationships in the village among men or women, but that does not mean, of course, that there were none. I simply might not have been privy to that information. Homosocial behaviors, however, were quite common among Nepali men, who are much more physically affectionate with one another in public than American men are; it was not unusual for me to see Junigau men sitting on one another's laps or holding hands. Such physical intimacy is less common among Junigau women, although many often sleep together and sit closely while combing one another's hair.

6. Contraception was not available in the village until the health post opened in 1993, and even then supplies were unreliable. A few villagers got birth control pills or Depo-Provera shots from clinics in Tansen, but there was widespread distrust of the possible side effects of such treatments. The most common (though still quite rare) form of birth control in the village is vasectomy, for which those Junigau men who are in the Indian Army report receiving a bonus.

7. The same consequences often face Nepali women who have been raped. While I have only heard of one possible rape in Junigau, which resulted in the woman's marriage with the alleged rapist, the cases I heard about from surrounding villages all resulted in the woman's suicide.

8. See Maggi (1998) for a description of Kalasha women's agency in decisions to stay in a marriage or elope with another man.

9. For the purposes of analyzing trends over time, I have divided first marriages into three time periods, roughly correlating to eras of distinctive literacy practices in the village: before 1960 (before construction of the school), 1960–82 (only primary and middle school available), and 1983–98 (high school available).

10. *Kalyāhā* literally means "quarrelsome person" (Turner [1931] 1990), which makes sense given the role matchmakers sometimes have to play in persuading a reluctant party to go along with the match.

11. Note that it is from the man's perspective that the type of marriage (matrilateral) is named. Anthropology's sexist past is betrayed in its conventions for labeling kinship systems.

12. As Bennett astutely remarks, however, "Women are never full ritual members of these patrilineal groups; rather they *are links between them*" (1983:165; emphasis in the original). Kathryn March makes a similar point in her dissertation (1979).

13. This low rate of actual first-cousin marriage answers those who might be concerned that such close marriages might lead to a higher incidence of genetic problems. I have observed no such genetic problems in Junigau.

14. These figures are through 1993 only; the update to the survey that I conducted in 1998 was shorter and did not ask about premarital kinship relationships. Nevertheless, it is my sense that these "inappropriate" matches are increasing in number.

15. "*sāino garbar bhayo, mishiyo, bigriyo, harāyo, khatam bhayo.*"

16. It seems to me that this return of a coin signifies a rejection of the practice of paying bridewealth for a woman, and, indeed, some people explained that the coin was returned because in Junigau men do not "pay a fee" (*bhāḍā tirne*) for their brides.

Chapter 5

1. Cf. Ahearn (1998). Other scholars have also noted similarly bawdy practices among the populations they study. See Hitchcock (1966:47); Narayan (1995:254); Shepherd (1982:262); Srivastava (1991:278–79); and Wadley (1994:58).

2. Indeed, on the survey I conducted among all ever-married residents of Junigau's central ward, none reported symmetrical use of forms of *you* between spouses on a regular basis. Such symmetrical usage does appear in love letters sometimes, however. Most commonly, a wife uses *tapaī* or *hajur* (very respectful forms) when speaking to her husband, while he uses *tā* (the lowest form of *you*) to address her. When I asked women why they addressed their husbands so respectfully, they often answered as Saraswati did: "Your husband is of all people—right?—the biggest/most important; yes or no?" I

answered diplomatically that I had no way of knowing, as I had no husband at the time. Women who have been married for years, however, sometimes resort to addressing their husbands using the lower forms of *you* in times of anger or when the men are drunk. Some of the older women regularly use *timī* (a middle-range familiar term) with their husbands, but their husbands inevitably use the lower *tā* in response. Shila Devi and Vajra Bahadur, whose courtship is presented in chapter 6, use slightly less asymmetrical terms: she uses *tapaī* with him, while he uses *timī* with her. Some women told me that they had heard that spouses in Kathmandu both use *timī* to address each other, but the women expressed skepticism that such tales were true. I myself have heard such usage in Kathmandu but never in the village.

3. I am translating the Nepali word *man* as "heart/mind." This is only a rough gloss for such a polysemic word. *man* refers to the site of one's emotions, the place inside oneself where one feels something. It can also, however, refer to the site of one's more cerebral opinions or thoughts. For this reason I am using the inelegant but more comprehensive term, *heart/mind*.

4. Anita Kumari's love of her husband is an excellent example of Bourdieu's "double negation," which "inclines agents to make a virtue of necessity, that is, to refuse what is anyway refused and to love the inevitable" (1977:77).

5. This incident presents just one example of the challenges—and shortcomings—of survey research. I attempted to confirm the responses individuals gave me by consulting others, listening to lengthy descriptions of events, and asking the same question in different ways, but no matter how hard I tried to check answers, I found (as do all survey researchers who are honest with themselves) that surveys are inevitably limiting and misleading. For this reason, I rely on narratives of marriage, love letters, and my many years of residence in Junigau for most of the material that appears in this book.

6. Capture marriage is also called marriage by abduction, marriage by capture, bride abduction, and bride theft by other ethnographers. I use the terms synonymously throughout this ethnography.

7. See Ahearn (1994:135–50) for a more detailed discussion of capture marriage in the anthropological literature.

8. Junigau residents do not keep careful track of their ages.

9. The word *rāḍī* can be translated as either "whore" or "widow" in Junigau, indicating the extent to which the words are synonymous in many villagers' minds.

10. In her book on Magars from Gulmi District, which is several days' walk to the northwest of Junigau, Lecomte-Tilouine claims that "all Magars" engage in cross-cousin marriage and also "always" choose their own spouses. Furthermore, she maintains that the wedding ceremony is performed without a religious specialist and consists mainly of a parental blessing. While 9 percent of Junigau Magars did marry their actual MBD/FZS cross-cousins, the rest of Lecomte-Tilouine's comments do not apply to Junigau: "La forme de mariage est, elle aussi, identique chez tous les Magar. Dans tous les cas, le mariage préférentiel avec la cousine croisée matrilatérale est pratiqué. Hormis cette préférence, l'union se fait selon le libre choix des jeunes gens parmi les partenaires pos-

sibles et la résidence natale de l'éspouse est très proche, souvent dans le même village. La cérémonie de déroule sans spécialiste religieux et consiste principalement en une bénédiction des époux par leurs parents" (1993:31).

11. *"māyā lāgyo."* This sentence could also be translated as, "I came to love him" or "I fell in love with him." Literally, it simply means "love [was] felt."

12. Here is further support for the view that marriage occurs not because of a particular religious ceremony but after sexual intercourse, either actual or symbolic (in the form of red powder applied to the part of the woman's hair).

13. *Mother's brother (māmā)* is the kinship term I use to address Rita Sara's husband.

14. This is yet another example of the truth of the saying popular in Junigau, "Weddings pull weddings" (*bihāle bihālāī tānchha*).

Chapter 6

1. For the complete correspondence of Shila Devi and Vajra Bahadur, see appendix A (available at <http://www.press.umich.edu/webhome/ahearn/index.html>).

2. A *chaupāri* is a stone sitting area built up around the base of two *bar-pipal* trees. In other areas of Nepal, it is called a *chautārā*.

3. *bar-pipal* trees are two banyan trees that are planted side by side, one male and the other female. Nepalis often conduct symbolic wedding ceremonies for the trees.

4. This date is based on the Nepali calendar. The year is 2047 (mid-April 1990 to mid-April 1991). The twelve months of the Nepali calendar start in mid-April and proceed in this order: Baisakh, Jeth, Asār, Sāun, Bhadau, Asoj, Kārtik, Mangsir, Pus, Māgh, Phāgun, and Chaita. Thus, this letter was written in the fourth day of the fifth month (Bhadau) of the year 2047, which corresponds roughly to a date in the last half of August 1990.

5. Repeated ellipses are common in Junigau love letters. I elongate them somewhat to differentiate them from pauses in a conversation (. . .) or omitted material (. . .).

6. Shila Devi and Vajra Bahadur had the speaking kinship relation (*bolne sāino*) of *māmā-bhānjī*, unmarriageable cross-cousins. The effect of this fictive kinship relation on their courtship will be discussed later.

7. Although this letter is the oldest surviving letter from their correspondence, it was not the first one Shila Devi and Vajra Bahadur exchanged. As is often the case in Nepal, the man initiated the correspondence, for, as Vajra Bahadur noted, using a common Nepali saying, "Who crows, the rooster, or the hen?" Vajra Bahadur wrote the first letter several weeks before this one, and several more exchanges preceded this letter. Shila Devi told me in 1998 that she had burned Vajra Bahadur's early letters, and Vajra Bahadur said he had also destroyed Shila Devi's early letters. The beginning of their courtship was rocky, they explained, and was frequently punctuated by breakups.

8. Respectful greeting.

9. Highest honorific form of *you*.

10. During the Bhai Tika festival, Junigau girls and women worship their brothers (actual and fictive) by putting red *ṭikas* on their foreheads and feeding them special foods. In exchange, the brothers give their sisters gifts of clothing.

11. Here Shila Devi uses *timī,* the familiar form of *you* rather than the honorific form for the first time in a letter.

12. Vajra Bahadur is probably referring here to the Laws of Manu, which present eight different kinds of marriage, including elopement and arranged marriage (cf. Kane 1974:517).

13. The familiar form of *you, timī,* continues throughout this paragraph.

Chapter 7

1. See Luke (1988) for an analysis of the Dick and Jane textbooks in a very different cultural context.

2. For further elaboration on Nepal's history and Nepali nationalism, see Burghart (1984); English (1985); Gellner et al. (1997); Höfer (1979); Hutt (1994); and Regmi (1978).

3. Translation mine. Unless otherwise noted, all excerpts from conversations, letters, books, or magazines are my own translations from the Nepali.

4. For a history of Nepal's education plans, see Bista (1991).

5. These selections were in English; I have not translated them.

6. The Pradhan Pancha was the village leader during the *panchāyat* era. After Nepal's 1990 democratic revolution, village *panchāyats* were replaced with Village Development Councils. For a succinct history of the *panchāyat* era, see Burghart (1994).

7. Excerpts from the English textbooks retain the spelling, punctuation, and usage of the originals.

8. S.L.C. stands for School Leaving Certificate, which is awarded to students who pass a national exam after finishing high school.

9. J.T.A. stands for junior technical assistant, a type of governmental agricultural extension agent.

10. *Namaskār* is a very respectful greeting that is accompanied by a gesture in which the hands are clasped, palms together.

11. For various case studies on Hinduism, ethnicity, and nationalism in Nepal, see Gellner et al. (1997).

12. National Planning Commission Secretariat (1992:22).

13. A *stupa* is a temple containing a relic from the Buddha's body or possessions.

14. Sarita and Bir Bahadur's courtship and love letters are analyzed in chapter 9.

15. The plethora of papers presented at the 1999 meetings also demonstrated the popularity of the newly flourishing field of the cross-cultural study of romantic love—an outcome, at least in part, of Jankowiak's (1995) groundbreaking volume. It is also not a coincidence, in my opinion, that cross-cultural manifestations of romantic love finally began to receive serious scholarly attention at a time when women were gain-

ing strength in terms of power and numbers in the academy. The two panels were "Modern Love: Local Practices of the Global Ideology of Companionate Marriage" and "The Politics of Romance: Situated Love in a Global World." Among the many fine papers presented at these sessions, the following were of particular relevance to this ethnography: Hirsch (1999); Maggi (1999); Parikh (1999); Rebhun (1999a); and Wardlow (1999).

16. See Onta (1996, 1997) for a description of *Deurāli*'s organizational structure and history.

17. This is certainly not the case with respect to property rights. Currently in Nepal, women are banned from inheriting land from their fathers unless they reach the age of thirty-five without getting married. See Gilbert (1992) and Kunreuther (2000) for two excellent analyses of the property rights of Nepali women.

18. See Pigg (2001) for a fascinating analysis of the discourse surrounding AIDS in Nepal.

19. These groups have no relation to the small groups of Maoists who fashion themselves after Peru's Shining Path movement. By 2000 the Maoist insurgency in Nepal had led to over one thousand deaths (Kumar 2000). As of this writing, Junigau residents remain unaffected and for the most part unaware of the Maoist movement.

20. The Nepali title, *Prem Patra,* could be translated as singular or plural. In the book, there are numerous love letters exchanged between the young protagonists rather than one special love letter, so the more appropriate translation is probably *Love Letters.*

21. Darjeeling has many residents who speak Nepali, and many wealthier residents of Nepal send their children to school there, so the setting of the novel probably appeals to Nepali speakers inside and outside of Nepal's official borders. The book itself was published in Varanasi, India, and was marketed to all of these Nepali speakers.

22. Compare this episode to the sentiments expressed in a 1990 letter from Vajra Bahadur to Shila Devi:

> In this world only you
> are mine and I am yours.
> I spill out the pains of my heart/mind only to you
> because you are my life friend.
> You can also spill out your own to me . . .

23. I was told that there are no love letter guidebooks written in Nepali.

24. The author of this book uses only the name, Manohar.

25. Movsesian even includes in his section "Love Paragraphs" some examples of how to write letters on the occasion of "Easter and Passover" or "Christmas and Hanukkah," but he does not mention any of the holidays celebrated by Hindus, Muslims, or people of other South Asian faiths.

26. Lest Western readers feel that such guidebooks full of trite models of love letters would be poorly received in their societies, I should mention that just before Valentine's Day in 1995 I found Michelle Lovric's (1995) *How to Write Love Letters* on prominent display at the Borders bookstore in Ann Arbor, Michigan. In it, Lovric writes, "This

book is for people who find it difficult to write letters, and it's also for people who would like to be better at it. It's for people who are in love (but who are tongue-tied in person), who may find, in the model letters following, a template for their thoughts that they can imprint with their own feelings" (9).

Chapter 8

1. The figures that follow are all for ever-married villagers. Among unmarried villagers (both male and female), virtually all are literate as a result of formal schooling.

2. According to UNESCO, Nepal's overall adult literacy rate in 1995 was 27 percent, while for women it was 14 percent and for men 41 percent (World Bank 1996:188, 200). The UNESCO definition of *literacy* differed, however, from that used by Junigau villagers. A literate person, according to UNESCO's definition, had to be able to read and comprehend a paragraph on the subject of everyday life.

3. The World Bank states that 85 percent of all appropriately aged Nepali girls were in primary school in 1993, as opposed to 100 percent of appropriately aged Nepali boys. The rates for high school enrollment in 1993 were 23 percent for girls and 46 percent for boys. The analogous figures for Junigau high school enrollment are somewhat higher. (Countrywide statistics for Nepal should be taken with a grain of salt, however, as there are considerable logistical obstacles involved in conducting a national survey.)

4. Because of nonexistent infrastructure, however, Nepal was only able to spend 65 percent of the allocated development budget in the first five year plan from 1956 to 1961 (Bista 1991:134). On the history of education in Nepal, see Dor Bahadur Bista's controversial book, *Fatalism and Development: Nepal's Struggle for Modernization* (1991). On the history and politics of Nepal during the Rana regime, see Regmi (1978). On state formation in Nepal and the impact of British rule in nearby India, see English (1985). Vincanne Adams's chapter, "History and Power in Nepal," provides an excellent overview of Nepali history from the eighteenth century to the 1990s (Adams 1998:30–81). For more information on Nepal during the *panchāyat* era, see Burghart (1994). On Nepal during and after the 1990 democratic revolution, see Adams (1998); Kondos (1994); and Hutt (1994). On nationalism, Hinduism, and ethnicity in Nepal, see Burghart (1984); Gellner et al. (1997); and Höfer (1979). There is a vast literature in the Nepali language on education, development, and the history of Nepal; interested readers should consult the journal *Studies in Nepali History and Society* as a starting point.

5. The stainless steel plates were intended to prevent the villagers from further denuding the nearby forest in order to make thousands of leaf plates every time there was a feast. Deforestation is one of Nepal's most serious problems, and it is constantly the focus of development programs on Radio Nepal. It is also featured in school textbooks. Even before the youth club was started, Junigau residents planted an entire eroded hillside with pine seedlings in an attempt to reforest their village.

6. National Planning Commission Secretariat (1992:12).

7. Newspapers were quite unpopular among Junigau college students. They were

written in prose that was difficult for villagers, even those attending college, to understand. Junigau young people on the whole evinced far more interest in the types of magazines described in the previous chapter (especially film magazines and those containing information about science and development) than they did in politics or current events.

8. Liechty writes of cinema viewing in Kathmandu:

As people's daily lives become more and more deeply invested in media consumption, the narratives, narrative logics, and images of media serve more and more as interpretive resources for life, ways to make sense out of life, and eventually methods to interpret and even represent life. This is the power of media realism: not to make media images real but to make lived-reality an increasingly mediated experience. (1998:122)

9. See Kratz (1995) on the negative agency of women.

Chapter 9

1. The complete text of Bir Bahadur's letters to Sarita are in appendix B (available at <http://www.press.umich.edu/webhome/ahearn/index.html>). Sarita did not realize I was interested in her letters as well as Bir Bahadur's until after she made the long trip from her marital home back to Junigau, where I was staying, and so she only brought Bir Bahadur's letters to me. During a future trip to Nepal, I hope to be able to copy the other side of the correspondence.

2. Bir Bahadur uses *tapaī*, an honorific form of *you* here.

Chapter 10

1. Although I never heard any Junigau residents predict that young women might use their literacy skills for writing love letters, in an autobiography first published in Indonesia in 1950, Minangkabau writer Muhamad Radjab remarks that Minangkabau girls were not permitted to attend school in the 1920s "because it was thought that they would just use their knowledge of writing to send love letters to boys" ([1950] 1995:160). I thank Karl Heider for bringing this reference to my attention.

2. Giddens argues that the abstract systems that emerge under modernity are not always alienating; sometimes they can be empowering: "the expansion of abstract systems creates increasing quanta of power—the power of human beings to alter the material world and transform the conditions of their own actions" (1991:138). While Giddens was primarily referring to abstract systems within the economy, one could also apply his insight to abstract systems of cultural thought, such as romantic love, that come to be seen by people as characteristic of modernity. I differ somewhat from Giddens, however, in that I remain agnostic as to whether or not a person's "power" actually increases under the abstract systems of modernity; what I have emphasized in this

ethnography is that Junigau residents *think* that love, as part and parcel of modernity, empowers them.

3. See Ernestine McHugh (1989) for an analysis of concepts of the person among the Gurungs, another Tibeto-Burman ethnic group of Nepal.

4. In the introduction to their 1992 volume, *Responsibility and Evidence in Oral Discourse,* Jane Hill and Judith Irvine argue that, "The allocation of responsibility is thus a centrally important aspect of social meaning constructed in interactional processes" (4).

5. The two Nepali phrases I have translated as "coercion" are *kar* and *bādhya.* The Nepali word for "consent" is *mañjur.*

6. As Bennett notes, romantic love represents "a shift in loyalties dangerous to the joint family and the patrilineal ideals it embodies" (1983:177). Karen Lystra found that love letters played a similar role in promoting a new kind of individualism in the United States in the nineteenth century. Romantic love as expressed in love letters had the effect, Lystra writes, of creating, "some special experience within an individual before marriage that was not shared by others," thus contributing to the formation not only of close conjugal bonds but of "American individualism" (1989:8–9). Although the contents of Junigau's love letters differ from those written by nineteenth-century Americans, the novel practice of exchanging such letters over a protracted courtship similarly reflects and contributes to changes in family patterns and power dynamics in the village.

7. Marriage to parallel cousins (even classificatory) is considered extremely taboo; as of this writing, it has never occurred in Junigau.

8. Indeed, Ortner notes that Spivak's own analysis of an Indian woman's suicide in 1926 contradicts her statement that the subaltern cannot speak (1995:189).

References

Abu-Lughod, Lila. 1986. *Veiled Sentiments: Honor and Poetry in a Bedouin Society.* Berkeley: University of California Press.

———. 1990. The romance of resistance: tracing transformations of power through Bedouin women. *American Ethnologist* 17 (1): 41–55.

———. 1993. *Writing Women's Worlds: Bedouin Stories.* Berkeley: University of California Press.

Abu-Lughod, Lila, and Catherine A. Lutz. 1990. Introduction: Emotion, discourse, and the politics of everyday life. In *Language and the Politics of Emotion,* ed. Catherine A. Lutz and Lila Abu-Lughod, 1–23. Cambridge: Cambridge University Press.

Acharya, Bhairav, Ramji Prasad Acharya, and Basanta Kumar Sharma Nepal. 1988. *Mahendra mālā: Kakshā Chha, Bhāsā Ra Sāmājik Sikshā Ekikrit Pāṭhyapustak* [Mahendra's Garland: Class Six, Integrated Language and Social Studies Lesson Book]. Ministry of Education and Culture, His Majesty's Government. Bhaktapur, Nepal: Janak Educational Materials Centre.

Acharya, Meena, and Lynn Bennett. 1981. *The Rural Women of Nepal: An Aggregate Analysis and Summary of Eight Village Studies.* Kathmandu: Center for Economic Development and Administration, Tribhuvan University.

Adams, Vincanne. 1998. History and power in Nepal. In *Doctors for Democracy: Health Professionals in the Nepal Revolution,* 30–81. Cambridge: Cambridge University Press.

Adhikary, Kamal Raj. 1993. The participation of the Magars in Nepalese development. Ph.D. diss., University of Texas.

Ahearn, Laura M. 1994. Consent and coercion: Changing marriage practices among Magars in Nepal. Ph.D. diss., University of Michigan.

———. 1998. "A twisted rope binds my waist": Locating constraints on meaning in a Tij songfest. *Journal of Linguistic Anthropology* 8 (1): 60–86.

———. 2000a. Agency. *Journal of Linguistic Anthropology* 9 (1): 9–12.

———. 2000b. True traces: Love letters and social transformation in Nepal. In *Letter Writing as a Social Practice,* ed. David Barton and Nigel Hall, 199–207. Amsterdam: John Benjamins.

———. 2001a. Language and agency. *Annual Review of Anthropology* 30:109–37.

———. 2001b. "We were kings here once": Gendered constructions of Magar ethnicity in a speech by Gore Bahadur Khapangi. *Himalayan Research Bulletin* 21 (1). Forthcoming.

Anderson, Benedict R. [1983] 1991. *Imagined Communities: Reflections on the Origins and Spread of Nationalism.* London: Verso.

Appadurai, Arjun. 1991. Afterword. In *Gender, Genre, and Power in South Asian Expressive Tradition,* ed. Arjun Appadurai et al., 467–76. Philadelphia: University of Pennsylvania Press.

———. 1996. Global ethnoscapes: Notes and queries for a transnational anthropology. In *Modernity at Large: Cultural Dimensions of Globalization,* ed. Arjun Appadurai, 48–65. Minneapolis: University of Minnesota Press.

Arnove, Robert, and Harvey J. Graff. 1987. *National Literacy Campaigns: Historical and Comparative Perspectives.* New York: Plenum.

Bakhtin, M. M. 1981. Discourse in the novel. In *The Dialogic Imagination: Four Essays by M. M. Bakhtin,* ed. Michael Holquist, trans. Caryl Emerson and Michael Holquist, 259–422. Austin: University of Texas Press.

Barton, David, and Nigel Hall. 2000. *Letter Writing as a Social Practice.* Amsterdam: John Benjamins.

Barton, David, and Mary Hamilton, eds. 1998. *Local Literacies: Reading and Writing in One Community.* New York: Routledge.

Barton, David, Mary Hamilton, and Roz Ivanič, eds. 2000. *Situated Literacies: Reading and Writing in Context.* New York: Routledge.

Basso, Keith H. [1974] 1989. The ethnography of writing. In *Explorations in the Ethnography of Speaking,* ed. Richard Bauman and Joel Sherzer, 425–32. 2d ed. Cambridge: Cambridge University Press.

Baynham, Mike. 1995. *Literacy Practices: Investigating Literacy in Social Contexts.* London: Longman.

Benjamin, Walter. [1923] 1992. The task of the translator. Trans. H. Zohn. In *Theories of Translation: An Anthology of Essays from Dryden to Derrida,* ed. Rainer Schulte and John Biguenet, 71–82. Berkeley: University of California Press.

Bennett, Lynn. 1983. *Dangerous Wives and Sacred Sisters: Social and Symbolic Roles of High-Caste Women in Nepal.* New York: Columbia University Press.

Berger, Peter L., and Thomas Luckmann. 1966. *The Social Construction of Reality: A Treatise in the Sociology of Knowledge.* New York: Anchor.

Besnier, Niko. 1995. *Literacy, Emotion, and Authority: Reading and Writing on a Polynesian Atoll.* New York: Cambridge University Press.

Bing, Janet M., and Victoria L. Bergvall. 1996. The question of questions: Beyond binary thinking. In *Rethinking Language and Gender Research: Theory and Practice,* ed. Victoria L. Bergvall, Janet M. Bing, and Alice F. Freed, 1–30. New York: Longman.

Bista, Dor Bahadur. 1991. *Fatalism and Development: Nepal's Struggle for Modernization.* Calcutta: Orient Longman.

Bourdieu, Pierre. 1977. *Outline of a Theory of Practice.* Cambridge: Cambridge University Press.

Boyarin, Jonathan, ed. 1993. *The Ethnography of Reading.* Berkeley: University of California Press.

Bright, J. S. N.d. *Lively Love Letters.* New Delhi: Goodwill Publishing House.

Brukman, Jan. 1974. Stealing women among the Koya of South India. *Anthropological Quarterly* 47 (3): 304–13.

Burghart, Richard. 1984. The formation of the concept of nation-state in Nepal. *Journal of Asian Studies* 44 (1): 101–25.

———. 1994. The political culture of *panchayat* democracy. In *Nepal in the Nineties,* ed. Michael Hutt, 1–13. New Delhi: Oxford University Press.

Caplan, Lionel. 1995. *Warrior Gentlemen: "Gurkhas" in the Western Imagination.* Providence, RI: Berghahn.

Chemjong, I. S. 1967. *History and Culture of the Kirat People.* Pt. 2. Kathmandu: Nepal Printing Press.

Clifford, James. 1986. Introduction: partial truths. In *Writing Culture: The Poetics and Politics of Ethnography.* ed. James Clifford and George E. Marcus, 1–26. Berkeley: University of California Press.

Collett, Nigel. 1994. The British Gurkha connection in the 1990s. In *Nepal in the Nineties,* ed. Michael Hutt, 98–105. New Delhi: Oxford University Press.

Collier, Jane Fishburne. 1997. *From Duty to Desire: Remaking Families in a Spanish Village.* Princeton: Princeton University Press.

Collins, James. 1995. Literacy and literacies. *Annual Review of Anthropology* 24: 75–93.

Cook-Gumperz, Jenny. 1986. Introduction: The social construction of literacy. In *The Social Construction of Literacy,* ed. Jenny Cook-Gumperz, 1–15. Cambridge: Cambridge University Press.

de Munck, Victor C. 1998. *Romantic Love and Sexual Behavior: Perspectives from the Social Sciences.* Westport, CT: Praeger.

de Sales, Anne. 1987. *Pāpini bibāh:* Le mariage de la mauvaise fille—essai d'identification d'une fête magar. *L'Ethnographie* 83 (100–101): 275–301.

Des Chene, Mary. 1991. A cultural history of the Gurkhhas, 1815–1987. Ph.D. diss., Stanford University.

Desjarlais, Robert R. 1992. *Body and Emotion: The Aesthetics of Illness and Healing in the Nepal Himalayas.* Philadelphia: University of Pennsylvania Press.

———. 1997. *Shelter Blues: Sanity and Selfhood among the Homeless.* Philadelphia: University of Pennsylvania Press.

Deurālī. 1996. Issues of 21 Bhadau 2053, 25 Asoj 2053, and 2 Kartik 2053.

Dickey, Sara. 1995. Consuming utopia: Film watching in Tamil Nadu. In *Consuming Modernity: Public Culture in a South Asian World,* ed. Carol Breckenridge, 131–56. Minneapolis: University of Minnesota Press.

Divakaruni, Chitra Banerjee. 1999. *Sister of My Heart.* New York: Doubleday.

DuBois, John W., and Stephan Schuetze-Coburn. 1993. Representing hierarchy: Constituent structure for discourse databases. In *Talking Data: Transcription and Coding in Discourse Research,* ed. Jane A. Edwards and Martin D. Lampert, 221–60. Hillsdale, NJ: Lawrence Erblaum.

Dumont, Louis. 1983. *Affinity as Value: Marriage Alliance in South India, with Comparative Essays on Australia.* Chicago: University of Chicago Press.

Eco, Umberto. 1979. *The Role of the Reader: Explorations in the Semiotics of Texts.* Bloomington: Indiana University Press.

———. 1990. *The Limits of Interpretation.* Bloomington: Indiana University Press.

Edwards, Jane A. 1993. Principles and contrasting systems of discourse transcription. In *Talking Data: Transcription and Coding in Discourse Research,* ed. Jane A. Edwards and Martin D. Lampert, 3–31. Hillsdale, NJ: Lawrence Erblaum.

English, Richard. 1985. Himalayan state formation and the impact of British rule in the nineteenth century. *Mountain Research and Development* 5 (1): 61–78.

Escobar, Arturo. 1991. Anthropology and the development encounter. *American Ethnologist* 18 (4): 658–82.

———. 1995. *Encountering Development: The Making and Unmaking of the Third World.* Princeton: Princeton University Press.

Fabian, Johannes. 1983. *Time and the Other: How Anthropology Makes Its Object.* New York: Columbia University Press.

Ferguson, James. 1990. *The Anti-politics Machine: "Development," Depoliticization, and Bureaucratic Power in Lesotho.* Minneapolis: University of Minnesota Press.

Finnegan, Ruth. 1988. *Literacy and Orality: Studies in the Technology of Communication.* Oxford: Blackwell.

Freire, Paolo. 1972. *Pedagogy of the Oppressed.* New York: Continuum and Penguin.

Freire, Paolo, and Donaldo Macedo. 1987. *Literacy: Reading the Word and the World.* South Hadley, MA: Bergin and Garvey.

Fricke, Thomas E. 1984. *Himalayan Households: Tamang Demography and Domestic Processes.* Ann Arbor: UMI Research Press.

Gardner, Katy. 1997. Mixed messages: Contested "development" and the "Plantation Rehabilitation Project." In *Discourses of Development: Anthropological Perspectives,* ed. R. D. Grillo and R. L. Stirrat, 133–56. Oxford: Berg.

Gellner, David N., Joanna Pfaff-Czarnecka, and John Whelpton, eds. 1997. *Nationalism and Ethnicity in a Hindu Kingdom: The Politics of Culture in Contemporary Nepal.* Amsterdam: Harwood Academic Publishers.

Ghimire, Vishwambhar. 1986. *Mahendra Mālā: Kakshā Dui, Bhāsā ra Sāmājik Sikshā Ekikrit Pāṭhyapustak* [Mahendra's Garland: Class Two, Integrated Language and Social Studies Lesson Book]. Ministry of Education and Culture, His Majesty's Government. Bhaktapur, Nepal: Janak Educational Materials Centre.

———. 1988. *Mahendra Mālā: Kakshā Ek, Bhāsā ra Sāmājik Sikshā Ekikrit Pāṭhyapustak* [Mahendra's Garland: Class One, Integrated Language and Social Studies Lesson Book]. Ministry of Education and Culture, His Majesty's Government. Bhaktapur, Nepal: Janak Educational Materials Centre.

Giddens, Anthony. 1991. *Modernity and Self-Identity: Self and Society in the Late Modern Age.* Stanford: Stanford University Press.

———. 1992. *The Transformation of Intimacy: Sexuality, Love and Intimacy in Modern Societies.* Stanford: Stanford University Press.

Gilbert, Kate. 1992. Women and family law in modern Nepal: Statutory rights and social implications. *New York University Journal of International Law and Politics* 24
(2): 729–58.

Goode, William. 1959. The theoretical importance of love. *American Sociological Review*
24: 38–47.

Goodwin, Charles, and Alessandro Duranti. 1992. Rethinking context: An introduction.
In *Rethinking Context: Language as an Interactive Phenomenon*, ed. Alessandro Duranti and Charles Goodwin, 1–42. Cambridge: Cambridge University Press.

Goody, Jack. 1986. *The Logic of Writing and the Organization of Society*. Cambridge:
Cambridge University Press.

Goody, Jack, and Ian Watt. 1963. The consequences of literacy. *Comparative Studies in
Society and History* 5:306–26, 332–45.

Gramsci, Antonio. 1971. *Selections from the Prison Notebooks of Antonio Gramsci*. London: Lawrence and Wishart.

Grillo, R. D. 1997. Discourses of development: The view from anthropology. In *Discourses of Development: Anthropological Perspectives*, ed. R. D. Grillo and R. L. Stirrat, 1–33. Oxford: Berg.

Grillo, R. D., and R. L. Stirrat. 1997. *Discourses of Development: Anthropological Perspectives*. New York: Berg.

Gupta, Akhil. 1998. *Postcolonial Developments: Agriculture in the Making of Modern
India*. Durham: Duke University Press.

Heath, Shirley B. 1983. *Ways with Words: Language, Life, and Work in Communities and
Classrooms*. Cambridge: Cambridge University Press.

Hill, Jane H., and Judith T. Irvine, eds. 1992. Introduction to *Responsibility and Evidence
in Oral Discourse*, 1–23. Cambridge: Cambridge University Press.

Himal. 1997a. Special issue on migratory labor in India (vol. 10, no. 1 [January-February]).

———. 1997b. Special issue on Gurkha soldiers (vol. 10, no. 4 [July-August 1997]).

Hirsch, Jennifer S. 1999. "Men go as far as women let them": Courtship, intimacy, and
the Mexican companionate marriage. Paper presented at the annual meetings of the
American Anthropological Association, 20 November.

Hitchcock, John. 1961. A Nepalese hill village and Indian employment. *Asian Survey* 1
(9): 15–20.

———. 1963. Some effects of recent change in rural Nepal. *Human Organization* 22 (1):
75–82.

———. 1965. Sub-tribes in the Magar community in Nepal. *Asian Survey* 5 (4): 207–15.

———. 1966. *The Magars of Banyan Hill*. New York: Holt, Rinehart and Winston.

Hobart, Mark. 1993. *An Anthropological Critique of Development: The Growth of Ignorance*. New York: Routledge.

Hobhouse, L. T. 1964. *Liberalism*. New York: Oxford University Press.

Höfer, Andras. 1978. A new rural elite in central Nepal. In *Himalayan Anthropology: The
Indo-Tibetan Interface*, ed. James Fisher, 179–86. The Hague: Mouton.

———. 1979. *The Caste Hierarchy and the State in Nepal: A Study of the Muluki Ain of
1854*. Innsbruck: Universitatsverlag Wagner.

Hoffman, John. 1984. *The Gramscian Challenge: Coercion and Consent in Marxist Political Theory.* Oxford: Blackwell.

Holland, Dorothy, and Debra Skinner. 1989. The linguistic mediation of gendered selves in Nepal. Paper presented at the American Anthropological Association annual meetings, Washington, DC.

———. 1995. Contested ritual, contested femininities: (Re)forming self and society in a Nepali women's festival. *American Ethnologist* 22 (2): 279–305.

Hutt, Michael, ed. 1994. *Nepal in the Nineties.* New Delhi: Oxford University Press.

Illouz, Eva. 1997. Introduction to the sociology of love. In *Consuming the Romantic Utopia: Love and the Cultural Contradictions of Capitalism,* 1–22. Berkeley: University of California Press.

Jankowiak, William, ed. 1995. *Romantic Passion: A Universal Experience?* New York: Columbia University Press.

Jeffery, Patricia, and Roger Jeffery. 1994. Killing my heart's desire: Education and female autonomy in rural North India. In *Women as Subjects: South Asian Histories,* ed. Nita Kumar, 125–71. Charlottesville: University of Virginia Press.

Jiro, Kawakita. 1974. *The Hill Magars and Their Neighbours: Hill Peoples Surrounding the Ganges Plain.* Vol. 3 of *Synthetic Research of the Culture of Rice-Cultivating Peoples in Southeast Asian Countries.* Tokyo: Tokai University Press.

Jones, Rex Lee. 1973. Kinship and marriage among the Limbu of eastern Nepal: A study in marriage stability. Ph.D. diss., University of California at Los Angeles.

Kairan Māsik. 1992. Vol. 9, no. 1, (*asār-sāun 2049* [July-August 1992]).

Kāmanā. 1996. Issue no. 104.

Kane, Pandurang Vaman. 1974. *History of Dharmasāstra (Ancient and Mediaeval Religious and Civil Law).* 2d ed., vol. 2, pt. 1. Poona, India: Bhandarkar Oriental Research Institute.

Kingsolver, Ann E. 1991. Tobacco, Toyota, and subaltern development discourses: Constructing livelihoods and community in rural Kentucky. Ph.D. diss., University of Massachusetts.

Kondos, Vivienne. 1994. *Jānā Sakti* (People Power) and the 1990 revolution in Nepal: Some theoretical considerations. In *Anthropology of Nepal: Peoples, Problems, and Processes,* ed. Michael Allen, 271–86. Kathmandu: Mandala Book Point.

Kovid, Prakash. 1990. *Prem Patra* [Love Letters]. Varanasi, India: Sarita Publishing.

Kratz, Corinne. 1995. Personhood and agency in Okiek marriage arrangement. Paper presented at the annual meetings of the American Anthropological Association, 16 November.

Krauskopff, Gisèle, and Marie Lecomte-Tilouine. 1996. *Célébrer le Pouvoir: Dasaī, une Fête au Népal.* Paris: CNRS Éditions.

Kumar, Dhruba. 2000. *Domestic Conflict and Crisis of Governability in Nepal.* Kathmandu: Center for Nepal and Asian Studies.

Kumar, Nita. 1994. Introduction. In *Women as Subjects: South Asian Histories,* ed. Nita Kumar, 1–25. Charlottesville: University Press of Virginia.

Kunreuther, Laura. 2000. Between love and property: The right to inherit in Nepal. Paper presented at the South Asia Center, Columbia University, 12 April.

Lāphā Traimāsik [Lapha Tri-monthly]. 1992–93. *Mangsir-māgh,* 2049 [November–January].

Lecomte-Tilouine, Marie. 1993. *Les Dieux du Pouvoir: Les Magar et L'Hindouisme au Népal Central.* Paris: CNRS Éditions.

Liechty, Mark. 1998. The social pattern of cinema and video-viewing in Kathmandu. *Studies in Nepali History and Society* 3 (1): 87–126.

Lindholm, Charles. 1995. Love as an experience of transcendence. In *Romantic Passion: A Universal Experience?* ed. William Jankowiak, 57–71. New York: Columbia University Press.

Lovric, Michelle. 1995. *How to Write Love Letters.* New York: Shooting Star.

Luke, Allan. 1988. *Literacy, Textbooks, and Ideology: Postwar Literacy Instruction and the Mythology of Dick and Jane.* London: Falmer.

Lystra, Karen. 1989. *Searching the Heart: Women, Men, and Romantic Love in Nineteenth Century America.* New York: Oxford University Press.

Macfarlane, Alan. 1979. *The Origins of English Individualism: The Family, Property, and Social Transition.* New York: Cambridge University Press.

———. 1986. *Marriage and Love in England: Modes of Reproduction, 1300–1840.* Oxford: Blackwell.

Machanda, Rita. 1999. Empowerment with a twist. *The Hindu,* 21 November. http://www.indiaserver.com/thehindu/1999/11/21/stories/13210619.htm.

MacLeod, Arlene Elowe. 1992. Hegemonic relations and gender resistance: The new veiling as accommodating protest in Cairo. *Signs: The Journal of Women in Culture and Society* 17 (3): 533–57.

Maggi, Wynne Rae. 1998. Our women are free: An ethnotheory of Kalasha women's agency, Ph.D. diss., Emory University.

———. 1999. Heart-struck: Love marriage as a marker of ethnic identity among the Kalasha of Northwest Pakistan. Paper presented at the annual meeting of the American Anthropological Association, 20 November.

Mannheim, Bruce, and Dennis Tedlock. 1995. Introduction to *The Dialogic Emergence of Culture,* ed. Dennis Tedlock and Bruce Mannheim, 1–32. Urbana: University of Illinois Press.

Manohar. N.d. *Love Letters.* New Delhi: New Light Publishers.

March, Kathryn S. 1979. The intermediacy of women: Female gender symbolism and the social position of women among Tamangs and Sherpas of highland Nepal. Ph.D. diss., Cornell University.

———. 1991. Points and counterpoints: Three daughters-in-law on the break-up of their patrilineal brother-husbands' joint household. Paper presented at the meetings of the Association of Asian Studies, Washington, DC.

Marx, Karl. [1853] 1978. The Eighteenth Brumaire of Louis Bonaparte. In *The Marx-Engels Reader,* ed. R. C. Tucker, 594–617. 2d ed. New York: Norton.

McCollum, Chris. 1998. American narratives of falling in love from the perspective of relational psychoanalysis. Paper presented at the Society for Psychological Anthropology Reunion, Emory University, 23 October.

McDougal, Charles. 1979. *The Kulunge Rai: A Study in Kinship and Marriage Exchange.* Kathmandu: Ratna Pustak Bhandar.

McElhinny, Bonnie. 1998. Genealogies of gender theory: Practice theory and feminism in sociocultural and linguistic anthropology. *Social Analysis* 42 (3): 164–89.

McHugh, Ernestine. 1989. Concepts of the person among the Gurungs of Nepal. *American Ethnologist* 16 (1): 75–86.

Meerendonk, M. 1960. *Basic Gurkhali Dictionary (Roman Script).* Kathmandu: Ratna Pustak Bhandar.

Ministry of Education and Culture, His Majesty's Government, Nepal. 1983. *My English Book Two: For Grade Five.* Bhaktapur, Nepal: Janak Educational Materials Centre.

———. 1989. *Mahendra Mālā: Kakṣā Chār, Bhāsā ra Sāmājik Siksā Ekikrit Pāṭhyapustak* [Mahendra's Garland: Class Four, Integrated Language and Social Studies Lesson Book]. Bhaktapur, Nepal: Janak Educational Materials Centre.

———. 1994. *Nayā Goreṭo* [New Path]. 15th ed. Kathmandu, Nepal: Gorkhapatra Sangsthan.

Mohanty, Chandra Talpade. 1991a. Introduction: Cartographies of struggle—third world women and the politics of feminism. In *Third World Women and the Politics of Feminism,* ed. Chandra P. Mohanty, A. Russo, and L. Torres, 1–47. Bloomington: Indiana University Press.

———. 1991b. Under Western eyes: Feminist scholarship and colonial discourses. In *Third World Women and the Politics of Feminism,* ed. Chandra P. Mohanty, A. Russo, and L. Torres, 51–80. Bloomington: Indiana University Press.

Molnar, Augusta. 1981. *The Kham Magar Women of Thabang.* Vol. 2 of *The Status of Women in Nepal.* Kathmandu: Centre for Economic Development and Administration, Tribhuvan University.

Movsesian, Ara John. 1993. *How to Write Love Letters and Love Poems.* Bombay: Jaico Publishing House.

Narayan, Kirin. 1995. The practice of oral literary criticism: Women's songs in Kangra, India. *Journal of American Folklore* 108 (429): 243–64.

National Planning Commission Secretariat, Central Bureau of Statistics. 1992. *Statistical Pocket Book, 1992.* Kathmandu: Ratna Offset Press.

Ong, Walter J. 1982. *Orality and Literacy: The Technologizing of the Word.* London: Methuen.

Onta, Pratyoush. 1996. Village weekly *Deurāli* celebrates 100th issue. *Everest Herald,* 13 June.

———. 1997. The other print media. *Kathmandu Post,* 13 June.

Ortega y Gasset, José. [1937] 1992. The misery and the splendor of translation. Trans. E. G. Miller. In *Theories of Translation: An Anthology of Essays from Dryden to Derrida,* ed. Rainer Schulte and John Biguenet, 93–112. Berkeley: University of California Press.

Ortner, Sherry B. 1981. Gender and sexuality in hierarchical societies: The case of Polynesia and some comparative implications. In *Sexual Meanings: The Cultural Construction of Gender and Sexuality*, ed. Sherry B. Ortner and Harriet Whitehead, 359–409. Cambridge: Cambridge University Press.

———. 1989. *High Religion: A Cultural and Political History of Sherpa Buddhism*. Princeton: Princeton University Press.

———. 1995. Resistance and the problem of ethnographic refusal. *Comparative Studies in Society and History* 37 (1): 173–93.

———. 1996. *Making Gender: The Politics and Erotics of Culture*. Boston: Beacon.

Ortner, Sherry B., and Harriet Whitehead, eds. 1981. *Sexual Meanings: The Cultural Construction of Gender and Sexuality*. New York: Cambridge University Press.

Parikh, Shanti A. 1999. What's love gotta do with it? Love letters and romance among youth in Uganda. Paper presented at the annual meetings of the American Anthropological Association, 19 November.

Parish, Steven M. 1994. *Moral Knowing in a Hindu Sacred City: An Exploration in Mind, Emotion, and Self*. New York: Columbia University Press.

Pigg, Stacy Leigh. 1992. Inventing social categories through place: Social representations and development in Nepal. *Comparative Studies in Society and History* 34 (3): 491–513.

———. 1996. The credible and the credulous: The question of "villager's beliefs" in Nepal. *Cultural Anthropology* 11 (2): 160–201.

———. 2001. Languages of sex and AIDS in Nepal: Notes on the social production of commensurability. *Cultural Anthropology* 16 (4). Forthcoming.

Pradhan, G. S. 1981. *My English Book Three: For Grade Six*. Kathmandu: Janak Educational Materials Centre.

Pratt, Mary Louise. 1986. Fieldwork in common places. In *Writing Culture: The Poetics and Politics of Ethnography*, ed. James Clifford and George E. Marcus, 27–50. Berkeley: University of California Press.

Quinn, Naomi. 1982. "Commitment" in American marriage: A cultural analysis. *American Ethnologist* 9:755–98.

———. 1996. Culture and contradiction: The case of Americans reasoning about marriage. *Ethos* 24:391–425.

Radjab, Muhamad. [1950] 1995. Village childhood: The autobiography of a Minangkabau child. In *Telling Lives, Telling History: Autobiography and Historical Imagination in Modern Indonesia*, ed. and trans. Susan Rodgers, 149–324. Berkeley: University of California Press.

Raheja, Gloria Goodwin. 1988. *The Poison in the Gift: Ritual, Prestation, and the Dominant Caste in a North Indian Village*. Chicago: University of Chicago Press.

———. 1994. Introduction: Gender representation and the problem of language and resistance in India. In *Listen to the Heron's Words: Reimagining Gender and Kinship in North India*, ed. Gloria Goodwin Raheja and Ann Grodzins Gold, 1–29. Berkeley: University of California Press.

Raheja, Gloria Goodwin, and Ann Grodzins Gold, eds. 1994. *Listen to the Heron's Words:*

Reimagining Gender and Kinship in North India. Berkeley: University of California Press.

Ramanujan, A. K. 1989. On translating a Tamil poem. In *The Art of Translation: Voices from the Field,* ed. R. Warren, 47–63. Boston: Northeastern University Press.

Rao, Aparna. 1998. *Autonomy: Life Cycle, Gender and Status among Himalayan Pastoralists.* New York: Berghahn.

Rebhun, L. A. 1995. Language of love in Northeast Brazil. In *Romantic Passion: A Universal Experience?* ed. William Jankowiak, 239–61. New York: Columbia University Press.

———. 1999a. For love and for money: Romance in urbanizing Northeast Brazil. Paper presented at the annual meetings of the American Anthropological Association, 19 November.

———. 1999b. *The Heart Is Unknown Country: Love in the Changing Economy of Northeast Brazil.* Stanford: Stanford University Press.

Regmi, Mahesh C. 1978. *Thatched Huts and Stucco Palaces: Peasants and Landlords in Nineteenth Century Nepal.* New Delhi: Vikas Publishing House.

Rosaldo, M. Z. 1980. The use and abuse of anthropology: Reflections on feminism and cross-cultural understanding. *Signs: The Journal of Women in Culture and Society* 5:389–417.

Rutherford, Blair, and Rinse Nyamuda. 2000. Learning about power: Development and marginality in an adult literacy center for farm workers in Zimbabwe. *American Ethnologist* 27 (4): 839–54.

Sapir, Edward. [1929] 1985. The status of linguistics as a science. In *Selected Writings in Language, Culture, and Personality,* ed. David G. Mandelbaum, 160–68. Berkeley: University of California Press.

Schiffrin, Deborah. 1994. *Approaches to Discourse.* Cambridge: MA: Blackwell.

Schwimmer, Brian E., and D. Michael Warren, eds. 1993. *Anthropology and the Peace Corps: Case Studies in Career Preparation.* Ames: Iowa State University Press.

Scott, James C. 1985. *Weapons of the Weak: Everyday Forms of Peasant Resistance.* New Haven: Yale University Press.

———. 1990. *Domination and the Arts of Resistance: Hidden Transcripts.* New Haven: Yale University Press.

Scott, Joan Wallach. 1986. Gender: A useful category of historical analysis. In *Gender and the Politics of History,* 28–50. New York: Columbia University Press.

Seidman, Steven. 1991. *Romantic Longings: Love in America, 1830–1980.* New York: Routledge.

Shepherd, Gary. 1982. *Life among the Magars.* Kathmandu: Sahayogi Press.

Shorter, Edward. 1977. *The Making of the Modern Family.* New York: Basic Books.

Sivaramakrishnan, K. 2000. Crafting the public sphere in the forests of West Bengal: Democracy, development, and political action. *American Ethnologist* 27 (2): 431–61.

Skinner, Debra, and Dorothy Holland. 1990. Good selves, angry selves: The formation of female gender identities in a mixed-caste Hindu community in Nepal. Paper presented at the annual Conference on South Asia, Madison, WI.

Skinner, Debra, Dorothy Holland, and G. B. Adhikari. 1994. The songs of Tij: A genre of critical commentary for women in Nepal. *Asian Folklore Studies* 53:259–305.

Skinner, Debra, Alfred Pach III, and Dorothy Holland. 1998. *Selves in Time and Place: Identities, Experience, and History in Nepal.* Lanham, MD: Rowman & Littlefield.

Spivak, Gayatri Chakravorty. 1988. Can the subaltern speak? In *Marxism and the Interpretation of Culture,* ed. C. Nelson and L. Grossberg, 271–313. Urbana: University of Illinois Press.

Srivastava, I. 1991. Woman as portrayed in women's folk songs of North India. *Asian Folklore Studies* 50:269–310.

Street, Brian. 1984. *Literacy in Theory and Practice.* Cambridge: Cambridge University Press.

———, ed. 1993. *Cross-Cultural Approaches to Literacy.* Cambridge: Cambridge University Press.

Thapa, M. S. 1993. *Prāchin Magar ra Akkhā Lipi.* [Ancient Magars and Alphabetic Writing]. Kathmandu: Vriji Prakashan.

Tiwari, R. C., R. S. Sharma, and Krishna Vikal. 1990. *Hindi-English Dictionary.* New York: Hippocrene.

Trautmann, Thomas R. 1981. *Dravidian Kinship.* Cambridge: Cambridge University Press.

Trawick, Margaret. 1990. *Notes on Love in a Tamil Family.* Berkeley: University of California Press.

Turner, Ralph Lilley. [1931] 1990. *A Comparative and Etymological Dictionary of the Nepali Language.* London: Routledge and Kegan Paul.

Vaidya, Ratna Das. 1982. *My English Book Four: For Grade Seven.* Kathmandu: Janak Education Materials Centre.

Wadley, Susan S. 1994. *Struggling with Destiny in Karimpur, 1925–1984.* Berkeley: University of California Press.

Wardlow, Holly. 1999. All's fair when love is war: Attempts at companionate marriage among the Huli of Papua New Guinea. Paper presented at the annual meetings of the American Anthropological Association, 20 November.

Watkins, Joanne C. 1996. *Spirited Women: Gender, Religion, and Cultural Identity in the Nepal Himalaya.* New York: Columbia University Press.

Williams, Raymond. 1977. *Marxism and Literature.* Oxford: Oxford University Press.

———. 1983. *Keywords: A Vocabulary of Culture and Society.* Rev. ed. New York: Oxford University Press.

Woost, Michael D. 1997. Alternative vocabularies of development? "Community" and "participation" in development discourse in Sri Lanka. In *Discourses of Development: Anthropological Pespectives,* ed. R. D. Grillo and R. L. Stirrat, 229–53. Oxford: Berg.

World Bank. 1996. *World Development Report 1996: From Plan to Market.* Oxford: Oxford University Press.

Yuvā Manch. 1996. Issue of Kartik 2053.

Index

References to illustrations and tables are in italics.